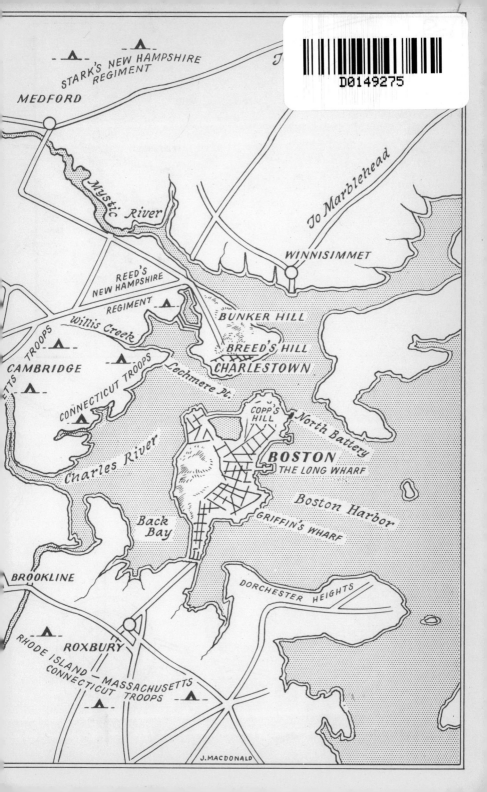

NOW WE ARE ENEMIES

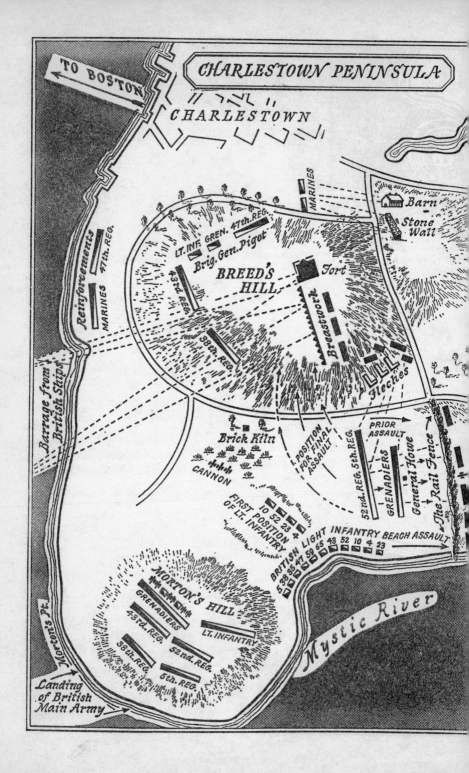

NOW
WE
ARE
ENEMIES

*The Story of
Bunker Hill*

THOMAS J. FLEMING

ST MARTIN'S PRESS
New York

TO CAMBRIDGE

Causeway

BUNKER

HILL

British
Forces

American
Forces

CHRONOLOGY

1745   Fort Louisburg on Cape Breton Island captured by American army.

1755   Braddock's defeat.

1755   American army defeats French at Battle of Lake George.

1758   British-American army defeated at Ticonderoga.

1758   British-American army recaptures Louisburg.

1759   British army captures Quebec.

1760   Canada surrenders. George III becomes King of England.

1762   Spain enters war on side of French.

1762   British-American army captures Havana.

1763   France and Spain surrender. Seven Years' War ends.

1765   Stamp Act crisis.

1766   Stamp Act repealed.

1767   Townshend Acts. Americans resist new taxes.

1770   British troops kill five Bostonians in riot.

1770   Townshend taxes repealed by Parliament except on tea.

1773   Boston Tea Party.

1774   First Continental Congress meets.

1775   Bloodshed at Lexington and Concord on April 19.

1775   Second Continental Congress meets on May 10.

1775   Battle of Bunker Hill, June 17.

The author would like to acknowledge the generous assistance given him by the staffs of the Massachusetts Historical Society, The Widener Library at Harvard University, the New-York Historical Society, The William L. Clements Library at the University of Michigan, and The New York Public Library in the preparation of this book.

The battle map showing the British and American forces, which appears as a two-page title, was drawn by James MacDonald, as was the end paper of Boston and Vicinity, 1775.

NOW WE ARE ENEMIES

I

"ALL'S WELL."

The cry of the watch aboard His Majesty's ship *Lively* saluted the darkness and silence which enveloped Boston Harbor. Beneath a moonless but star-rich sky, a soft southwest wind mixed the scent of early summer greenery with the seacoast's salt tang. If ever an hour seemed to justify this routine report from the lips of that dutiful British marine, it was this one, the midnight of June 16, 1775. Yet the cry, as it drifted on the water to be echoed and re-echoed by the watch on other ships—from the battleship *Glasgow* with its tiers of cannon to the small frigate *Falcon*—carried within it an ominous irony.

All was well in the heavens and on the natural earth. But for the men and women who walked this corner of the globe, a corner which the man of England on the *Lively*'s quarterdeck still called new, all was distinctly not well. Across the harbor Boston was an occupied city; soldiers with fixed bayonets patrolled the empty streets, and sentries stood guard on wharves and at checkpoints on the continental side of the once busy port, sealing it off by land and sea. Hundreds of houses were silent and dark, abandoned by their owners. In hundreds of others men and women had gone to bed hungry. Boston was also a city under siege. Over 15,000 armed, angry citizens were entrenched outside the city gates, their campfires winking through the night like vigilant baleful eyes. Already food was scarce, especially for those who did not have the money to pay for it and had to depend on the reluctant generosity of the army of occupation.

Across the harbor from Boston, and a mere 100 yards off the *Lively*'s bow, was the village of Charlestown, "the mother of the colony." The pioneers from old England had built their first crude shelters here 150 years ago and they had prospered until their wharves, together with Boston's, had cleared 1,000 ships a month. But in the last sixty days Charlestown's citizens, terrified by the heavy guns of the British fleet frowning upon their homes and shops, had fled into the country to live on the charity of relatives and friends.

Suddenly in the empty streets of Charlestown there were moving figures. In single file fifty men with muskets at the ready hugged the dark sides of the vacant houses, stopping every few feet to listen for the sound of a hostile footstep. Quickly they split into groups of ten and fanned out until they had prowled past every one of the town's 600 buildings and assured themselves they were alone. Minutes later they reassembled by the Town Meeting House. "Domingo," the password for the night, came softly from their lips as squad after squad formed up under the eyes of stern-faced Captain John Nutting of Pepperell, Massachusetts. Forty of the grimly determined soldiers he was commanding had followed Nutting from their farms around Groton and Pepperell. Ten were strangers from Connecticut. A year ago, if a man had told any one of them that he would soon find himself prowling the streets of an empty seaport town, ready to slay men who spoke the same language and revered the same King, he would have laughed incredulously.

Across the harbor in silent Boston, a few people were still awake. One of them was a dark, heavy-set man, over six feet tall, with a rather thick nose and snapping black eyes. His name was William Howe, and he sat in the study of his rented house enjoying a glass of port while he pondered a map of Boston and its surrounding countryside.

William Howe was a major general in the British army. But in many ways he was less a stranger to Massachusetts than those Connecticut men who crouched beside Captain John Nutting near the Charlestown meeting house. Little more than fifteen years ago all New England had drunk toasts to Howe's courage. In the night of September 13, 1759, he had led twenty-four volunteers up the vertical face of the Quebec cliffs and overpowered the French troops stationed on the heights. Behind him had come his commanding officer, James Wolfe, with the rest of the British army. The astonished French had awakened in the morning to find 3,000 men drawn up in battle formation on the supposedly inviolable Plains of Abraham. While Wolfe smashed the French assault in front, Howe, with 400 light infantrymen, bluffed to a standstill a relieving army of 2,000 French attacking from the rear. In three hours the British Empire in America dramatically doubled in size, and 100 years of French and Indian terror along New England's frontier came to an end at last.

After the war Howe's military reputation had carried him into Parliament, where he regularly sided with the "friends of America" who opposed the policies of George III and his ministers. To this formidable combination of military glory and political sympathy must be added the affection and admiration Americans felt for his two older brothers, Richard and George Augustus Howe.

"Black Dick," named for the swarthy complexion the Howes all shared, was one of the best-known admirals in the Royal Navy. Off Nova Scotia he had fired the first shot in the world war against France and Spain which his brother William had helped win at Quebec. After a battle Lord Richard would go below and talk with his wounded men, often ordering food and liquor from his own mess for them—a rare gesture in a class-conscious, rank-ridden age, and one that endeared him to democratically inclined Americans.

The oldest brother, George, had been called by no less a genius than Wolfe, "the noblest Englishman that has appeared in my time and the best soldier in the army." He also had the family ability to bridge the gaps of rank and class. When he came from England in 1758 to rally the Americans from a series of shattering French defeats, he was hailed as a miraculous change from a succession of British generals who insisted on treating "colonials" as inferiors and fighting the French and Indians with the parade-ground tactics of European battlefields.

George Howe threw away his gold braid and cumbersome uniform and wore frontier buckskin. He treated Americans as equals and frankly asked them to teach him all they knew about wilderness fighting. He even went out with Robert Rogers and his rangers on their patrols "to learn [wrote Rogers] our methods of marching, ambushing, retreating, etc. . . ." An even better view of him comes from a provincial carpenter: "It was not extravagant to suppose that every soldier in the army had a personal attachment to him, he frequently came among the Carpenters and his maner was So easy and fermiller, that you loost all that constraint or diffidence we feele when addressed by our Superiors whose manners are forbiding."

On July 5, 1758, George Howe was leading his American rangers in a skirmish with French and Indian irregulars near Fort Ticonderoga when a bullet struck him in the heart. Only a few minutes before, one of his warmest admirers, Major Israel Putnam of Connecticut, had begged him not to expose himself so needlessly to danger. All New

England mourned him, and the citizens of Boston spontaneously voted to erect a statue in his memory.

Now, seventeen years later, George Howe's youngest brother had come from England to find Boston besieged by 15,000 Americans. In their eyes he had come as an enemy, a betrayer of old trust and friendship. Nor was this the only irritation to William Howe's political conscience. His own constituents in the borough of Nottingham, back in England, had written him a most unfriendly letter on the eve of his departure for America telling him they took a dim view of his mission. They particularly reminded him that when he had stood for re-election to Parliament in 1774, he had promised Nottingham's voters that he would never, under any circumstances, accept a commission to serve against "our American brethren."

"If you should resolve, at all events to go," wrote Howe's Nottingham correspondent, "I don't wish you may fall as many do; but I cannot say I wish success to the undertaking."

Howe defended himself earnestly in a return letter. "My going thither [to America] was not of my seeking. I was ordered, and could not refuse without incurring the odious name of backwardness to serve my country in distress. So contrary are men's opinions here, to some with you that instead of the grossest abuse, I have been most highly complimented upon the occasion by those who are even averse to the measures of Administration. Every man's private feelings ought to give way to the service of the public at all times, but particularly when of that delicate nature in which our affairs stand at present."

In Howe's eyes, he had not come to America as an enemy. His own political party, which was in violent opposition to His Majesty's Government's American policy, had approved his acceptance of the King's commission. He saw himself, through his family's tradition of friendship, as uniquely equipped to settle the explosive dispute that was alienating 3,000,000 loyal American subjects, without compromising British pride and honor. King George III had proclaimed himself willing to extend the olive branch as well as the sword, and William Howe was convinced (and other men hoped) that he could wield both these instruments better than any other soldier in the empire.

Howe had sailed hoping he would need to do no more than brandish his sword and his equally shining military reputation to make the Americans more amenable to negotiation. But when he arrived in Boston and found himself confronted by an armed rebellion, he had been forced to put aside his diplomat's role for the time being. The legate of a great empire does not talk peace without first proving he can win the war. It was imperative, therefore, to end this embarrassing siege of Boston as quickly as possible. From the moment he arrived three weeks earlier with two fellow major generals, Henry Clinton and John Burgoyne, Howe had gone to work on a battle plan. The day after tomorrow it would go into operation.

The 15,000 colonial besiegers were encamped in an irregular nine-mile semicircle which ran from Roxbury on the south through Cambridge in the center to Medford on the north. Cambridge was the headquarters of the American army as well as the depot for their scanty supplies of ammunition and food. Though he was outnumbered five to one, Howe intended to launch a daring attack on this nerve center. The assault was to begin at dawn on Sunday, June 18, the day after tomorrow. Under the covering guns of the fleet Howe was to lead a brigade of 1,500 men in an amphibious landing on Dorchester Point. From there he would move rapidly to secure the heights on this narrow peninsula which looked down upon Boston from the south, then move swiftly out to smash the flimsy American defenses at Roxbury.

Major General Henry Clinton meanwhile was to launch another attack from boats landing on the banks of Willis Creek opposite the American center at Cambridge. Leaving a few hundred men to protect his flank at Roxbury, Howe planned to sweep around Back Bay with the rest of his brigade, while General Clinton was securing the heights above Charlestown, which also frowned threateningly down upon Boston from the north. If the situation then looked favorable he would lead the combined brigades against the center of the American army in Cambridge.

Here the colonists would have to commit their raw troops on open fields where Howe was confident his superbly disciplined regulars would roar through them like a juggernaut. With their organization annihilated, their stores and ammunition destroyed, the whole makeshift American army would evaporate into the woods whence it came. The siege of Boston would be over, the armed rebellion would be shattered. Then William Howe, bearer of the olive branch and friend of Americans, would step forward. He would offer amnesty to all who laid down their arms, help negotiate a generous peace and be back in London, the toast of court and Parliament, before the end of the year.

William Howe put the map away, finished his port and began undressing for bed. It was, he told himself with justifiable confidence, a good plan. All it needed was the presence of that elusive goddess called luck to bring it to a pitch of smashing perfection. Howe had good reason to believe the goddess would be with him. She had yet to fail him on a battlefield.

His reverie was interrupted by a knock on the door.

"General Clinton wishes to speak with you, sir," said Howe's aide, Captain George Sherwin.

"Send him up," Howe said.

A moment later Major General Henry Clinton burst into the room. A paunchy, fair-haired, fussy man, there was some-

thing unsoldierlike about him—but appearances are decep-
tive. He had distinguished himself on European battle-
fields and had a keen military mind. He was also no stranger
to Americans. He had grown up in New York, where his
father had been colonial governor from 1741 to 1751, and his
first military experience had been in the New York militia.

"Good evening, General," Howe said. "You are just in
time for a nightcap."

"No time for nightcaps," Clinton said excitedly. "I have
just been out reconnoitering, and I suspect that the Americans are entrenching on Charlestown Heights."

"In large force?" Howe asked.

"It's impossible to tell in the darkness. But some of our
sentries have heard a great deal of movement."

"They have had pickets out there for some time," Howe
said.

"I think it is a large force. We should give them no time
to entrench. I told General Gage that we should prepare
now for a landing at dawn, close to the neck of land, and
take them in the rear."

"What did General Gage say?"

"It is probably just their sentries changing—or if it is an
entrenching party, it would be better to see what they have
done in the morning and make plans accordingly."

William Howe stared out his study window into the darkness. Ten years of peaceful pleasures in London made him
look with a certain distaste on dawn attacks. They meant a
sleepless night of preparations . . . and then Gage could
as easily be right as Clinton. What if there were nothing on
Charlestown Heights but a company of farmers crouched in
a ditch? They would look a little foolish landing regiments
and artillery on the beach, under a barrage from the ships,
to clean out a squad of fifty frightened bumpkins. Besides,
the whole army was going into action the day after tomorrow. Lose a night's sleep now, and they could lose a half

day's fighting from overtired men on Sunday. William Howe shook his head. "I am inclined to agree with Gage. Better to wait until morning and see what we are dealing with. I doubt if it will be anything we can't flush out with four companies of marines."

"You . . . are probably right," Clinton said. "I am only thinking of Sunday's operation. I would hate to see it disrupted by an unexpected engagement."

"Of course, of course," Howe said. Clinton was hypersensitive to anything which suggested criticism of his ideas. "But I hardly think it will be the case. The rebels have yet to make an offensive gesture. They are obviously waiting for us to make the first move."

Henry Clinton went to bed, soothed and reassured, and slept soundly. So did William Howe and his aide, Captain Sherwin. For the young captain, it was the last sleep from which he would wake as a living man. For the two generals, it was the last night they would sleep soundly for many years.

In the darkness above Charlestown, on a steep-sided hill which was variously called Green's Pasture, Breed's Pasture, Charlestown Heights and Bunker Hill, three men were arguing violently. Thanks to an efficient spy system, they were all keenly aware of William Howe's plan to break the siege of Boston. They had a plan of their own—a plan which they hoped would checkmate William Howe's offensive before it started. But now they could not seem to agree on details.

The tallest of the debaters was William Prescott. A lean farmer from Pepperell, Massachusetts, with steady blue eyes and firm unwavering mouth, he was a man who carried himself like a soldier at all times and disliked talk as much as he liked action. Now forty-three, he had fought as a lieutenant in the colonial regiments which had helped the British take the Nova Scotia fortress of Louisburg from France in

1759. His cool courage and qualities of leadership had caught the eyes of the commanding British officers and he had been offered a commission in the Royal Army—a rare compliment for an American. Prescott had refused it and returned to his farmer's life in Pepperell. But he had never lost his interest in military matters. He had remained active in the colonial militia and was an avid reader of available books on the science of war.

Beside the tall colonel was a shorter, more heavily built man. Gray-haired, square-jawed, fifty-three-year-old Israel Putnam was as outspoken as Prescott was reserved, as excitable as the Massachusetts farmer was imperturbable. Throughout all New England, especially in his home state of Connecticut, his exploits against the Indians and the French had made him a living military legend. More than one British officer asleep across the harbor in Boston was a warm personal friend with whom he had shared the dangers of a dozen campaigns. William Howe's brother George had died in Putnam's arms at Ticonderoga.

The third man was Colonel Richard Gridley, the most gifted engineer in the New World. Without him William Howe's brilliant exploit on the heights of Quebec in 1759 might have ended in a bloody debacle. It was Gridley's engineering skill that had enabled Wolfe to drag two cannons up the perpendicular cliffs—and it was Gridley who personally directed their fire, which wreaked havoc in the ranks of the bewildered French. Until a few months ago Gridley had held the rank of colonel in the British army. Then came an ominous letter from England asking him where he would serve if the bitterness between the mother country and the colony of Massachusetts Bay exploded into violence. Gridley's answer was blunt. "I have never drawn my sword except on the side of justice, and justice lies I believe with my countrymen." Instantly the half pay which he received during time of peace was severed.

These three Americans, so different in talent and temperament, were arguing about a problem which could only be solved by a local geographer. Prescott had received from Artemas Ward, commander in chief of the army of Massachusetts, verbal orders to march three regiments to Charlestown peniusula, and "fortify Bunker's Hill." Unfortunately, there were three hills on the long vaguely triangular peninsula.

The first was at the very tip, a nondescript little rise called Morton's Hill, barely thirty-five feet high. The second, where the arguing Americans stood, was sixty-seven feet high, with a circular summit and an abrupt slope on the south descending into Charlestown village; it was about a third of a mile from Morton's Hill and about a mile and a half from the narrow neck of land which connected the peninsula to the mainland. The third—largest and highest—was northwest of the second hill and ran for 300 yards down the center of the peninsula, ending less than a half mile from the Neck. This, Colonel Prescott kept insisting, was Bunker Hill. The hill on which they were standing was a completely distinct but unfortunately nameless height, and he had no orders to fortify it.

Putnam swore a military oath. He was a brigadier general only in the army of Connecticut, which gave him no authority over Prescott, who held his colonel's commission from Massachusetts. But he outranked Prescott in prestige. "I tell you, Colonel, it would be a waste of time to put men on that hill. First of all we have no cannon that can reach the shipping in the harbor from it. We will be no annoyance to them. The regulars may just let us sit there like a bunch of squirrels on a branch. And if they do come after us the hill can't be defended one half as well as this one."

"I agree with General Putnam," Richard Gridley said. "Particularly in regard to defense."

"I want to build fortifications on both hills," Putnam

said. "But we must begin here. The regulars cannot tolerate cannon here if they want to stay in Boston."

"I assure you it's the best decision, Colonel Prescott," Gridley said. "General Putnam and I went over this ground very carefully only a week ago."

Other officers, most of them Massachusetts men, got into the argument on Putnam's side. They assured Prescott that the hill on which they were standing was also called Bunker by many people. The summits of the two hills were a half mile apart, but the slopes were somewhat connected by a saddle between them which was more elevated than the rest of the peninsula. Still Prescott hesitated. He was not the sort of man who liked to make decisions on hearsay. But there was not a soldier in the expedition who was from either Boston or Charlestown.

Richard Gridley settled the debate with a snort of exasperation. "It is past midnight, gentlemen. Let us begin somewhere soon or these men will have no cover to fight behind in the dawn."

"We begin here," Putnam said.

Prescott nodded and strode across the summit of the hill to the northern slope where 900 men sprawled on the damp grass awaiting orders. Three hundred were his own regiment, all men from Groton and Pepperell. He had no doubts about them. He had trained and drilled them himself and, more important, he knew every one of them personally. They had all been guests at his spacious farmhouse where, like his father before him, he maintained a tradition of openhanded hospitality.

He was not so sure of the rest. Three hundred were from the county of Essex, under the command of Lieutenant Colonel James Bricket, a doctor turned soldier. Their colonel, James Frye, was ill with the gout, and they had marched without him. Bricket had no military experience. How well would his men fight without Frye, the man who was sup-

posed to lead them? A third regiment, three companies short
was commanded by middle-aged Ebenezer Bridge. Prescott
had his doubts about him as a soldier, too. He had more
confidence in wiry Lieutenant Colonel Moses Parker, the
second in command, who was a veteran of more than twenty
battles with the French. Their major, twenty-three-year-old
John Brooks (another doctor turned soldier) also had a good
military reputation. Attached somewhat vaguely to Prescott's regiment was a company of New Hampshire soldiers
under Captain Reuben Dow; they were there mainly to certify that the expedition had the approval of their province's
leaders. Finally, there were 200 Connecticut men under
muscular, thirty-six-year-old Thomas Knowlton. He had
served under Putnam against the French and was Putnam's
"Favorite Captain." But he had told Putnam to his face that
this expedition was madness and they were certain to be cut
off and annihilated. Only personal loyalty to "Old Put" had
persuaded him to come.

They were all—officers and men—probably the most unmilitary looking soldiers ever assembled to fight a major
battle. Only Prescott wore a uniform—a light blue coat and
a three-cornered blue hat. The rest wore their everyday
farm clothes. Their leather trousers, or small clothes, resembled knickers and fastened just below the knee. Their
long loose coats and waistcoats all had the oversized fit of
homemade garments and were dyed in a dozen irregular
colors, pressed from the bark of oak, sumac and other trees
found in New England's hills and swamps. On their heads
were large, round-topped, broad-brimmed hats; on their legs
heavy wool stockings which descended into cowhide shoes,
ornamented by large buckles. There were no boots—
those were for the rich.

For two hours they had waited, first on Bunker Hill and
now on this nameless rise, while their officers debated and
they muttered and whispered nervously among themselves.

"They say that Putnam would march right into a cannon's mouth," said Asa Pollard of Billerica.

"He can march. I'll watch," said Peter Boynton of Andover, with a nervous laugh.

"I'll put my trust in the colonel," said Peter Brown, Prescott's company clerk. "He's not the kind of man to march us out here and leave us."

Not until they had crossed the narrow isthmus known as Charlestown Neck did they have the vaguest idea where they were going or why. But their suspicions had been keenly aroused when they had mustered on Cambridge's green common at six o'clock and President Samuel Langdon of Harvard University had appeared and offered a fervent prayer for their success. They had waited until darkness fell before beginning their two-and-one-half-mile march. Prescott had led the way, with two sergeants carrying masked lanterns. A few hundred yards from Charlestown Neck they had met Israel Putnam and a detachment of Connecticut troops leading two wagons filled with entrenching equipment.

Now, Colonel Prescott loomed above them issuing crisp, clear orders. Detachments trotted to the wagons at the foot of the hill and began distributing the picks and spades. Other men began lugging up bunches of twisted branches called fascines and empty hogsheads which when filled with dirt would, hopefully, stop the largest cannon ball the British could fire. On the summit of the hill they found Colonel Gridley sketching out the shape and size of the entrenchment with a pick.

Prescott ordered Captain Hugh Maxwell of his regiment to join Captain Nutting's party in the deserted village of Charlestown. Maxwell was to patrol the waterfront along the whole south shore of the peninsula and to report instantly the least sign of alarm. In this bitter conflict which divided sons against fathers, it was almost impossible to keep a military secret. The British had their spies in Cambridge just as the Americans had eyes and ears in Boston. Those ships that rode so quietly at anchor could be packed with armed marines ready to spring ashore and fall upon these amateur soldiers before they could exchange their picks and shovels for their guns.

Meanwhile on the summit of their nameless hill the young farmers went furiously to the work on the soft summer earth. Professional soldiers they were not, but professional swingers of picks and wielders of shovels they most certainly were. Years of clearing rocks and tree stumps from their flinty New England farms were on their side. But even for men so gifted with the pick and shovel it soon became evident that the fort was a major undertaking. Gridley's plan called for an oblong structure about 160 feet long and 80 feet wide with earthworks into which the strengthening fascines and hogsheads would be carefully packed. The walls were to be six feet high, at least a foot thick. Firing platforms had to be constructed inside. Also in the plan was a solid breastwork which would run from the northern wall to a swamp at the foot of the hill.

At first the Americans were slowed by orders to dig with caution; the clang of a pick on a concealed rock could easily be heard by the watch aboard the *Lively*. But as soon as the magnitude of the job became apparent these orders were abandoned. Half the men worked for an hour while the other half stood guard. Prescott insisted on this precaution although Gridley complained they would never be able to complete both the breastwork and the fort by morning. Prescott bluntly told him the breastwork would have to wait until the redoubt was completed. If they hoped to have these raw farmers make a stand against the finest soldiers in the world they must have some cover from which to fight. With this Israel Putnam was in agreement. "Americans are much afraid of their legs," he had roared at the hesitant commander in chief,

Artemas Ward, in the council of war. "Cover them and they will fight forever."

Around and around the oblong hole in the earth Prescott prowled, stopping now to exchange a word with his nephew Benjamin who was a sergeant in his regiment, now to prod a slacker with an urgent phrase. Occasionally he threw aside his coat and hat and stepped into the hole with a shovel himself. Majors, captains, lieutenants followed his example, working side by side with their men.

"Dig men, dig," Prescott said again and again. "Dig for your lives."

He meant every word of it.

These Massachusetts men from Groton and Concord and Billerica and their Connecticut and New Hampshire cousins from Pomfret, Ashford and Hollis did not realize it, but with every swing of the pick, every heave of the shovel, they were creating a moment in history which would radically alter the next two centuries. Two years ago there was not a man among them who would have hesitated to drink a toast to King George III on his royal birthday. A dozen years ago when the Peace of Paris had sealed the doom of the French empire in the New World, they had all, in the words of John Adams, "gloried in the name of Englishmen." Now, like a river running in flood, a jumble of events and men had swept them to the crest of this hill where in tomorrow's sunlight many of them would stain with their blood the earth they now dug, and mingling with it would be the blood of other men who also called themselves Englishmen. In the roar of cannon and muskets would die the last faint hope that war—and a hundred years of hatred and suspicion—could be avoided.

Inevitably the event which turns history in a new direction becomes shrouded in myth and rumor. It becomes the tool of propagandists on both sides. The hatred and grief and bitter pride which come later are read back into the first momentous day. Nowhere is this mournful truth more evident than in that pivotal struggle which history calls the Battle of Bunker Hill. The very name was changed, in part for propaganda purposes. The real story of what happened has been lost in a galaxy of myths. There is the myth of the outnumbered American sharpshooter, and the myth of the well-equipped but robot British regular. There is the myth of George III's arrogance and American hatred for royal tyranny. There is the myth of British military stupidity, and innate American martial genius.

As bad as the myths is the simplification. Bunker Hill lives, if it exists at all in the average memory, as a sort of semicomic charade in which a nameless little band of Americans on a hilltop shoot at a line of advancing British, knock some down and march away, gaily playing "Yankee Doodle." A day so important deserves more than this parody of the truth, in every citizen's memory. The men who fought, British and American, deserve more than the anonymity into which they have lapsed in most history books. In fact, it is no exaggeration to say that only by understanding the minds and emotions of the men who fought can the whole truth about Bunker Hill be grasped.

The toiling Americans on their nameless hill (which, for clarity, we shall now begin to call Breed's Hill—the name it later received) and the brilliant major general across the harbor in Boston are by no means the only actors in the drama which will reach a bloody climax tomorrow. There are many other men and women we must meet, before the guns begin to fire. Some of them will neither fight nor die. But as suffering spectators, they add their own important commentary to the day's greatness. Others, who will fight, and perhaps die, we must meet individually, as baffled or angry, fearful or hesitant participants, few of whom realized how profoundly they were creating history with their sweat and blood.

2

CHIEF among these participants was a portly, courteous man who paced an oak-lined study in Province House, the official residence of the Governor of Massachusetts, while William Prescott and Israel Putnam argued on Breed's Hill. In many ways fifty-four-year-old Thomas Gage could lay more claim to American affection than William Howe. He lacked the younger general's military brilliance, but Gage had spent eighteen years of his life in the New World. Among his many American friends he could count George Washington. Gage and the Virginian were among the few who fought well in General William Braddock's disastrous defeat in the western wilderness near Fort Duquesne in 1755; and for some years afterward they maintained a friendly correspondence. Gage had fought beside Israel Putnam in another campaign.

Thomas Gage had also been one of the few British officers who, like Lord George Howe, decided to alter the army's tactical thinking. In this direction Gage had gone even further than Howe, recruiting and commanding the first colonial regiment in the British army—the Royal Americans. It was no small feat for a British officer to recruit provincials; Americans had a profound distaste for regular army discipline. Not long after he became colonel of this light-armed battalion, trained for wilderness fighting, Gage married beautiful, headstrong Margaret Kemble, daughter of one of the most prominent families in New Jersey. All but one of their eleven children were born in America. Through his wife's relatives, the Schuylers, the Van Cortlandts and the De Lanceys, Gage had a wider circle of American friends than any British soldier on the continent. He even became an American landowner, purchasing 19,000 acres in New York's Oneida County.

For the last nine years of his service in America, Gage had been commander in chief of His Majesty's forces in the New World. They were, scarcely without exception, years of turbulent dispute between the colonies and mother country. Twice the British Parliament had tried to tax its thirteen dependencies along the Atlantic seaboard, and twice a wave of riots and boycotts against English goods had forced the ministers of King George III to back down with humiliating haste. Throughout the turmoil Gage had been the man in the middle. With his soldiers he could have tried to ram the taxes down American throats by arresting rioters, cowing the critics of Parliament into silence. But he had never failed to act with notable restraint and a strict regard for American rights under the English constitution. No better description of his achievement exists than the words of a testimonial from the mayor and council of New York, given to Gage when he left for England in 1773. The official dinner at which it was presented included George Washington among the many distinguished guests.

"Yours was the arduous task to command an army in that critical hour when the several branches of the empire, rent by unnatural discords, seemed to be upon the point of dissolving the union to which they owe their safety, their glory and their happiness: and yours was the honor to direct in that storm, not only with wisdom and firmness, but with that magnanimity and prudence so happily suited to the exigencies of the time: and with that affectionate tenderness to the true interest of the public which never fails to add more lustre to the character of a general than can be derived from all the splendid exploits of arms."

At the same time, throughout his long tenure as commander in chief, Gage had watched with growing concern the deterioration of British authority in America. We must remember that Thomas Gage was distinctly a member of Britain's ruling class. His father had been the first Viscount Gage of Castle Island, Baron Gage of Castlebar in the Irish peerage, and for thirty-three years a member of Parliament and a man about town. The general's elder brother, William, had inherited the paternal titles and parliamentary seat and had for many years served as Paymaster of the Forces, one of the most lucrative and influential patronage posts in the government.

For all his natural and acquired friendship, Gage inevitably saw America with the eyes of a man for whom London was the center of the world, and Boston and New York provincial outposts. He did not like what he saw happening to British prestige in these outposts. As early as 1770, he was denouncing the king's ministers for asserting Parliament's powers in grandiose terms and taking no effective steps to enforce them. "You have yielded by bits," he wrote, "and in such a manner, as it appeared that everything was constrained and extorted from you: such a conduct could not fail to encourage people here to commit every extravagance to gain their ends, and one demand has risen upon another."

In another letter he wrote: "Nothing will avail . . . but a very considerable force and that force empowered to act. If that is done at once . . . matters may still end without bloodshed. But if you . . . make a show only of resistance, it is the opinion of many you will draw them into arms. Better therefore to do nothing."

There were few men in the empire who had the knowledge or the courage to criticize British policy toward America so acutely. But Gage was a soldier, not a politician, and his advice was ignored. Parliament continued to assert its powers and wring its hands when Americans balked. Americans, on their side, were slowly driven toward total exasperation. It soon became evident to more than a few intelligent observers that it would not take a large spark to cause an explosion.

The spark had been struck while Thomas Gage was home in England on leave. If the Americans set the blaze, Britain supplied the powder and the fuse. In their ignominious retreat from their last attempt to raise money in the colonies, Parliament had repealed all its taxes except one: a three-cent tax on tea. This, George III and those who agreed with his policy of "firmness" had insisted on keeping to "maintain the right." The colonists, who had wrecked the earlier taxation schemes by refusing to buy any goods with a parliamentary tax on them, simply continued to refuse to drink English tea. This did not mean they stopped drinking tea, a beverage they, like all good Englishmen, profoundly loved. They simply smuggled what they wanted from Holland. Tea piled up in English warehouses to the tune of some 18 million pounds.

One of the heaviest losers in this clash of wills was the East India Company, which had, since Queen Elizabeth's days, a gigantic monopoly on the commerce of the Indian and Pacific Oceans, between the Cape of Good Hope and the Straits of Magellan. In 1773 the company came before Parliament and announced it was on the brink of bankruptcy. The company's advocates laid much of the blame for their financial condition on the American boycott against their tea, long one of their most profitable imports from the East. The truth was much more complex. The company was a tangle of corruption and mismanagement;

between 1732 and 1772 their gross profits had averaged 120 per cent of their costs. But aside from the fortunes the company executives managed to accumulate, the overhead also included staggering sums for bribes to men in high political office. More than one of these well-greased palms belonged to members of Parliament. Others in both Lords and Commons owned East India stock, which was rapidly sinking out of sight. The government's own financial credit was also entangled; the crown owed the East India company £3,200,-000, which it was in no position to pay.

The answer to this impending disaster, Parliament decided, lay not in reform of the East India Company, but in unloading the company's tea on the American colonies. Without too much thought, Lords and Commons hurriedly arranged to give the company the right to sell the mountains of tea in its London warehouses at a cut rate—in America only. To push the operation in a profitable direction, they eliminated the export duty ordinarily paid in England. Thus the company was enabled to sell its tea in America at half the price the colonists were paying for tea smuggled from Holland. The three-cent colonial import duty, however, Parliament retained—just to remind the Americans that they still had "the right."

Thus was the gunpowder provided by Parliament. The East India Company, with perfect consistency, now proceeded to insert the fuse by bungling its end of the job as totally as it had botched British diplomacy in India. They parceled out the licenses to sell their cut-rate tea not to established tea merchants, but to political favorites such as the two nephews of Massachusetts Governor Thomas Hutchinson. Every shade of opinion, from the most conservative businessman in New York to the wildest radical in Boston, promptly united against the measure. If Parliament could thus disrupt an established branch of business, what was to prevent them from doing the same thing to merchants dealing in sugar, cotton, lead or wool?

When the first shipments of parliamentary tea arrived in America, the colonists were waiting. In New York some of the cases were smashed open and dumped into the ship's hold; in Charleston, South Carolina, it was stored in a dark cellar of the customs warehouse, and an angry mob made sure it never came out. It soon spoiled. In Philadelphia, the captain of the ship wisely decided not to try unloading.

But Boston, which had for over a decade led the continent in defiance, arranged for a more total rejection. About eight o'clock on Thursday night, December 16, 1773, a war whoop was heard in the streets and several hundred men, thinly disguised as Mohawk Indians, thundered down to Griffin's Wharf, where three ships carrying tea were waiting to unload. While thousands stood on the shore and watched, the pseudo-redskins hacked open 342 chests of tea and dumped them into Boston Harbor.

Nothing could have been devised to irritate the sensibilities of King and Parliament more totally. The issue, as they saw it, was considerably larger than the three-cent tax on tea. The tax was a symbol of Parliament's authority in America—authority which the Americans had been defying for a decade with partisan slogans such as "No taxation without representation." Half the cities in England itself had no representatives in Parliament, and they did not think their liberties as Englishmen were abrogated. Moreover, England had just won a world war against France and Spain, which made her incontestably the most powerful empire on the globe; what did the word empire mean, if some malcontents in a distant corner could perversely ignore its laws? Five years ago the crown had had to send troops into Boston to protect the lives of public officials. Now the Boston Tea Party—a unique combination of defiance and destruction of private property, a crime which the eighteenth century often punished by death—was too much. King and Parliament exploded. Boston must be taught a lesson once and for all, or Great Britain must give up the last vestige of authority in America.

From the American point of view, the issue was also much larger than the tax on tea. Their resistance was part of their contention that Parliament did not have the right to arrange the business lives of Americans for the profit and pleasure of men in London. As the Bostonians saw it, their resistance to the Tea Act was not essentially different from their earlier imbroglios—it was only slightly more strenuous. The Americans sat back, confident that when British businessmen saw the turmoil the Tea Act was causing, they would put pressure on Parliament to restore the status quo and that august body would promptly back down as it had done before. British businessmen in 1775 were not much different from businessmen today; they had little or no interest in abstract rights, and when politicians attempting to exercise these rights interfered with the business of business—profits —the politicians heard from their merchant constituents in a tone and content similar to this message from an irate Yorkshireman, sent in an earlier crisis:

"Our trade is hurt; what the devil have you been doing? For our part we don't pretend to understand your politics and American matters, but our trade is hurt; pray remedy it, and a plague on you if you won't."

Unfortunately the most influential man in England was not so interested in running the nation in a businesslike way. George III was intensely concerned with principles and ideals, and he had a tendency to see himself as the only man in the realm who took these matters seriously. In the King's view, the Boston Tea Party had violated the fundamental principles of the British constitution, and His Majesty was emphatically in favor of doing something about it. The trouble was, he did not know much about these peculiar Americans who kept sending him messages protesting their loyalty while breaking his laws. Inevitably, as it pondered the problem, the royal mind turned to General Thomas Gage. Here was a man who ought to know Americans better than any other responsible official in the government. On February 4, 1774, Gage was summoned to an interview which was to have momentous consequences in his own and many other lives. He had been for firm measures. Now was certainly not the time to change his thinking. Americans, he told the King, "would be lyons, whilst we are lambs." If Government took "the resolute part," they would be "very meek." The earnest monarch asked him how many troops would be needed to keep order in Boston while the tea party warriors and the leaders of the rebellious "faction" were punished. Gage said four regiments—about 1,500 men— would be ample. Gage also said he was "ready to return at a day's notice" if the King needed him in America.

These words carried Thomas Gage a giant step closer to becoming a general sent on a diplomat's mission—a mission doomed, from the moment it was conceived, to lead Gage to his harassed midnight pacing in Province House and his American friends to their grim work on the summit of Breed's Hill. In a letter to his chief minister, Lord North, George III declared the general's language "was very consonant to his character of an honest determined man." Unfortunately for Gage and the cause of peace, he had spoken before Parliament had made up its mind exactly how to punish Boston. It was a thorny problem. Sending a royal commission to root out the tea party offenders was a waste of time. Last year the citizens of Providence, Rhode Island, had turned on the captain and crew of the revenue cutter *Gaspee,* which was wreaking havoc on their smuggling operations, and had burned it to the water. Royal commissioners had been sent by the angry home government, and they had cooled their heels in Providence for months without turning up so much as a single witness to the affair, although eight boatloads of men participated in the attack.

Then someone suggested punishing the town of Boston as a whole. There were precedents in British law to support the idea. The ministry snatched it up and, having done nothing for too long, now proceeded to do too much too quickly. The Boston Port Bill sailed through both houses of Parliament by huge majorities. As of June 1, the harbor would be closed for commerce and the capital of the colony would be shifted to Salem, until the East India Company was reimbursed for their tea and the Royal Governor of Massachusetts was satisfied that law and order were restored in Boston.

Not satisfied with this exorbitant punishment, which scarcely fitted the crime, the ministry proceeded to remodel the government of Massachusetts. No longer was the Governor's Council, the upper house of the colony's legislature, to be selected by vote of the lower house. The council would be appointed by the Governor. The salaries of the judges, sheriffs and other law-enforcement officials would no longer be in colonial control—they would be paid by the crown. To protect government servants from supposedly prejudiced local juries, the Governor was given the power to transfer any soldier, revenue officer or other official accused of a crime to England, or another colony, for trial. Troops were to be quartered not only in empty warehouses and abandoned buildings, as in the past, but in inhabited dwellings, at the expense of the colony. Finally, all town meetings, the heart and soul of Massachusetts democracy, were unconditionally barred, without official permission.

Each of these measures had been discussed at various times by Englishmen interested in reforming the patchwork system of colonial government. Gage himself had suggested appointing royal councilors and paying official salaries through the crown almost ten years before. Massachusetts, Connecticut and Rhode Island were particularly criticized because their systems were too democratic for prevailing British tastes. In those days, a certain amount of democracy was considered a good idea, but too much supposedly opened the state to control by the mob. Events in Boston had amply confirmed this opinion. But to ram through these governmental reform measures in an atmosphere of rage and punishment was the worst possible diplomacy. The first victim of this bad judgment was Thomas Gage.

The King liked Gage. Lord North, the chief minister, made a point of liking what the King liked. It was almost inevitable that North should suggest Gage as the best man to restore order in Massachusetts. At the same time North quailed at sending a general and four regiments without some kind of window dressing to soften the government's intentions. It smacked too much of an act of war—the one thing North wished to avoid. The solution was supplied by Thomas Hutchinson, then Governor of Massachusetts. He asked for a leave of absence from the harassments of his job, and North readily persuaded the King to appoint Gage in his place. It was a neat maneuver. Massachusetts would have to welcome Governor Gage in peace or embark on open rebellion. The Governor could make sure the Coercive Acts were strictly executed, and if he ran into trouble, he could readily call on his alter ego, General Gage, for help.

Gage could hardly back out of the job, after his pledge to the King. But he could not muster any enthusiasm for the assignment. As a moderate man who knew Americans well, he must have realized the government had gone too far in the direction of firmness. In fact, he probably suspected before he went that the ministry's firmness was largely vocal, as it had been in the past. The Boston Port Bill punished that obstreperous town alone; the other acts took on the whole province of Massachusetts. Gage had said he would keep order among Boston's 18,000 inhabitants with four regiments; but he would not dream of taking on the 400,-000 citizens of Massachusetts with such a puny force. Obviously the government labored under some basic misconceptions about the situation in Massachusetts.

Foremost was the idea that the trouble was limited to the city of Boston. Another conviction, bolstered by some experience, was the probability that Boston would not fight back. In 1768, Gage, as commander in chief, had been ordered by the government to send two regiments to Boston, and there had been some talk of armed resistance. But Gage made sure the troops were accompanied by a formidable armada. One ship of the line and seven frigates formed up in battle order within musket shot of the shore, and the troops landed without so much as a shout of protest.

But by far the greatest misconception, shared by Gage himself and almost everyone else in England, was the belief that the trouble in Boston was the work of a "faction." William Howe had defended his decision to go to America with this argument. "One word for America," he wrote his Nottingham critics. "You are deceived if you suppose there are not many loyal and peaceable subjects in that country. I may safely assert that the insurgents are very few, in comparison to the whole." The common people were, in the prevailing view of the times, open to the appeal of a skilled demagogue. They had no opinions of their own, and the only problem they presented was one of control. The faction, aided by the mob, had frightened the majority of sober, loyal, responsible citizens into silence. Arrest, bribe or otherwise silence the demagogues, control the mob, and the good people would resume control of the colony, the passions of the multitudes would cool and peace would rapidly ensue.

It was, from a distance of 3,000 miles, a thoroughly logical theory. But Thomas Gage must have had some qualms about its validity on May 17, 1774, the day he reached Boston. Not one of his troopships had arrived; he was armed with nothing but the act of Parliament closing the port. Instead of a howling mob, he was met at the dock by an honor guard of well-drilled, smartly uniformed Boston cadets, led by no less than John Hancock. Church bells rang, guns boomed in welcoming salute and in spite of windy rainy weather the citizens of Boston dutifully lined the streets to welcome the new Governor. There was not a breath of disturbance, although Boston already had the grim news of the Port Bill.

That evening a banquet was served in Gage's honor in Faneuil Hall. Samuel Adams, John Adams, John Hancock, Benjamin Church and every other leader of the "faction" was there, and the toasts to George III were numerous. Only once, when Gage offered a toast to the retiring governor, Thomas Hutchinson, was there a moment of embarrassment: the banqueters gave a long low hiss.

The next day Gage found out a little more about the tactics he was to face for the next year. Before dawn a silversmith named Paul Revere was on his big gray horse, pounding south to New York and Philadelphia with Massachusetts' appeal for the support of her sister colonies. Before noon a Boston town meeting was in solemn session, presided over by Samuel Adams. Several prominent citizens rose and suggested a collection to pay for the tea; they even offered to start the ball rolling with substantial contributions of their own. They were brushed aside—politely and firmly. The meeting spent its time deliberating how to ease the blow of the Port Bill on the people whom it would throw out of work.

As the troops arrived and set up their tents on the common, Gage waited hopefully for more law-abiding citizens to come forward. He assured everyone who came to him for advice that no mob would tar and feather any friend of government while he was in Boston. But the results were depressing. Only 130 citizens volunteered to pay for the tea. It was worth £18,000, an astronomical sum in colonial Boston. A man with an income of £45 a year was considered wealthy. Obviously there was no hope of achieving this quick solution to the quarrel. Gage also tried to drum up support in the town meetings to abolish the Boston Committee of Correspondence, that highly effective propaganda and agitation machine. Once more the friends of government got nowhere.

If Boston refused to back down an inch, perhaps Massachusetts as a whole would prove more reasonable. Gage called a meeting of the legislature for June 5 and found that body, which included representatives from every county in the province, equally uncooperative. They refused even to consider paying for the tea.

Meanwhile the Boston Port Bill had gone into effect at noon on June 1. Thanks to Paul Revere and his hard-riding friends, the entire continent observed the day in mourning. In Boston all business came to a standstill, bells tolled and the people adjourned to their churches where they prayed for deliverance and heard fiery exhortations from their ministers, which Gage and the friends of government found shocking. "Pulpits," wrote one indignant loyalist, "were converted into gutters of Sedition." Virginia declared a day of fast, and Philadelphians shuttered their houses and muffled their church bells.

Even more alarming to Gage was the determination other colonies displayed to support Boston in her hour of need. "Don't pay for an ounce of the damned tea," wrote one Christopher Gadsen of South Carolina, as he forwarded 200 barrels of rice, with a promise of 800 more to follow. Wilmington, North Carolina, raised £2,000 within a week, and a ship and crew volunteered to carry the money to Boston free of charge. Israel Putnam drove 100 sheep almost as many miles from his Connecticut farm; his neighbors sent over 500 more. Marblehead sent 224 quintals of "good eating fish, one and three quarters casks of olive oil, and thirty-nine pounds, five shillings and sixpence in cash." Salem, long Boston's rival at sea, vowed it would take no advantage of Boston's situation, offered to load and unload Boston cargo and declared Boston merchants could enjoy the use of their wharves and warehouses free. Even newly conquered French Quebec sent 1,000 bushels of wheat.

On June 17, 1774—exactly one year to the day before Bunker Hill—the Massachusetts legislature voted 120 to 12 to send delegates to a continental congress in Philadelphia. The same day a Boston Town meeting eliminated, finally and completely, the idea of paying for the tea and voted to set up common tables to feed the poor.

Gage found some consolation in a prompt pledge of loyalty from the Episcopal Church. But they were a minority in a sea of Congregationalism. Far more encouraging was a letter which he received on June 21 signed by all the lawyers and judges of the Worcester County courts with one exception. These gentlemen, led by Colonel Timothy Ruggles, denounced "discord and confusion" and promised to do everything in their power "to support the execution of the laws and render your Excellency's administration prosperous."

Here at last was some solid evidence that the infection of disloyalty could yet be confined to Boston. Worcester was 40 miles from Boston—a full day's journey in 1774—hence less likely to be influenced by the radical politics of the capital . . . so Gage reasoned. On July 5 he was optimistic enough to write his superior, Lord Dartmouth, Secretary for the Colonies: "There is now an open opposition to the faction carried on with a warmth and spirit unknown before, which it is highly proper to cherish, and support by every means; and I hope it will not be long before it produces very salutary effects."

3

UP ON Breed's Hill the total refutation of Gage's summer-time optimism was making steady progress. Already Prescott's farmers had dug out the center of the American fort and had begun the laborious process of packing the walls with the fascines and dirt-filled hogsheads. Nothing more than a geographical survey of these shirt-sleeved toilers was needed to see how totally wrong Thomas Gage and his government had been when they assumed that Boston alone was the seat of rebellion and the rest of New England was either loyal or at least indifferent. Most obvious, of course, was the presence of the Connecticut and New Hampshire men. But even among the Massachusetts contingent not a single man in this midnight expedition was from Boston. On the contrary, most were from towns and counties as far away as Worcester, and even farther. Prescott's Pepperell and Groton men lived on the New Hampshire border. The Frye regiment had recruits from a dozen small towns in the large northern county of Essex—Andover, Haverhill, Tewksbury—all semi-isolated little democracies who normally looked to their own seaports, Salem, Gloucester, Newburyport, rather than Boston for leadership. The Bridge

regiment came from the web of towns around Concord—
closer to Boston—but by no means a suburb in an age when
roads were bad and a farm supplied a man with almost all
the necessities of life.

More significant than geography were the words of the
tall, tough colonel now in command of these furiously toiling
men. On July 4, 1774, the day before Gage wrote optimisti-
cally to London, Prescott had sent forty bushels of grain to
Boston with a letter urging the Bostonians "to stand fast in
the common cause." A few weeks later he sent another letter,
which tells more about the spirit of resistance throughout
Massachusetts than pages of statistics.

> "Be not dismayed nor disheartened, in this great day of
> trials. We heartily sympathize with you and are always ready
> to do all in our power for your support, comfort and relief;
> knowing that Providence has placed you where you must
> stand the first shock. We consider that we are all embarked
> in one bottom and must sink or swim together. We think if
> we submit to these regulations all is gone. Our forefathers
> passed the vast Atlantic, spent their blood and treasure, that
> they might enjoy their liberties, both civil and religious, and
> transmit them to their posterity. Their children have waded
> through seas of difficulty, to leave us free and happy in the
> enjoyment of English privileges. Now, if we should give them
> up, can our children rise up and call us blessed? Is not a
> glorious death in defence of our liberties better than a short,
> infamous life, and our memory to be had in detestation to
> the latest posterity? Let us all be of one heart, and stand
> fast in the liberties wherewith Christ has made us free."

The "salutary effects" of opposing the so-called Boston
faction all but exploded in Gage's face the moment he attempted to extend his authority to the entire colony of Massachusetts. The turning point came less than a month after
the high tide of the Governor's optimism, when the acts of
Parliament altering the colony's charter arrived on August

6, 1774. On August 9 a county convention gathered in
Worcester and drew up a set of resolutions declaring that
the people of Massachusetts owed no obedience to the English Parliament, that the charter of the province was the
basis of their allegiance to the King and that any attempt to
vacate the charter would have a "tendency to dissolve the
union between Great Britain and the province."

If this was hardly the language of loyalty, it was still only
language and could be regarded as nine-tenths bluster. On
September 1, 1774 Gage found out the colonists were prepared to act as tough as they talked. Part of the trouble
came from his eagerness to "spirit up the friends of government." In attempting to make something out of the almost nonexistent loyalist minority, he spent a great deal of
time listening to their advice. Unfortunately, the loyalists,
already harassed by seeing friends tarred and feathered and
other friends chased out of their homes in the middle of
the night by patriot mobs, were not inclined toward moder-
ation. So it came to pass that Gage received a letter from
William Brattle, the major general of the Massachusetts
militia and an aged but ardent loyalist. General Brattle informed the Governor that the townships had for some weeks
been removing their gunpowder from the colony powder
house in Charlestown and storing it at home. There was,
Brattle reminded Gage, not a single gunpowder factory in
all Massachusetts. One way of cutting off an armed revolution before it occurred was, obviously, to keep all the powder
in government hands. Gage decided this was a very sound
suggestion.

Shortly before dawn on September 1, the Governor General sent 260 men across the harbor to Charlestown. They
were back before breakfast with 250 half barrels of powder
—all that was left in the magazine. At the same time another detachment made a quick trip to Cambridge and returned safely with several cannon which that township had

recently purchased. What happened next gave Gage the fright of his life.

The story of the seizures spread through Massachusetts and Connecticut like a tornado, swelling every mile. Within two days 20,000 armed men were on the march for Cambridge, exchanging wild tales of Boston in flames, British ships bombarding from the harbor, the town of Cambridge looted, raped and ruined by a brigade of redcoats. This spontaneous army dispersed only after the American leaders assured them that no injury had been done and Gage had acted within his rights as Governor. Israel Putnam, who had alarmed the entire province of Connecticut, led his men home with the Cromwellian advice to Massachusetts to "keep a strict guard over the remainder of your powder; for that must be the great means, under God, of the salvation of our country."

So shaken was Gage by the "powder alarm" that he was driven to what seems, at this distance, an almost pitifully desperate act. A day later, as he was walking up the main street to have dinner with Brigadier General Robert Pigot, Gage let Brattle's letter fall out of his pocket. An American promptly found it and took it to the resistance leaders. That night, a mob visited Brattle in his house and the old man made it to Boston in his nightshirt only one jump ahead of them. Even Boston, patrolled by British troops, was not safe enough for him, and he did not stop until he was behind the walls of Castle William, three miles out in the harbor. More than anything else he did in Boston, this feeble gesture toward reconciliation showed the impossibility of Gage's position. If he did not take the advice of the loyalists, he would never hope to "spirit them into opposition." If he took their advice, he was, obviously, alienating himself from the vast majority of the colony. Revealing the letter and the source of the decision to seize the powder did nothing to boost Gage's standing with the Americans who still hoped for a peaceful settlement. It only confirmed their dark suspicion that the loyalists had the Governor completely bamboozled.

If Gage still had illusions about confining the infection to Boston the last shred must have vanished when the judges tried to open the province's courts on September 6. Few changes had been made in the judiciary. Gage had taken pains to leave the same men who had served in previous years as elected officials. But now they were royal appointees and this made all the difference to the Americans. Again, it was supposedly uncontaminated Worcester that led the way. Timothy Ruggles, the judge of the Court of Common Pleas who had been the guiding spirit behind the loyalty letter in June, appeared in Boston and frankly told Gage it would be worth his life to appear in Worcester to open the court. Two other judges with more courage put in an appearance. They found 6,000 armed men lining the streets of Worcester. Through these silent ranks the justices, the court officers, the lawyers and every other person who had signed the loyalty letter to Gage were forced to march as penitents, stopping every few feet to read aloud their recantations. On the courthouse steps the justices signed a pledge to refrain from "all judicial proceedings . . . on account of the unconstitutional act of the British Parliament, respecting the administration of justice in this province."

At this time Worcester also produced a canny suggestion which swiftly changed the military balance of power in the province. At least half the colonels of Massachusetts' thirty militia regiments were loyal. The Worcester County Convention suggested that all militia officers resign the commissions they had held in the name of the crown. The local officers promptly took the hint; they had no desire to be marched through the "ranges of the people." The Worcester County Convention then reorganized their militia into seven regiments, with the towns electing company officers who in turn would elect the field officers. They also directed the officers to enlist a third of their men to be ready to act at "a minute's notice." Thus the minutemen came into existence, not in Boston, that supposed seat of rebellious faction, but in Worcester, forty miles inland.

The other counties snapped up the idea of bringing democracy into the militia, and in a few weeks every militia officer in the province was forced to resign and new officers were elected on the Worcester model. None were loyalists.

The last straw, as far as Gage was concerned, was the action of the legislature. Gage had summoned them to meet at Salem on October 5. He then issued a proclamation countermanding his summons because of "the extraordinary resolves which have been passed in many of the counties." The legislature ignored him, met anyway and resolved themselves into a "Provincial Congress, to be joined by such other persons as have been or shall be chosen for that purpose to take into consideration the dangerous and alarming situation of public affairs in this province, and to consult and determine on such measures as they shall judge will tend to promote . . . the peace, welfare and prosperity of this province."

In three months, Thomas Gage found every supposition on which his mission had been based utterly demolished. There was no majority of citizens to support the government in the name of Parliament. There was no unruly mob who could be sent flying in a single bayonet charge. Without firing a shot, or molesting a single British soldier, the Americans had effectively deprived him of the power to govern the province of Massachusetts. The faction reigned supreme —because they were not a faction. They were the majority of the people.

Even before the legislature became the Provincial Congress and took over the government of Massachusetts outside Boston, Gage saw clearly that he and the home government had completely misjudged the situation. On September 25 he wrote to his friend, Lord Barrington, the secretary of the army, that the Intolerable Acts had been taken as a challenge not only in Massachusetts but in all America. A week later he told this same Lord that Britain could not have her own way with America except by conquering, "and to do that effectually, to prevent further bickerings, you should have an army near twenty thousand strong composed of regulars, a large body of good irregulars such as the German Huntsmen, Canadians, etc. and three or four regiments of light horse, these exclusive of a good and sufficient field artillery."

On November 2 he put his advice in even stronger language: "If you resist and not yield [to the American demands] that resistance should be effectual at the beginning. If you think ten thousand men sufficient, send twenty, if one million is thought enough, give two; you will save both blood and treasure in the end. A large force will terrify, and engage many to join you, a middling one will encourage resistance, and gain no friends. The crisis is indeed an alarming one and Britain had never more need of wisdom, firmness and union than at this juncture."

Unfortunately it was a juncture in history at which Britain lacked each of these qualities to an incredible degree. The Lords in Parliament, the Gentlemen in Commons, the members of the Cabinet and George III himself were utterly incapable of uniting on a coherent, consistent policy about America. The King was for strong measures but his chief minister, Lord North, desperately hoped for reconciliation. Lord Dartmouth, the secretary of state for the colonies, was a gentle, earnest Methodist who had donated generously to help found a college in New Hampshire, which that province had gratefully named after him; he looked on the drift toward war with horror. But he was weak and North was worse than weak, he was a rationalizer who voted with the majority, especially when that majority included George III.

The men who made the most noise in the cabinet and in Parliament were Lords who had never seen America but were convinced, on the basis of past performances, that the colonists could not fight. Beyond doubt, Americans had sometimes behaved deplorably in earlier wars, deserting by the score and displaying unbelievable ineptitude at military organization and efficiency. The economic opportunities of the New World and the American tradition of personal independence combined to make army life, with its harsh discipline and low pay, singularly unappealing to the average colonial. Only the most shiftless and maladjusted succumbed to the recruiters. But when the emergency was great, and their best men responded to the call to arms, the Americans had fought well enough. The British war party conveniently forgot these successes.

Loudest of all the American critics was the Earl of Sandwich, First Lord of the Admiralty. He predicted that the Americans would "never meet our people in fair conflict." Only when firing from behind rocks and trees or when raised to a frenzy by their "poisonous rum" would they offer any semblance of battle. "Have we not conquered the French and the Spaniards," he asked Parliament one day, "and shall we be afraid of a body of fanatics in New England, who will bluster and swell when danger is at a distance, but when it comes near, will like all other mobs throw down their arms and run away?" He compared the Americans to the Bengalese, "also fanatics, but it is well known that a few of our troops will rout the greatest number of them." Completely carried away by his own twisted rhetoric, he declared: "Were I in General Gage's situation and heard that 20,000 New England men were coming against me, I should wish that they were rather thirty or forty thousand." The more rebels, reasoned His Lordship, the greater the stampede.

Viscount Townshend, one of Wolfe's lieutenants before

Quebec, ironically lamented the fate of the army or navy officer sent to America, since he would have no chance to earn a bit of glory by honest fighting, but "would have nothing to do but burn, sink and destroy." Lord Rigby declared he "should disdain to treat with America. It was romantic to think they would fight. It was an idea thrown out to frighten women and children. There was more military prowess in a militia drummer." Colonel James Grant, who had fought in America, testified in the House of Commons that "they would never dare face an English army, and did not possess any of the qualifications necessary to make a good soldier." Another loud talker, General Alured Clarke, vowed that he could march from one end of America to the other with four regiments and geld every male without meeting serious opposition.

Most bloodthirsty was Lord George Germain, who saw in the impending conflict a chance to regain the reputation he had lost in the Seven Years' War. For refusing to advance at the bloody battle of Minden in 1759 he had been expelled from the Privy Council, declared unfit to serve the King and branded a coward. For the next sixteen years he had devoted himself to worming his way back into royal favor and had largely succeeded. He had recently regained his seat in the Privy Council and now began pushing for Dartmouth's job as colonial secretary. "Roman severity" was his formula for dealing with the Americans. If they fought back he recommended stripping them of every semblance of representative government and turning the whole continent over to a military legate who would run it from Rhode Island; this, the most democratic of all the colonies, Germain would abolish completely and turn into an army base. When he was not outlining such monstrous schemes, Germain was with Sandwich, declaiming in Parliament on colonial cowardice, moral depravity and boorishness.

Along with these misconceptions there was a fundamental

disagreement on how to cope with the problems of military strategy in an empire suddenly become global. Lord Barrington, the secretary of the army, was determined to maintain a strong force in England to defend the homeland against the French, who were making menacing noises. He argued for a sea war which would blockade the American coast and reduce the colonies to their knees by wiping out the overseas trade on which their prosperity depended. Sandwich, as Admiralty Lord, took a completely opposite position. Americans must be taught a lesson, he maintained; they must acknowledge, with blood if necessary, the military superiority of the mother country. Only a resounding defeat on land could accomplish this necessary chastisement. He was also anxious about reports that the French were building a substantial new fleet, and was determined to keep the bulk of his navy in home waters. Sandwich had more personal influence with the King. The sea blockade was never seriously considered.

Instead, Gage was left to shift for himself in Boston with barely 1,500 men to subdue a province which could, if pressed to an extreme effort, put 100,000 men in the field. Three thousand miles from home, dependent for orders on men who did not have an answer to the problem, all he could do was play desperately for time and pursue a totally negative policy of not starting a war.

Gage had been sent out as a combination soldier-diplomat. The very nature of his job, and the nature of the man chosen for it, was a symptom of the basic indecision afflicting the home government. Somehow, Lord North and his friends hoped they would or could simultaneously frighten the Americans and negotiate with them. It was inevitable that Gage's wisdom in the situation should be more military than diplomatic. On September 2, the day after the powder alarm, he began fortifying the approaches to Boston. To the colonists it was an ominous move. To Gage it was a simple matter of self-preservation. In 1774, Boston was more island than peninsula. Its only link to the mainland was the strip of earth called the Neck. Any attack from provincial Massachusetts would have to come over this narrow passage, and Gage was determined to discourage all hope of success. Various committees headed by leaders of the opposition came to Gage and warned him that it was a warlike gesture. They insisted they did not have the slightest intention of attacking British troops. Military preparations in the countryside were purely defensive. Gage received these committees with typical courtesy and assured them that he, in turn, had no intention of attacking Americans. His fortifications were purely defensive and were not planned to cut Boston off from the rest of Massachusetts.

About this time, Gage abandoned the four-regiment theory and sent urgent messages to New York, Quebec and elsewhere for every available soldier. There were not many available. Two regiments, the Tenth and the Fifty-second, came from Quebec, and two more, the Eighteenth and the Forty-seventh from New York. Two companies of the Sixty-fifth were scrounged from Newfoundland, and 400 marines headed by Major John Pitcairn came ashore from the warships *Asia* and *Boyne*. The marines were ordered by the cabinet—the only gesture of material support Gage was to receive for the next five months. The other troops he gathered on his own initiative.

Gage all but stripped the continent of soldiers to reinforce Boston. He left only two companies in New York, a regiment in Quebec and a handful of companies in forts scattered from Florida to the Ohio country. These desperate measures brought his strength to 3,500 men.

As for cutting Boston off from Massachusetts, this was the least of Gage's worries. During the next five months, he must at times have wished he could cut the sullen city off and let it drift out to sea, while he took his chances against the rest of the province. The citizens of Boston, his own soldiers and even his wife conspired to make life difficult for the man whom George III called "the mild general." The Americans made elaborate and at first successful efforts to persuade the enlisted men to desert. Another favorite sport was separating soldiers from their muskets. The Americans did a brisk business buying them from the underpaid privates who would then report them stolen. Sometimes it was easier, or cheaper, to get a man drunk and then relieve him of his gun. Everyone became adept at smuggling guns and ammunition past the guards at the Neck. The patriots even managed to dismantle four cannon belonging to the Boston Cadet Company and get them safely to Cambridge, where they were promptly christened the Adams after Samuel and John. Another group of gunrunners stripped a battery of cannon on the Charlestown shore, hid them in the town and carried them into the country one by one.

Gage made no attempt to molest the American weapons smugglers, even when he caught them with more than their share of the goods. One doughty farmer was trundling his wagon of hay through Boston gate; the sentries thought it was a little odd to see hay coming out of Boston. Underneath it they found 19,000 musket balls, which they promptly confiscated. The outraged Yankee stormed back into Boston and went to Gage at Province House to protest the seizure of his "private property." That Gage tolerated such temerity was a tribute to his desperate desire "to avoid a bloody crisis as long as possible."

His own troops were not inclined to cooperate with him. Nor were Boston's tough ropewalkers, longshoremen and other laborers who had been thrown out of work by the Port Bill. "The liberty boys," as they were called, prowled the streets after dark, ready to pick a fight with British soldiers, officers included and in fact preferred. "Bloodyback," they would sneer as a group of soldiers walked by. Few

weeks passed without at least one incident which could
have erupted into a city-wide riot. One Samuel Dyer, whom
Gage had sent to England for trial on charges of luring
soldiers to desert, reappeared in town on October 18, a free
man for lack of evidence. He promptly got into a brawl with
two British officers and twice aimed a pistol at them, which
misfired. Dyer then resorted to the sword and wounded one
officer slightly. On November 12 another pair of officers did
battle with a party of Americans armed with spiked poles,
and one of the officers, a captain, was wounded. In another
brawl a few weeks later noses and ears were clipped off by
swinging swords.

Gage did everything in his power to restrain his men as
their irritation over these clashes mounted. Martial law had
not been declared, so the troops were legally answerable to
the laws of Boston. The harassed Governor General was determined that the strictest observance of British justice
would be the order of the day. He punished lawbreakers
among the troops far more severely than Boston handled its
own criminals and repeatedly reminded his men that they
were not police and had no right to interfere in the business
of Bostonians as long as they were not blatantly preparing
for war. One night a British sentry remained stiffly at attention while a second-story man coolly looted a nearby house
right in front of his eyes. When asked why he did nothing,
the soldier gravely replied that he was only obeying General
Gage's orders.

Gage also listened patiently to a long line of individual
citizens who claimed they had been injured or insulted by his
soldiers. The people of Boston were not shy about standing
up for their rights. One day General Frederic Haldimand,
Gage's second in command, was startled to find a delegation
of children on his doorstep. It seemed that Haldimand's orderly had thrown ashes on the hill outside the general's
quarters and ruined the local sleigh riding. They declared

that they and their fathers had coasted on the hill since the founding of the colony and demanded the damage be repaired immediately. Haldimand good-humoredly told his orderly to make the necessary repairs. When he reported the complaint to Gage, the Governor sighed and said mournfully, "It is impossible to *beat* the notion of liberty out of these people. It is rooted in 'em from their childhood."

Gage's concessions to the people of Boston did not endear him to his men. As professional soldiers they had little sympathy for the colonial cause and utter contempt for American military pretensions. Thirty-two-year-old Earl Percy, Colonel of the Fifth Regiment and Acting Brigadier General, wrote to his father on November 25, 1774: "The people here are the most designing, artful villains in the World. They have not the least idea of either Religion or morality." In another letter, he describes the Bostonians as braggarts who "talk much and do little . . . are in general made up of rashness and timidity. Quick and violent in their determinations, they are fearful in the execution of them, unless, indeed they are quite certain of meeting little opposition and then, like all other cowards, they are cruel and tyrannical. To hear them talk, you would imagine that they would attack us and demolish us every night. And yet whenever we appear they are frightened out of their wits." Percy's father, the powerful Duke of Northumberland, had strong sympathies for America. If the young Earl felt this way it was inevitable that the rest of the army would have a low opinion of Gage's policy of refusing to strike the first blow.

They began to dislike him even more than they disliked the Americans. In conversation they referred to him as "Tommy" and wrote countless letters home complaining about his supposed timidity and indecision. Several firebrands confided even more violent opinions to private diaries. Lieutenant John Barker of the Fourth Regiment wrote: "In compliance with the request of the selectmen

General Gage ordered that no soldier in the future should appear in the street with his sidearms. Is this not encouraging the inhabitants in their licentious and riotous disposition? Also orders are issued for the guard to seize all military men found engaged in any disturbance whether aggressors or not; and to secure them, till the matter is enquired into. By whom? By villains that would not censure one of their own vagrants even if he attempted the life of a soldier; whereas if a soldier errs in the least, who is more ready to accuse him than Tommy?"

As the months dragged by the conduct of the troops steadily deteriorated in spite of all Gage's efforts. On January 1 the same Lieutenant Barker informed his diary: "Nothing remarkable but the drunkenness among the soldiers which is now got to a very great pitch; owing to the cheapness of the liquor a man may get drunk for a copper or two." The officers did not set their men a very good example. They formed burlesque congresses and marched in mock procession in the streets absurdly dressed to represent the colonial leaders. On the Queen's birthday a banquet was held and from the balcony of a tavern toasts to Lord North and other members of Parliament were announced in stentorian tones while in the street a squad of soldiers fired salutes.

Another party of officers broke the windows of John Hancock's home and hacked down the railing in front of it with their swords. When a country bumpkin named John Ditson was caught trying to buy a gun from a soldier, the officers of the regiment tarred and feathered him in the guardhouse and paraded him through town in a cart, with a band playing "Yankee Doodle." March 15 was declared a day of fast by the Provincial Congress and the people of Boston went solemnly to their churches that morning. The King's Own Regiment proceeded to pitch two tents outside the chapel in the West End of Boston and play their drums and fifes throughout the service while their colonel looked on approvingly.

Meanwhile Gage continued his policy of defensive military preparations. After fortifying the Neck he began building defenses on four main heights inside Boston—Beacon Hill, Copp's Hill, Barton's Point and Fort Hill, to repel attacks from the water or from within the town itself. He also sent officers in disguise into the country to find out what was going on in the various towns and map the important roads. They usually returned more rapidly than they departed, often bringing with them the few loyalists who had dared to give them shelter.

Far more successful were Gage's efforts to find out what the American leaders were thinking and doing by the use of some cash of the realm. He obtained the services of plump Dr. Benjamin Church, one of the most ardent patriots, and a member of the Committee of Safety, the executive arm of the Provincial Congress which was governing Massachusetts beyond Boston Neck. Other informants sent Gage valuable data about where the colonists were concealing their military stores and supplies. The main depot was obviously Concord, a village about sixteen miles from Boston. By the beginning of April, 1775, Gage's intelligence was good enough to keep him alert to the most minor movements of the patriot leaders. Every trip Paul Revere made was carefully noted, and usually Gage knew why he made it.

Meanwhile Gage continued what conciliatory gestures were available to him. He replied courteously when the First Continental Congress asked him to stop fortifying Boston, defending his decision in terms of what the colonists had done to force him into it. When the Congress' petition to the King, calling for a redress of American grievances, was published, Gage wrote to Peyton Randolph, the president, and congratulated him on the moderate and temperate tone of this earnest document.

Mrs. Gage was also one of the General's problems during these tension-ridden months. Before she sailed from England to join him, she had told a friend that she was dubious about the ministry's whole project and hoped her husband would never become "the oppressor of her countrymen." Margaret Gage was an outspoken woman and the general must have heard plenty of pro-American propaganda at breakfast, lunch and dinner. Mrs. Gage was also very social and as the first lady of the province entertained frequently. Admiral Graves, in command of the fleet in the harbor, had brought his wife from England and set her up in a house on shore. Graves was something of a pompous ass and no friend of Gage's; he undoubtedly encouraged Mrs. Graves when she proceeded to entertain as if she, and not Margaret Gage, were the first lady of Massachusetts. The rivalry between the two households was a standing joke in the Boston garrison.

In England, meanwhile, there was mounting dissatisfaction with Gage. The King and his ministers were still in the four-regiments phase of official thinking and only became exasperated when Gage wrote them letter after letter telling them the real truth. Significantly, none of Gage's letters was ever revealed to Parliament during this time. The ministry was obviously afraid that these gentlemen, who were far more sensitive to the feelings of the country, would repudiate a policy which was leading to a major war. Parliament was more than willing to underwrite four regiments but ten times that many men would hardly make sense to guardians of the public purse, when the goal was enforcing a three-cent tax on tea. The King and his ministers were also annoyed at Gage because he had not tried anything novel or daring which might have eliminated the American problem in one bold stroke. What this feat could have been must remain vague. The problem was realistically soluble in only two ways—both of which Gage had suggested: retaliation with maximum force or graceful surrender to American demands. Nothing in Gage's orders suggested he should experiment on his own. He was all too aware that if he made a wild move and failed, he would have been the scapegoat—and if he succeeded the ministers would have taken all the credit. With admirable persistence, Gage kept handing the problem back to the people who had created it. After months of inaction, they finally came to a semi-decision.

On January 25 Lord Dartmouth met Gage's predecessor, Thomas Hutchinson, in London and told him that "measures were now determined with respect to America." The measures were not put on board a ship until February 22 because Lord North wanted to make one last effort to conciliate the colonies and, with perfect inconsistency, also to make sure that Parliament was ready to go as far toward war as the ministers. Early in February Massachusetts was declared in a state of rebellion by a heavy majority. Next came a bill restricting the trade of New England to Great Britain and, even more destructive, barring New England ships from the Newfoundland fishing grounds. Both these measures were deathblows to the economies of the four New England provinces and to Massachusetts in particular. Next came Lord North's Conciliatory Resolution which stated that any American colony which consented to vote money, through its own assembly, for public—empire—usage would be exempt from taxation by Parliament. The Conciliatory Act squeaked through by a narrow margin; it was, at best, a sop to Lord North's conscience and at worst, as the Americans saw it, a scheme to divide the colonies.

Certain of the support of a Parliament which had no knowledge of the real situation in America, the ministry ordered the pliant Lord Dartmouth to send his "secret" let-

ter of instructions to Gage. It arrived on April 14. In it Dartmouth lectured Gage for his inactivity and told him "force
should be repelled by force." With a total disregard for military realities, he informed the general that "a smaller force
now, if put to the test, would be able to encounter them with
greater probability of success than you might expect from a
greater army.

"The only consideration that remains is, in what manner
the force under your command may be exerted to defend the
constitution and restore the vigour of the government,"
Dartmouth went on. "The King's servants also believe that
the first and essential step toward reestablishing government
would be to arrest the principal actors and abettors in the
Provincial Congress."

The arrest part of this order Gage completely ignored.
He knew it would start a full scale civil war. But he could
not ignore the entire dispatch, which told him in unmistak-
able terms to take the offensive. Still, Gage hoped that he
could manage a limited offensive, without bloodshed. By
what seemed at the time a happy coincidence, one of his informers, probably the patriotic speechmaker Dr. Church,
had just sent him a lengthy report on the impressive amounts
of food, guns and ammunition the patriots had gathered at
Concord. Moreover, the Provincial Assembly had adjourned
on April 15 to await replies from the neighboring colonies of
Connecticut and New Hampshire to their call for a New
England "army of observation." The traitor urged Gage to
seize the Concord supplies with a column from Boston. It
would serve the double purpose of all but disabling any
army the provincials might form—and of discouraging New
Hampshire and Connecticut from taking so formidable a
step toward war.

Thus, on the night of April 18, Gage launched his fateful
secret mission to Concord—700 men under Colonel Francis
Smith and Major John Pitcairn. Paul Revere and other

alarm riders quickly made it a secret no longer, and in the dawn the marine major, heading the advance guard, found some seventy minutemen straggled in a nervous line across the Lexington green, five miles from Concord. The Americans had been up all night and many of them had been drinking away the hours in nearby Buckman's Tavern. The British regulars had been marching all night and were in no mood to let this group of amateur soldiers get in their way. Why this puny band of militia attempted to stop the British is a major mystery. Earlier in the year Gage had sent a detachment out to Salem to confiscate some cannon. The citizens of that town had turned them back with a determined show of force. The Lexington men may have hoped to do the same thing. Instead a shot was fired, the troops at the head of the British column fired a volley and charged with the bayonet. Before the cursing Major Pitcairn could get them under control, seven Americans lay dead on the village green.

The British proceeded to Concord and destroyed some stores and a few cannon which the Americans had not succeeded in hiding during the night. Before the regulars began their return march the news of Lexington had aroused all Massachusetts and militia companies were streaming in from miles around. The original British detachment of 700 would almost certainly have been destroyed by the avenging swarms of minutemen, who poured a ferocious fire on them from the nearby woods and stone walls. Gage however had prudently sent Earl Percy with another 1,000 men to protect their line of march, and the exhausted conquerors of Lexington stumbled behind Percy's fresh troops and collapsed on the ground for an hour with their tongues hanging out, "like so many spent dogs."

Even Percy—with over 1,500 men—had trouble getting back to Boston. He saved himself by making a last-minute decision to avoid Cambridge, where a whole new contingent of colonials was waiting for them, and retreated onto Charlestown peninsula where the guns of the fleet covered him.

Percy and his men spent that night building a flèche (a two-sided walled fortification) on the western end of Bunker Hill in expectation of an early morning American attack which did not materialize. The next day Gage withdrew them to Boston. He simply could not spare the number of troops it would have taken to garrison the peninsula of Charlestown properly. At any moment Boston itself could rise all around him. There was also the possibility of an attack across the Neck or by water from the west.

Meanwhile companies of minutemen poured into Cambridge from all over Massachusetts and from Connecticut, Rhode Island and New Hampshire. An army of 15,000 men appeared within the week, only a musket shot away from Gage's sentries. So the mild general found himself after months of semi-peace with a semi-war on his hands. Now, sixty days later, it was about to become all-out war. Thomas Gage had less than a half dozen hours before this last, painful fact was announced to him by history.

As he paced his study floor he must have wondered despairingly why his advice was still untaken. London had sent him three generals, but only a dribble of reinforcements. His army was still on the short side of 5,000 men. If he had any consolation, it could only be in the words of the great Chatham, who had led England to victory over France and Spain a decade before. Months ago the aging lion, his vigor sapped by a long illness, rose in the House of Lords to denounce the ministry's policy and defend Thomas Gage. "I cannot but feel with the most anxious sensibility for the situation of General Gage and the troops under his command. Thinking him as I do a man of humanity and understanding, and entertaining as I ever shall the highest respect, the warmest love for the British troops, their situation is unworthy—penned up, pining in inglorious inactivity, they are an army of impotence; you may call them an army of safety and of guard, but they are in truth an army of impotence and contempt, and to render the folly equal to the disgrace they are an army of irritation and vexation.

"But I find the report creeping abroad that the ministers censure General Gage's inactivity. Let them censure him. It becomes their justice and their honor. I do not mean to censure his inactivity; it is a prudent and necessary inaction; but it is a miserable condition where prudence is a disgrace and where it is necessary to be contemptible. His tameness, however disgraceful, cannot be censured; for the first drop of blood shed in a civil and unnatural war would be a wound beyond all cure. When I hear General Gage censured for inactivity, I must retort with indignation on those whose intemperate measures and improvident councils have betrayed him into his present situation."

But England was not listening—neither to her great men nor to her faithful servants of more modest talents, such as Thomas Gage.

4

ON THE dark summit of Breed's Hill, the American fort was taking final shape. The southern side, facing Boston and the village of Charlestown, had a redan, or sharply projecting angle, which was designed to hold cannon. The eastern side, facing the sea, commanded the more gradual slope of the hill. There was an entrance in the rear, or western side, and in the northeastern corner there was a sally port, protected by a blind, through which the defenders could, if they chose, launch a counterattack on the enemy. The sally port was also designed to permit men to pass out of the fort to man the breastwork, which was to run parallel to the eastern side of the fort to the base of the hill. As yet, however, not a single spadeful of earth had been expended on this vital part of the defense. Prescott still insisted that the redoubt must be completely finished first; this meant that firing platforms of wood and earth had to be constructed inside; the floor must be smoothed and all parts of the walls raised to the same height and equally strengthened. More than a few of the officers and men must have wondered why the colonel insisted on perfection from men toiling in the dark against a fearful deadline. They would find out, in the dawn.

Prescott and his soldiers were not the only Americans working through the night. In Watertown, about a dozen miles away, a handsome blond-haired man, who looked young enough to be Prescott's son, was grappling with a different, but equally serious set of problems. His name was Joseph Warren and he was the president of the Massachusetts Provincial Congress.

During the sixty momentous days which had elapsed since the first blood was shed at Lexington and Concord, this thirty-four-year-old physician had shouldered the awesome responsibility of leading his fellow Massachusetts citizens through a strange political wilderness. The senior leaders of Massachusetts resistance, John Adams, Samuel Adams and John Hancock, were enroute to Philadelphia for the Second Continental Congress when Gage struck at Concord. They were badly needed in Philadelphia to defend the armed defiance with which Massachusetts had met the British challenge. But at the same time, never was there more need for gifted leadership in Massachusetts.

The army which had rushed headlong into Cambridge on April 19 was an utterly disorganized collection of untrained farmers, constantly on the verge of melting away. In England, ex-Governor Thomas Hutchinson told Edward Gibbon, who was more interested in the decline of Rome than the troubles of Great Britain, that "unless fanaticism got the better of self preservation, they (the people) must soon disperse, as it was the season for sowing their Indian corn, the chief subsistence of New England." Even more disturbing were the problems of creating a government to run a province of 32,000 square miles containing 400,000 people. How should this government conduct itself? Was it to raise the Pine Tree Flag of Massachusetts and announce independence from England? Should it be an agent of peace and submission—and disperse the army? These were crucial decisions. The eyes of America were on Massachusetts, scrutinizing her every move. In the First Continental Congress, moderate men had arisen and angrily denounced New England. The disputatious Puritans were accused of fomenting rebellion and aiming at independence, a word which even so staunch an advocate of American rights as George Washington regarded with revulsion.

The Massachusetts Provincial Congress, which hastily met in Concord two days after Lexington, was keenly aware of these problems. But they had not the slightest hesitation about choosing Warren as the man who they believed could handle them with the proper combination of restraint and courage. On April 23, the committee in charge of proposing a new president for the absent John Hancock announced the "vote was full for Dr. Warren."

Warren was an aristocrat—his family had been in Massachusetts since 1659. His father was a well-to-do farmer, and both Joseph and his younger brother John were Harvard graduates. In 1764 Joseph married Elizabeth Hooton, "an accomplished young lady with a handsome fortune," according to the wedding announcement printed in the Boston *Gazette.*

More than any other figure who strode across the revolutionary stage, Warren gave his devotion to the American cause simply because he believed in it. Others believed as passionately, of course; but for Samuel Adams political agitation was a profession which had rescued him from a debtors' prison; James Otis had deep grievances against the royal government because of their mistreatment of his father; John Hancock was a millionaire merchant who made much of his money from smuggling and owed the British Revenue Service over £100,000 in fines; as a lawyer, John Adams was naturally drawn into the political arena. Warren, as a doctor, could have remained aloof, as many of his fellow physicians in Boston did. They were the only class in Massachusetts who were not pressured to join the cause.

But as early as 1767 the handsome young doctor "undertook a serious examination of the right of Parliament to tax the colonies" and became deeply convinced that American grievances were just. From that day he gave every spare moment of his life to the struggle. "Neither resentment," wrote one man who knew him, "nor interested views, but a regard for the liberties of his country induced him to oppose the measures of the Government. He stepped forward into public view, not that he might be noted and admired for a patriotic spirit, but because he *was* a patriot." This open, direct honesty was one of the two keys to Warren's character. The second was courage. John Adams once said Warren's courage "would have been rash absurdity, were it not tempered by self control." One of the many ironies with which the drama of Bunker Hill is interwoven is the choice of Warren as Massachusetts' leader at this climax of England's attempt to ram its legislative decrees down colonial throats by force.

Making money out of medicine did not particularly interest Warren. He regularly served Boston's poor for nothing, and when his young wife presented him with four children in almost as many years, he sometimes found himself pressed for cash. Politics also deprived him of many well-to-do patients, although his good looks were said to persuade more than a few loyalist ladies to forget his friendship with Sam Adams and summon him to their bedsides. But the young doctor's generosity with his medical skill and his enthusiasm for the American cause endeared him to the Boston working class, who played a vital role in the resistance. One of the doctor's closest friends was burly Paul Revere, leader of the tough "Northenders." It was Warren who brought Revere into the exclusive Long Room Club, made up of Harvard graduates, scholars, men of wealth and affairs. The Warren-Revere friendship became an important link between the intellectual leaders of the American resistance and the rough and tumble rank and file, who provided the raw courage and muscle. On the day after the Boston Tea Party their names were linked in a street ballad:

> *"Our Warren's there and bold Revere*
> *With hands to do and words to cheer*
> *For liberty and laws."*

No one knows for certain whether the rugged artificer and the debonair doctor were among the pseudo-Indians. But it is likely. Warren never failed to prefer "the post of danger." After the Provincial Congress met, in defiance of Governor Gage's proclamation, and rapidly became the government of Massachusetts, Adams and Hancock did not deem it safe to remain in Boston. Warren continued to practice medicine and politics there until—and even after—the very last moment of peace. He took over Sam Adams' job as head of the Boston Committee of Correspondence which played a vital role in rallying the rest of the continent to the city's support. There was little doubt, once the Provincial Congress began collecting taxes and arranging (on paper at first) for the creation of an army, that its very existence was high treason. On November 15 Gage issued a proclamation declaring the congress an unlawful body and "tending to riot and rebellion." Yet Warren, a member of the congress, frequently visited Governor Gage at Province House.

He liked Gage. In a letter to his friend Josiah Quincy written in November, he says: "I have frequently been sent to him on committees, and have several times had private conversations with him. I have thought him a man of honest, upright principles, and one desirous of accommodating the difference between Great Britain and her colonies in a just and honorable way." But Warren's relationship to Gage was already distorted by the feeling that the Governor was under the influence of the loyalist extremists. A few lines further, in the same letter, he describes Gage's proclamation as "the work of that malicious group of harpies whose disappointments make them desirous to urge the Governor to drive every thing to extremes."

Warren's wife died in 1774 and he sent his four children to live with his mother in Roxbury, on the outskirts of Boston. Thereafter he gave himself totally to medicine and politics, with one exception. This was the time he set aside for Miss Mercy Scollay, daughter of John Scollay, one of Boston's selectmen. Throughout the year, he visited this young lady often enough to become engaged to her. There are no surviving records of the courtship, but since Mercy's father was in vigorous political agreement with Warren and the young doctor had by several testimonies considerable charm, it was probably not a difficult conquest.

How he found any time to give to his fiancée, or to politics, is a tribute to Warren's devotion to both, because medicine occupied a major portion of his waking hours. He was the first doctor in Massachusetts to institute a regular training course for young men who apprenticed themselves to him. (There was no medical school in America at the time.) His practice was large. He rarely made less than twelve calls a day and on a busy day he went as high as twenty. His daybook records professional visits at the houses of John Hancock, Samuel Adams (whose son was one of Warren's pupils) and John Adams, where he was particularly beloved. Adams' oldest son, young John Quincy, revered him as a second father; Warren's medical skill had saved his right hand when it was threatened by a severe fracture of the forefinger and other doctors had recommended amputation.

Night after night, after demanding days crowded with medicine, Warren worked at politics, advising resistance committees from Paul Revere's Northend, conferring with members of his Masonic Lodge, where he rapidly became the Grand Master, toiling on Committee of Correspondence letters or participating in the strenuous debates of the Long

Room Club, where the leaders hammered out the policy of resistance. Slowly but steadily Warren matured into the best kind of political leader—a man who knew and genuinely liked the people yet preserved the steady temper and discerning mind of the aristocrat.

Warren emerged as a major American spokesman not long after Hancock and the two Adamses departed for the First Continental Congress. On September 5, 1774, the county of Suffolk, of which Boston was the seat, held a convention, as counties all over Massachusetts were doing. Warren, as chairman, presented a series of resolutions which were simultaneously the strongest condemnation yet made of Great Britain's conduct—and the deepest avowal of America's fundamental loyalty to the crown. The first resolution acknowledged George III as justly entitled to the loyalty of every American. Then the acts of Parliament were condemned, one by one, for violating the charter of the province, the British constitution and the laws of nature. The resolutions proclaimed the need for total resistance to these acts—but declared that Americans intended to act merely on the defensive—"so long as such conduct may be vindicated by reason and the principles of self preservation, but no longer." They pledged submission to such measures as the "wisdom and integrity of the Continental Congress" might recommend for the restoration of their rights, and for the renewal of "the union between Great Britain and the colonies, so earnestly wished for by all good men." Finally they called upon their fellow Bostonians to refrain from "routs, riots or licentious attacks upon the property of any persons whatsoever" but by a steady opposition, "to convince these enemies that in a contest so important, in a cause so solemn, their conduct should be such as to merit the approbation of the wise, and the admiration of the brave and free of every age and of every country."

These Suffolk Resolves were rushed to Philadelphia by

Paul Revere. They arrived as the First Continental Congress was in the midst of an agonizing debate on how to effect a compromise with the conservatives, who were anxious to concede a great deal to England for the sake of peace. The president read them aloud and the room burst into "spontaneous applause." Congress instantly passed a vote of full approval, and for the first time New England men began to hope that the other colonies would stand behind them. In his diary John Adams wrote that night: "This day convinced me that America will support the Massachusetts or perish with her."

Warren's courage—and his profound thoughts on the solution to the bitter struggle—were dramatically fused on March 5, 1775, when he gave the oration commemorating Massacre Day. This was the colorful name Samuel Adams gave to the day in 1770 when a squad of British soldiers came to the rescue of a single sentry who was being pelted with ice and stones by a riotous Boston mob. They fired into the crowd, killing five. Each year one of the resistance leaders led a mass meeting at Old South Church to keep the memory of these somewhat dubious martyrs alive. This year, 1775, with Boston once more patrolled by British troops, the gathering had suddenly shifted from mere political propaganda to a meaningful symbol of the colony's determination to resist Parliamentary oppression. The British officers in Gage's garrison decided to attend in force, supposedly to make sure that no insult was offered to their uniforms. Rapidly, the meeting began to loom as the incident which would begin the war. Gage ordered his entire army to remain in their barracks, ready for action. The working class friends of Warren swore that if anyone tried to harm him, blood would flow. Many other friends strongly advised Warren not to attend, or if honor forced him to appear, to say nothing that could be construed as even slightly incendiary.

That night, Warren appeared before the packed meeting

house. Over forty British officers, armed with their swords and pistols, sat in the first few rows and on the pulpit steps. They had been shown every courtesy; the front row seats had even been reserved for them. Solemnly, Warren announced the topic: "On the dangers of standing armies in time of peace." The speech was a masterful review of the history of America's relations with the mother country, dwelling, with grim emphasis, on the five men who had lost their lives in the earlier occupation of Boston and its implications in their present time of trouble. Midway through the oration, a young officer sitting on the steps held up five pistol bullets in the palm of his hand. Without faltering Warren coolly dropped his handkerchief over them. Throughout the speech, officers hooted objections to his points, but he ignored them and closed with a declaration which silenced them more effectively than any direct reply could have done.

"An independence of Great Britain is not our aim. No: our wish is, that Britain and the colonies may, like the oak and ivy, grow and increase in strength together. But whilst the infatuated plan of making one part of the empire slaves to the other is persisted in, the interest and safety of Britain as well as the colonies require that the wise measures recommended by the honorable the Continental Congress be steadily pursued, whereby the unnatural contest between a parent honored and child beloved may probably be brought to such an issue as that the peace and the happiness of both may be established upon a lasting basis. But if these pacific measures are ineffectual, and it appears that the only way to safety is through fields of blood, I know you will not turn your faces from our foes, but will undauntedly press forward until tyranny is trodden under foot, and you have fixed your adored goddess, Liberty, fast by a Brunswick's side, on the American throne."

In Warren's able mind, and his equally able actions, we see in perfect focus the American position during 1775. Nowhere has there yet appeared that vituperation which Thomas Jefferson was to shower on George III in the Declaration of Independence. The House of Brunswick was, to predominately Protestant America, a royal line which was a bulwark of religious liberty. They were, in spirit if not in blood, in direct descent from William of Orange, who had, at the invitation of the English Lords, marched from Holland to seize the English throne in the "Glorious Revolution" of 1688. Catholic James II had aroused the nation with his attempt to turn back the clock and restore the old religion. In New England, peopled by dissenters who could not tolerate the slightly Roman style of the Episcopal Church, 1688 was a sacred year, and its Parliament, which had defied the absolutist King in the name of that unwritten document, the British constitution, was revered by Americans as a perfect example of how the people could assert their natural rights against tyranny.

The American view of the situation in England was deeply colored by this devotion to George III. In their eyes, the King was a good, kind, honest sovereign who loved his subjects in North America with a particular benevolence. (George had, in fact, early in his reign sent many warm words of praise and gratitude across the Atlantic, to buoy up Americans in the war against France.) As Warren and his compatriots saw the situation it was not the King who was persecuting the colonies—it was his ministers and the arrogant majority in Parliament. When the Americans excoriated Gage and his soldiers in pamphlets and newspaper editorials, they regularly referred to the British as the "ministerial army"—carefully separating George III from responsibility for the troops' obnoxious presence.

As the Americans saw it, the only way to get rid of the ministers was by resistance to their policy, the more forcible the better. This would accomplish one of two things: the ministry might collapse and a new ministry friendly to

Americans would come into power, or George III would be moved by the desperation of his beloved colonists to dismiss his corrupt ministers and restore harmony.

These were forlorn hopes. At a distance of 3,000 miles the Americans completely misjudged the character of George III—and knew equally little about the realities of English politics. George III and his advisers on their side of the Atlantic had even less accurate information about the Americans. To appreciate completely the twists and turns of ignorance and misjudgment which brought William Prescott and his men to Breed's Hill, we must cross the Atlantic and take a closer look at the King and his government. We will also see a great American fighting in the heart of London for the same peace which Thomas Gage and Joseph Warren were struggling to preserve in Boston.

What was George III really like? Here is a picture of the young King written by Lord Waldegrave, who had been his governor, shortly before he ascended the throne.

"His religion is free from all hypocrisy, but is not of the most charitable sort; he has rather too much attention to the sins of his neighbor.

"He has spirit, but not of the active kind; and does not want resolution, but it is mixed with too much obstinacy.

"He has great command of his passions, and will seldom do wrong, except when he mistakes wrong for right; but as often as this shall happen it will be difficult to undeceive him because he . . . has strong prejudices.

"He has a kind of unhappiness in his temper, which if it be not conquered . . . will be a source of frequent anxiety. Whenever he is displeased, his anger does not break out with heat and violence; but he becomes sullen and silent and retires to his closet; not to compose his mind by study or contemplation, but merely to indulge the melancholy enjoyment of his own ill humor. Even when the fit is ended, unfavorable symptoms very frequently return, which indicate that on certain occasions his Royal Highness has too correct a memory."

This was a mediocre man—with certain defects of character which were particularly unfortunate in the ruler of a great empire. The American situation called for improvisation. There was much plain common sense in the colonial argument that they could not tolerate having their business lives legislatively controlled by a body of men who had neither knowledge of their affairs nor interest in their needs. But the idea of the semi-independent dominion bound to the mother country, not by legislative authority but by loyalty to the crown, lay in the future and was simply beyond George III's narrow political conceptions. His only talent was for clinging to the obvious and traditional with the perseverance of a mollusk. Far from being the benevolent would-be savior of his American subjects, he had been brooding in his "too correct memory" for over a decade about their disobedience.

In a letter to Arthur Lee, the agent for Massachusetts in England, Joseph Warren defended the American position by arguing that in fighting for the constitution, Americans were in reality fighting for the King, "for the King is annihilated when the constitution is destroyed." Earnest George III was fighting the Americans for the very same reason—to rescue the British constitution from annihilation. His motive was not, as disillusioned Americans later believed, a wish to restore the power of divine right absolutism to the British monarchy. The idea of being an absolute king would have terrified George III. He clung to the British constitution, as he clung to ministers and advisers throughout his long life, because he had absolutely no confidence in himself. "If Lord North can see with the same degree of enthusiasm I do the beauty, excellence and perfection of the British Constitution as by law established and consider that if any one branch of the Empire is allowed to cast off its dependency that the others will infallibly follow the example . . . he will resolve with vigor to meet every obstacle or the state will be ruined."

To George III the essence of the British constitution lay in the existence and operation of Parliament. If Parliament was annihilated, the constitution was destroyed. The colonists, by refusing to obey the acts of Parliament, were for all practical purposes annihilating that august body. For what was Parliament if its laws were ignored? The Americans were striking at the very essence of British government and George III saw it as his duty to strike back. As early as November, 1774, he was writing to Lord North: "I am not sorry that the line of conduct seems now chalked out . . . the New England governments are in a state of rebellion. Blows must decide whether they are to be subject to this country or independent."

Once George III achieved an idea, not even a revolution could shake him out of it. He was, in fact, convinced it was an admirable royal quality. "I never assent until I am convinced what is proposed is right and then. . . . I never allow that to be destroyed by after-thoughts which on all subjects tend to weaken, never to strengthen the original proposal." In the King's opinion the parliamentary retreat from the Stamp Act, the first attempt back in 1765 to tax the colonists was "the fatal compliance" which opened the doors for the following decade of defiance.

A minister who attempted to argue with such a man was speedily suspected of every bad quality, from weakness to disloyalty. The King preferred ministers like Lord North, who believed saying yes was part of their ministerial duty. There were reasons for this compliance, which went beyond Lord North's pliable personality. In 1775 the British government was not the limited monarchy we know today. The King was in charge of the executive branch of the government and his duties and powers corresponded, roughly, to those the President now handles in the United States. This, in itself, was more than enough power to overawe a man of North's backbone. But in 1775 George III had by an accident of history also become the chief power in Parliament. Political parties as we understand them today had yet to be born. England was split into four or five "factions," some revolving around a noble Lord such as the Marquis of Rockingham, some around a class (the country squires) and roughly one-third of Parliament around the King who, through his executive power, had innumerable jobs, from cabinet posts to lucrative sinecures, to dispense among those who supported him.

George III had a great hatred for this "rule of factions" which was undoubtedly hampering a consistent government policy toward the multiple problems of running an empire. Every cabinet was a shaky coalition incapable of accomplishing anything constructive for fear of offending one of its supporting splinter parties. Unfortunately, George's solution, to unite all the factions under himself, the "patriot King," tended to place in power mediocrities like himself, who were not members of a faction because they had no particular political principles to inspire them.

Slowly but inevitably, in the decade since the Seven Years' War with France, the real political power in England slid into George's incapable hands. It was not a power consciously sought for its own sake. The King's one desire was to make Parliament true to itself and to England's tradition of firmness and pride. The vacillation toward the Americans was, in his opinion, disgracefully unbecoming to the rulers of a great empire. He was, in this mission, painfully conscious of his own inadequacy. "I act wrong in most things," he once wrote, in a moment of objective self-analysis. Only his sense of duty kept him to his difficult and unrewarding task.

It is a baffling, largely forgotten picture, this confrontation of George III and America which emerges from a fresh look at the history of the year 1775. Nowhere else could the patriot King find the loyalty offered him in America. Ireland was as usual a seething mass of discontent and rebellion. Only thirty years before thousands of Highland Scots had risen against his father, George II, and had been crushed with ghastly slaughter at Culloden. So little were the Scots pacified that when the ministry began searching for reinforcements to send General Gage, the suggestion to send Highlanders was immediately dismissed, because they would be all too liable to join the Americans in revolution. England itself had a multitude of grievances against the house of Brunswick. As Lord Mayor in 1774 the City of London had elected John Wilkes, a man who had made a career of scurrilously attacking George III, had been hounded out of the country once by the King's friends and even refused his seat in Parliament, although he had been legally elected.

But we must remember that we are looking backward on the scene with the always wiser eyes of hindsight. There was, between the King and America, the gulf of the Atlantic, making genuine communication impossible. There were no good-will tours or summit conferences. It took four months to exchange letters between England and America—and the letters the King received were invariably from government servants such as Thomas Gage, or Royal Governors such as Thomas Hutchinson. When Hutchinson landed in England, the King was so anxious to see him, the ex-Governor was ushered into the royal closet without being given a chance to change his clothes. The King talked with him for two hours, and the accuracy of the information he received is best demonstrated by the letter George III wrote to Lord North later in the day: "I have seen Mr. Hutchinson, late Governor of Massachusetts, and am now well convinced they will soon submit. He owns the Boston Port Bill has been the only wise and effectual method."

One other hope, equally forlorn, was frequently on American lips in those troubled months: their friends in Parliament would come to the rescue and overturn the ministry. On February 20, 1775, Warren wrote to Arthur Lee, "It is not too late to accommodate the dispute amicably. If there is any wisdom in the nation, God grant it may be speedily called forth! Every day, every hour, widens the breach. A Richmond, a Chatham, a Shelburne, a Camden, with their noble associates, may yet repair it and it is a work which none but the greatest of men can conduct."

These men were all noble lords in opposition to George III. But they were a mere shadow of the great alliance which had brought the present royal family to the throne. They were vigorous in oratory, but politically they were impotent, divided and uncertain about workable alternatives to the policy of the current ministry. All they could really offer America was encouragement, and this they had given liberally since the beginning of the quarrel. Almost ten years ago Isaac Barré, the Irish colonel who had fought beside Wolfe and Howe at Quebec, hailed the colonists' resistance to the Stamp Act and called them "Sons of Liberty." The American associations then forming to boycott British goods promptly adopted the name. The great Chatham also rejoiced in American opposition, declaring that "three millions of people so dead to all the feelings of liberty as voluntarily to submit to be made slaves would be very fit instruments to make slaves of all Englishmen." But words were no longer enough, and the Americans' "friends" simply did not have the votes to come to Massachusetts' rescue.

There was in England in 1775 one man who had a solution to the quarrel. His name was Benjamin Franklin and his answer was based on an "imperial vision" which transcended the dreams of Britain's most grandiose empire builders. At this time Franklin had been in England for seven consecutive years, serving as agent for Pennsylvania and Massachusetts and as the quasi-official representative of all the colonies in their quarrel with Parliament's authority. No one was a firmer advocate of American rights. His testimony before Parliament was a major factor in the repeal of the Stamp Act. At the same time, Franklin had a profound affection for the mother country, an affection which was animated by a magnificent vision of English-American destiny. Years before, when the crisis was in its early, relatively harmless stage, he wrote to his Scottish friend, Lord Kames: "I have long been of the opinion that the foundations of the future grandeur and stability of the British Empire lie in America and though like other foundations they are low and little seen they are nevertheless broad and strong enough to support the greatest political structure human wisdom ever yet erected." At that time the idea of independence struck him as an utterly alien thought. When an English friend, Charles Pratt, remarked that for all their loyalty and affection some day the Americans would set up for independence, Franklin insisted: "No such idea was ever entertained by the Americans nor will any such ever enter their heads unless you grossly abuse them."

Franklin's friendship with William Strahan is perhaps the best illustration of his love for England. Fellow printers, they had corresponded for over a dozen years before Franklin came to London in 1757. After their first meeting, Strahan wrote to Mrs. Franklin: "I never saw a man who was, in every respect, so perfectly agreeable to me." Later, when Franklin was reluctantly considering a trip home, and Strahan was doing all in his power to persuade him to stay, Franklin wrote: "You might easily prevail on me to do anything." The Englishman tried, with Franklin's hearty approval, to arrange a marriage between his son and Franklin's daughter, Sally. Only Mrs. Franklin's dread of sea voyages prevented the match. Strahan printed many of Franklin's writings, including some sharp attacks on the government's policy.

As trouble between the colonies and the crown deepened, Franklin found himself assaulted on both sides. To some radicals in Massachusetts he was considered "too much of an Englishman." In England he was regarded by many as the prime mover in the seditious plot against established government. He was viciously attacked before the Privy Council by the king's attorney general, Wedderburn, in a tirade which was described as "incompatible with the principles of law, truth, justice, propriety and humanity." But Franklin stayed on the job, refusing to allow personal venom to interfere with what rapidly became an all-absorbing mission. In the universities and learned societies where he was received as a fellow scientist and scholar, in coffeehouses where he was hailed as a literary genius, in the outer and inner rooms of Parliament where his political skill was considered second to none, among the merchants and bankers of London where he was greeted as a hardheaded fellow businessman, this amazing American, then sixty-eight, indefatigably argued his country's case and found hundreds of honorable Englishmen more than willing to listen.

In that critical July with Boston occupied by troops and its commerce ruined, he wrote repeatedly to America that the ministry did not represent the British people. "The friends of liberty here," he wrote to Thomas Cushing, speaker of the Massachusetts Assembly, "wish we may long preserve it on our side of the water that they may find it there if adverse events should destroy it here. They are therefore anxious and afraid lest we should hazard it by premature attempts in its favor. With regard to the sentiments of people in general here concerning America I must say that we have among them many friends and well-wishers. The dissenters are all for us and many of the merchants and manufacturers. There seems to be even among the country gentlemen a general sense of our growth and importance, a disapprobation of the harsh measures with which we have been treated and a wish that some means may be found of perfect reconciliation. A few members of Parliament in both Houses, and perhaps some in high office, have in a degree the same idea, but none of these seem willing as yet to be active in our favor lest adversaries should take advantage and charge it upon them as betraying the interests of this nation." Even when old friends such as Strahan voted in Parliament with the royal party against the American cause, Franklin remained basically optimistic. Although he held out no hope of any immediate change in the feelings or policies of England he urged his friends in America to bear "a little with the infirmities of her government as we would with those of an aged parent."

At the same time Franklin's letters expressed a first note of disillusion with George III. For almost fifteen years the philosopher had played a large role in convincing his fellow Americans that the young monarch was supremely fair, trustworthy and full of the most tender sentiments toward his American subjects. Now on February 14, 1774, he wrote to his son: "Between you and I the late measures have been I suspect very much the King's own, and he has in some cases a great share of what his friends call firmness. Yet by some painstaking and proper management the wrong impressions he has received may be removed which is perhaps the only chance America has for obtaining soon the redress she aims at."

News of the First Continental Congress gave Franklin fresh hope. The coolness, temper and firmness of the American proceedings, "the unanimity of all the colonies in the same sentiments of their rights and of the injustice offered to Boston and the patience with which those injuries are at present borne without the least appearance of submission, have a good deal surprised and disappointed our enemies. The tone of public conversation which has been violently against us begins evidently to turn."

He was also heartened by the colonial decision to import no more British goods. It was a similar measure which had brought the repeal of the Stamp Act. "If the non-consumption agreement should become general and be firmly adhered to," he wrote home, "this ministry must be ruined and our friends succeed them from whom we may hope a great constitutional charter to be confirmed by King, lords and commons whereby our liberty shall be recognized and established as the only sure foundation of that union so necessary for our common welfare."

Meanwhile his mind was full of the danger of imminent violence. "I am in a perpetual anxiety," he wrote on October 6, 1774. "Unless the mad measure of mixing soldiers among other people whose minds are in such a state of irritation may be attended with some sudden mischief or an accidental quarrel, a personal insult, an imprudent order, an insolent execution of even a prudent one, or twenty other things may produce a tumult unforeseen and therefore impossible to be prevented in which such a carnage may ensue as to make a breech that can never afterwards be healed."

Franklin did not realize how prophetic these words were when he wrote them. He merely redoubled his efforts to find help for America in the highest places. Through friends of friends he wangled an interview with Lord Chatham. "That truly great man," he wrote home, "received me with an abundance of civility. He inquired particularly into the situation of affairs in America, spoke feelingly of the severity of the late laws against the Massachusetts and expressed great regard and esteem for the people of that country who he hoped would continue firm and united in defending by all peaceable and legal means their constitutional rights." Unfortunately, Chatham, like Churchill, was a great wartime leader but his independence caused him trouble in peacetime politics. He had no friends to rally around him in Parliament.

Franklin himself had no illusions about the quality of Parliament. During the elections of 1774 he wrote to his friend Cushing, "As most of the members are bribing or purchasing to get in, there is little doubt of selling their votes to the minister for the time being to reimburse themselves. Luxury introduces necessity even among those that make the most splendid figures here. This brings most of the Commons as well as Lords to market and if America would save for three or four years the money she spends in the fashions and fineries and fopperies of this country she might buy the whole Parliament, ministers and all." Nevertheless Franklin spent hours with Chatham who was preparing his own solution to the quarrel. He assured the great man of America's admiration and suggested points of agreement that would be acceptable to the Continental Congress. Chatham's plan, although it did not agree at all points with Franklin's ideas, had many major virtues. He held that only Americans could tax Americans and that the charters of the colonies were inviolable. He proposed that the Continental Congress be made official and permanent, that Parliament suspend for the present the acts which the colonists complained were ruining them.

The great drama of conciliation reached a climax for Franklin on the day Lord Chatham presented his plan to the House of Lords. Here is what happened in Franklin's own words: "On Wednesday, Lord Stanhope at Lord Chatham's request called upon me and carried me down to the House of Lords which was soon very full. Lord Chatham in a most excellent speech introduced, explained and supported his plan. When he sat down Lord Dartmouth rose and very properly said it contained matter of such weight and magnitude as to require much consideration and he therefore hoped the noble earl did not expect the lordships to decide upon it by immediate vote but would be willing it should lie upon the table for consideration. Lord Chatham answered readily that he expected nothing more. But Lord Sandwich who rose in an impetulant vehement speech opposed its being received at all and gave his opinion that it ought to be immediately rejected with the contempt it deserved, that he could not believe it to be the production of any British peer, that it appeared to him rather the work of some American, and turning his face towards me who was leaning on the bar said he fancied he had in his eye the person who drew it up, one of the bitterest and most mischievous enemies this country had ever known. This drew the eyes of many lords upon me, but as I had no inducement to take it to myself I kept my countenance as immovable as if my features had been made of wood.

"Lord Chatham in his reply to Lord Sandwich took notice of his illiberal insinuation that the plan was not the person's who had proposed it, declared that it was entirely his own . . . that it had been heretofore reckoned his vice, not to be out to take advice, but he made no scruple to declare that if he were the first minister of this country and had the care of settling this momentous business he should not be ashamed to publicly call into his assistance a person so perfectly acquainted with the whole American affair as the gentleman alluded to and so injuriously reflected on: One, he was pleased to say whom all Europe held in high estimation for his knowledge and his wisdom and ranked with our Boyles and Newtons, who was an honor not to the English nation only but to human nature. I found it harder to stand this extravagant compliment than the preceding equally extravagant abuse, but kept it as well as I could to an unconcerned countenance as not conceiving it to relate to me."

Several other lords rose to speak in favor of Chatham's plan, but the King's ministers and several other enemies of Franklin and America, including Lord Hillsborough, formerly secretary of colonial affairs, rose to agree with Sandwich. The vacillating Dartmouth collapsed and announced that he was ready to reject the plan at once if the House so desired.

"Lord Chatham's bill," Franklin wrote bitterly to a friend four days later, "though on so important a subject and offered by so great a character and supported by such able and merited speakers, was treated with as much contempt as they would have shown to a ballad offered by a drunken porter."

5

AT ABOUT 3:00 A.M. Israel Putnam mounted his horse and rode back to American headquarters at Cambridge, leaving William Prescott in command on Breed's Hill. The Massachusetts colonel promptly ordered Major John Brooks to accompany him and descended to the village of Charlestown, where Captains Nutting and Maxwell and their men were standing guard by the ferryway. Neither captain had anything to report. Not a sound had reached their ears other than the call of the watch aboard the British ships and the more distant calls of sentries in Boston. But Prescott was not reassured. With Brooks he personally prowled along the harbor shore, listening for the stroke of a muffled oar, a muttered order. But they too found nothing but silence.

For a moment, before he turned back to his men on the hill, the taciturn colonel may have stood motionless, staring through the night at the dark mass of Boston's houses and hills on the other side of the harbor. If he had accepted the commission offered him at Louisburg fifteen years ago, he might be asleep over there, a captain or a major in His Majesty's service. His caution demonstrated how thoroughly he respected the abilities of those professional soldiers. Even now, if young Major Brooks had asked him, Prescott would have freely admitted the British army was the best in the world. Why did he dare to challenge them with that uniformless, untrained band of farmers sweating away on the hill above him?

For Prescott and those like him, direct men of action, the conflict had become something far more fundamental and less abstruse than taxation without representation. Courage was the question he was grimly determined to settle on Breed's Hill tomorrow with his raw recruits. Part of his feelings went back to the reason he had refused his Royal Army commission. Like George Washington and almost every other American who had seen military service in the various wars against the French and Indians, Prescott bitterly resented the second-class-soldier status which the British had imposed on provincial officers. The lowliest lieutenant with a regular commission outranked American colonels and generals whose commissions were from their provincial governments. This old resentment, which suggested that home-born Englishmen were somehow better men than their provincial brothers, had been volcanically reawakened by the present crisis. Every insult that was offered to American courage by lords in Parliament or British officers in Boston taverns brought the fighting blood of men like Prescott and Israel Putnam to a bitter boil.

Equally infuriating was the vituperation showered on them by their own countrymen. All the Americans who were, either in spirit or in fact, with Prescott on Breed's Hill called themselves Whigs, proudly aligning themselves with that English party which had for over 100 years defended individual liberty against the encroachments of the crown. Lord Chatham was a Whig, as was that other great friend of America, Edmund Burke, whose speech on conciliation, long an oratorical model for American schoolboys, was as ignored by Parliament as Chatham's plea.

The men in opposition to the Whigs, and traditionally in support of the royal prerogative, were called Tories both in England and America. But any resemblance between the British and American versions of the two parties ended in the names. In England each was split into incoherent factions. In America they were far more internally united, and their clashes were inestimably more harsh. Moreover the argument had nothing to do with the traditional Whig defense of the rights of Parliament against the rights of the crown. Parliament itself was being defied by Warren and his party and this, argued the American Tories, was treason. Hence they spared no adjectives when talking about the Whigs. Their feelings were further soured, as we have already seen, by their extreme minority position and the ungentle handling many of them received from Whig mobs. The dispute rapidly reached depths of bitterness which no American, ten years before, would have thought possible.

One Tory writer called on the citizens of Boston to abolish the Committees of Correspondence in the following terms: "I have watched the plant until it became a great tree; the vilest reptiles that crawl upon the earth are concealed at the root; the foulest birds of the air rest upon its branches." Attacks on the characters of the Whig leaders were particularly vicious. They were called "calves, knaves and fools, men whose ambitions wantonly opened the sources of civil discord." They were regularly told that they deserved a rebel's fate—the gallows—and the Tories cheered openly at every threatening gesture Gage made. One visitor to Boston told how "riding into town I found the Neck beset with soldiers; the cannon hoisted; and many Tories on the Neck and many more going up to see the encampment with the greatest pleasure in their countenances." A Tory minister, Dr. Samuel Peters, wrote a fellow loyalist in Connecticut: "I am in high spirits. Six regiments are now coming from England and sundry men of war. So soon as they come, hanging

work will go on, and destruction will first attend the seaport towns."

Few loyalists were really so bloodthirsty. But no one
among them repudiated the loudmouths and head-hunters,
and their extremists' views were accepted for the majority.
The bitterness divided families and destroyed friendships.
Prescott himself was one of the victims. His sister Elizabeth
was married to Abijah Willard, a man who had once been a
close friend and fellow soldier. Willard could not in conscience resist royal authority, and he and his wife became
increasingly disturbed when Prescott accepted his post as
colonel in the revised militia and began drilling and training his men. One night Willard visited Prescott in his Pepperell mansion and told him how much his sister dreaded
the thought of him being "taken in arms" and hanged as a
rebel. Prescott sprang up in a blaze of fury. "It is probable
that I will be taken in arms," he said. "But I will never be
taken alive. The Tories will never have the satisfaction of
seeing me hanged."

But Prescott, no matter how fierce his individual determination, was only a soldier under orders. He was not risking his life, and the lives of 900 men, out of personal pique.
To understand what brought them to Breed's Hill, we must
see the effect of the mounting political bitterness on other
Americans—in particular Joseph Warren. We must also appreciate the enormous impact of the situation created by the
day of Lexington and Concord.

Joseph Warren was one of the few people in Boston who
struggled against the rancor between Whig and Tory, although he was a prime target for some of the worst epithets.
One of the most frequent Tory cries was that the leaders of
the Massachusetts resistance were nothing but "mechanics
and country clowns." Because his father had been a farmer,
Warren was accused of being a former "milk boy" who was
risking everything to rise in society. Others called him a

"rascally apothecary." Elsewhere he and Sam Adams were linked as "desperate bankrupts," and "men of the baser sort." Yet Warren was always ready to "do kind offices to those who had different sentiments about the cause in which he was engaged." Warren was simply too generous and direct to be mean. He remained on the friendliest terms with Dr. James Lloyd, under whom he had studied medicine, although the older physician was a staunch loyalist.

But one brand of insult Warren could not bear was the frequent Tory attempts to frighten the Whigs or impugn their courage. Printed broadsides warned of an overwhelming army of 15 or 18 thousand Canadians and Indians ready to be let loose on Massachusetts and Connecticut. Again and again the Tories harped on the utter folly of the undisciplined colonial rabble attempting to resist British regulars. "Our country is without money, stores or necessaries of war —without one place of refuge or defence," wrote one pamphleteer. "If we were called together, we should be a confused herd without any disposition to obedience, and without a general of ability to direct or guide us."

Among his friends, Joseph Warren could not conceal how deeply these taunts at American courage enraged him. "They say we will not fight," he said once to his pupil, William Eustis. "By God I hope I die up to my knees in British blood." Living in Boston, Warren was also exposed to the jibes of the younger British officers who, after his Massacre Day oration, singled him out for particular attention. One day, as he was passing the town gallows, a group of young officers was standing nearby. Someone said: "Go on, Warren, you'll go to the gallows soon enough." Warren whirled in a fury, "Which of you said that?" he snarled. A duel would have been inevitable if one of them had admitted it, but they all maintained an insulting silence.

This vituperation did as much to damage the hopes of peace as the acts of Parliament, especially when men like

Warren, who saw Gage frequently, became more and more convinced that the governor was wholly under the influence of the Tory extremists. Small wonder then that for all his hopes of peace, when the moment came Warren was more than ready to act.

It was he who organized the scraps of intelligence picked up by Revere and his friends as they loitered around Boston on April 18 and correctly determined that Gage was planning a night march to Concord to seize the stores and disarm the Americans. Warren gave Revere his orders to ride and sent him and his now forgotten partner, William Dawes, out of Boston moments before sentries sealed off the town on all sides. The next morning, when the news of Lexington reached Boston, Warren made one visit—to a lady who was close to giving birth—then called his assistant, William Eustis, and ordered him to take care of the delivery and handle any other patients who might call for him. He took the ferry to Charlestown where he had a horse waiting. In the ferry he told another Bostonian: "They have begun it—that either party can do; and we'll end it—that only one can do." Unlike Samuel Adams, who professed to be over-joyed with the sound of guns at Lexington but refused to have anything to do with the fighting ("We are the cabinet," he said sternly to John Hancock when the more bellicose merchant began cleaning his musket), Warren was in the thick of the fierce fighting along the Lexington road. In West Cambridge he and General Heath were, in the general's words "several times very much exposed," and a ball clipped away Warren's earpiece, which gentlemen of the time wore to keep their wigs in place. But the young doctor only shook his head, laughed and returned to the task of rallying the militiamen for another attack. In the words of one historian of that memorable day, "the people were delighted with Warren's cool collected bravery and already considered him as a leader whose gallantry they were to admire and in whose talents they were to confide."

After Lexington, Warren's first action as the president of the Massachusetts Provincial Congress was a fervent call for the support of his fellow Americans. Dispatch riders thundered south through Connecticut and New York and north to New Hampshire with Warren's electric message.

"The barbarous murders committed on our innocent brethren on Wednesday the 19th instant have made it absolutely necessary that we immediately raise an army to defend our wives and our children from the butchering hands of an inhuman soldiery. . . . We conjure you, by all that is dear, by all that is sacred, that you give all assistance in forming an army. Our all is at stake. Death and devastation are the instant consequences of delay."

The same day, April 20, Warren wrote a letter in a far different tone to General Gage.

"Sir, the unhappy situation into which this colony is thrown gives the greatest uneasiness to every man who regards the welfare of the Empire or feels for the distresses of his fellowmen. But even now much may be done to alleviate these misfortunes which cannot be entirely remedied, and I think it of the utmost importance to us that our conduct be such as that the contending parties may entirely rely upon the honor and integrity of each other for the punctual performance of any agreement that shall be made between them. Your Excellency I believe knows very well the part I have taken in public affairs. I ever scorned disguise. I think I have done my duty. Some will think otherwise. But be assured sir, as far as my influence goes, everything which can reasonably be required of us to do shall be done and everything promised shall be religiously performed."

Warren then suggested an agreement whereby all those who wished to leave Boston would be permitted to do so, and anyone outside Boston who proposed to side with the royal government would be permitted to enter. He ended the letter with words of sorrow and regret which were a grim comment on the bitterness aroused by Tory attacks.

"I have many things I wish to say to your Excellency and most sincerely wish that I had broken through the formalities which I thought due your rank and freely told you all I knew or thought of public affairs, and I must ever confess whatever may be the event that you generously gave me such an opening as I now think I ought to have embraced, but the true cause of my not doing it was the vileness and treachery of many persons around you who I supposed had gained your entire confidence."

With these words Warren gave Thomas Gage a magnificent opportunity to end the plunge toward all-out war before it built up irresistible momentum. A more flexible man than Gage would have promptly invited Warren to a conference and proved to him, with words and actions, that the government was willing to listen to both sides. But nature, and long years in the peacetime army, had made a formalist of Thomas Gage. Perhaps, also, he had clung so long to his policy of not making a bold gesture that he could not change, he could not bring himself to risk the censure of his superiors in London by throwing aside formalities and going directly to Warren. Ponderously, in reply to Warren's letter, Gage pointed out that the Provincial Congress was an illegal body. For him, the Governor, to receive its president would be a tacit recognition of its legality. All communication between them would therefore have to be conducted by the selectmen of Boston.

Two days later this best hope of reconciliation was gone forever. Men and events were in tumultuous motion and Warren, the moderate still hoping for peace, found himself almost totally absorbed in complex preparations for war.

Armed men were pouring into Cambridge. They had to be fed, housed, organized into a semblance of an army. Some British stores at Roxbury were seized and the kitchens of Cambridge were stripped of food, pots and pans. Harvard College's kitchens were pressed into service. Warren "did wonders in preserving order among the troops," one writer reported. Many of the houses in Cambridge were deserted and strict measures were taken to prevent any looting. Warren also attended the deliberations of the Council of War, a group of military leaders which included William Heath, the leader along the Lexington road, William Prescott, John Whitcomb and Artemas Ward who had played a large role in organizing patriot resistance in Worcester. He was the exceptional judge who had refused to sign the Tory loyalty letter to Gage. Ward had been appointed general of the paper army which the Provincial Congress had projected, just before Gage struck at Concord. He was afflicted with "bladder stone" and had been sick in bed when the express rider galloped through his home town of Shrewsbury with news of the fighting, but he had flung himself on a horse and ridden all night to reach Cambridge on the morning of the twentieth.

A few moderates, such as Timothy Pickering of Salem, did not think the formation of an army was necessary. But they were quickly dismissed. Already Colonel John Thomas was standing guard at Roxbury, outside Boston Neck, with a makeshift regiment. The council promptly sent him reinforcements and ordered entrenchments thrown up on all roads leading into the country from Boston. Sentries were posted, and two days later the lines were extended to Medford, north of Boston, to form a semicircle around the port, with Cambridge in the center. General Gage was effectively besieged.

Other New England colonies sprang to the aid of Massachusetts. New Hampshire minutemen were on the march the day after Lexington. Israel Putnam was at work on his farm when an express rider thundered past shouting the news. Without even taking off his leather apron, he sprang on his horse, aroused the militia in the nearby towns, ordered them to follow him and then rode the same horse 100 miles without a stop to arrive in Cambridge on April 21. Two thousand Connecticut men arrived a few days later. Rhode Island voted on April 25 to send a 1,500-man "Army of Observation" which was soon enroute. But Massachusetts, which had as many as 10,000 militiamen in Cambridge the day after Lexington and, as the largest province, was expected to raise the bulk of the army, ran into trouble.

A militiaman did not consider himself a regular soldier. Since the foundation of the colony he had been required by law to turn out to resist the enemies of the province or township. But he was never expected to stay in the field for a long campaign. He was strictly an emergency soldier, and although the emergency these militiamen had come out to combat was unique, they did not feel it changed their status. Before the horrified eyes of Warren and the other leaders, they began to go home by the hundreds before the end of the week. On April 21 the Committee of Safety, at Warren's urging, had voted to enlist an army of 8,000 men. But the resolution required the stamp of the Provincial Congress, which was moving at a much more deliberate pace. Only four days after Lexington, Artemas Ward was frantically writing to the congress: "If I have not enlisting orders immediately I shall be left all alone. It is impossible to keep the men here, excepting something be done." The congress came alive and on the same day voted to raise an army of 13,600 and issued "beating orders" to a number of men with military reputations who had their authority to beat drums in towns throughout the province and enlist men for the army until the first of the year. Since they were anxious to keep all the veterans of the French wars on the scene, preferably as officers, the company size was reduced to fifty-nine men and a regiment was limited to ten companies. Again, the congress was following the established custom. In England recruiting parties used the same system during emergencies. Unfortunately, when time was a crucial element, it was not a very workable system, since an officer could not be commissioned until he completed his company, or regiment—a process which might take several weeks.

By the first week in May, the American camp was so depleted—the officers with "beating orders" had also left to do their recruiting—that the Provincial Congress debated evacuating Cambridge and moving their small supply of stores and ammunition farther into the country. Only the lines before Boston Neck at Roxbury would have been maintained. Ward and the Council of War decided instead to call in all the men enlisted thus far, whether their regiments and companies were complete or not. On May 10, therefore, express riders carried this order throughout the province:

"In Committee of Safety, Camb. May 10, 1775
"Sir:
"As we are meditating a Blow against our restless Enemies —We therefore enjoin you as you would Evidence your Regard for your Country, forthwith upon the Receipt of this Order to repair to the Town of Cambridge with the Men inlisted under your command.
"We are, etc.
Benja. Church, Junr.
Chairman"

Dr. Church was on General Gage's secret service payroll, but this did not prevent him from rising high in the councils of the unsuspecting Americans. Warren "did not have the greatest affection for him" but others regarded him with great admiration. As chairman of the Committee of Safety he actually had more practical power than Warren, who was encumbered by the slow-moving congress. Church now proceeded to attempt a very neat maneuver with this marching letter which was, of course, intended only for recruiting officers in towns outside the American lines. He sent a copy of it to General Thomas in his fortifications before Roxbury. Thomas, a veteran soldier, read it as an order. The Committee of Safety had authority over the movements of the army at all times. But he was also intelligent enough, as a general, to realize that an evacuation of the American lines at Roxbury would be an invitation to total disaster. The British would only have to rush a regiment into town, man the fortifications which the militiamen had so painfully constructed over the last two weeks and the whole American right flank would be turned, Cambridge would have been untenable and the Americans would have had to fall back all the way to Concord.

Warren, as president of the Provincial Congress, was the only man in Massachusetts who outranked Church at this time. Instead of marching his men to Cambridge, Thomas sent a messenger galloping to Warren at Watertown where the congress was in almost continuous session. Warren rushed back an instantaneous reply.

"I have this moment received your letter, the Contents very much surprised me, as I had been absent from the Committee of Safety all Day I could not at first understand the matter, but upon Enquiry I find the Committee gave orders that all recruiting Officers should repair to Cambridge with the men they had enlisted, but the sending the Order to your Camp was certainly a very great Error, as it was designed only for those Officers who are in the Country, absent from Camp.

"Your readiness to obey Orders does you great Honor and your prudence in sending to Headquarters upon receiving so extraordinary an Order convinces me of your Judgment."

Warren already had some suspicions about Church. Two days after Lexington the latter had coolly announced that he was going into Boston. Even Warren, for all his courage, was aghast: "Are you serious, Dr. Church? They will hang you if they catch you in Boston." But Church was determined and Warren gave him his reluctant permission, suggesting that he bring back medicine for the Lexington wounded if he escaped the noose. Thirty-six hours later, the plump doctor returned with medicine and a story of being taken prisoner, hustled to Province House and interrogated angrily by Gage. But Paul Revere, who had long been suspicious of Church, learned not long after from one of his Boston informants that Church and Gage were seen in public conversing "like persons who had been long acquainted." Warren took no action—the evidence was largely hearsay—but he undoubtedly resolved to keep an eye on his fellow physician in the future and steer him away from responsible positions.

Church was, by no means, the only suspected double-dealer. Letters poured in to the Committee of Safety daily giving names of local citizens supposedly in correspondence with Gage. Warren simply did not have time to investigate Dr. Church. There were too many other things to worry about. Chief on Warren's agenda in the first week after Lexington was the compilation of a thorough account of the skirmish. He knew it was vital to get the story of the first bloodshed before the people of America and England in a version favorable to Massachusetts. For three days members of the Committee of Safety interviewed witnesses at the scene of the fight; justices of the peace accompanied them and administered oaths to the deponents; a notary public certified the good faith of the justices of the peace. Testimony was even obtained from captured British soldiers.

Warren may have known that historians, sifting these accounts, would find some of them wildly partisan. But there was no time to be scrupulous about minute details. What the young doctor wanted to communicate was there—the essential truth that the British had struck the first blow—that they had sent armed men into the countryside on a mission of war.

In their eagerness to get a report to the other colonies, the Committee of Safety compiled a narrative without waiting for the sworn depositions from Cambridge to arrive. The writer was no less than the double-dealing Dr. Church who, straining to certify his patriotism, told the story in almost absurdly naïve terms, painting the Americans as totally innocent victims and the British as barbarous plunderers.

Warren permitted the Church version to go out to the colonies, but he was obviously dissatisfied with it and a week later, using the material from the depositions, he himself composed a version of the fight to be sent to England. His account was far more restrained and accurate than the Church report. He ended it with a direct appeal to the English people, which once more showed Warren's desperate wish to settle the quarrel peacefully and justly, before it was too late.

"We cannot think that the honour, wisdom and valour of Britons will suffer them longer to be inactive spectators of measures in which they themselves are so deeply interested; measures pursued in opposition to the solemn protests of many noble Lords, and expressed sense of conspicuous Commoners, whose knowledge and virtue have long characterized them as some of the greatest men in the nation . . . We sincerely hope that the great Sovereign of the Universe, who hath so often appeared for the English nation, will support you in very rational and manly exertion with these Colonies, for saving it from ruin; and that in a constitutional connection with the Mother Country, we shall soon be altogether a free and happy people."

Warren put his manuscript on board the light, fast Salem schooner, *Quero,* with orders to beat Gage's official report, which had already sailed on the *Sukey.* The Yankee captain, sailing without cargo, reached England two weeks before Gage's heavier packet and Warren's story of Lexington created a sensation throughout the British Isles. One Englishman, John Horne, was so moved by the document that he raised £100 for the widows and orphans of "Our beloved American fellow subjects, who, faithful to the character of Englishmen, preferring death to slavery, were . . . inhumanly murdered by the King's troops at or near Lexington and Concord." Some historians have seen Warren's work as a masterpiece of propaganda. It was. It reinforced among a substantial portion of the English people the already widespread conviction that the government was embarking on an unjust and unnecessary war. But the word propaganda had not yet been invented. Warren was, on the contrary, passionately sincere in his wish for peace and in his hope that English friends could rally support for America.

Meanwhile, Warren was busy negotiating with General Gage to permit the Whigs and their friends to leave Boston. In this crucial exchange, Gage continued to blunder badly. All negotiations were conducted through the selectmen of Boston, with inevitable delays and confusion.

Even here, Gage could have demonstrated his magnanimity by freely permitting all those who wished to leave Boston to depart unconditionally. But once more the diplomat and the general became inextricably entangled. He first demanded a large concession. Before anyone could leave, he wanted to remove one of his nagging fears—that Boston would rise at his back. He demanded that all the citizens in the town surrender their weapons to him. Warren advised the Bostonians to agree and they promptly deposited in Faneuil Hall 1,778 muskets, 634 pistols, 973 bayonets and 38 blunderbusses. Satisfied, Gage announced that the gates of Boston were open. Warren, on his side, sent word throughout the province that anyone who wished the protection of the "Ministerial Army" would be free to enter Boston unmolested.

In the first four days almost 4,000 Bostonians poured across the Neck, to be resettled as refugees in the towns around Boston. The Tories inside the city became vastly alarmed. They went to Gage and demanded him to stop the evacuation. If it continued at its present pace, the town would be empty of everyone but Tories and British soldiers, and then what would prevent the rebels from burning it around their ears? They were also forming a loyalist "regiment" of some 200 men, and Timothy Ruggles, who was now called a general, threatened to disband them if Gage did not take his advice. Reluctantly Gage agreed—and threw away his last chance to convince Warren and the rest of Massachussetts that he was not entirely under Tory domination.

Gage could not abrogate the agreement; he had the Bostonians' guns which they had surrendered in good faith; all he could do was make it more and more difficult to obtain official passes to depart. Where it was originally a matter of minutes, it now became hours and days. Whole families were not permitted to depart. An older son or a father was retained on some pretext and others were forbidden to take their possessions with them. The evacuation slowed to a trickle and then stopped entirely.

For Warren, who knew intimately so many Bostonians, Gage's breach of trust was doubly bitter. "General Gage has trepanned the people of Boston," he wrote to Samuel Adams. Warren's fiancée, Mercy Scollay, and her family were among those whom Gage detained; though there is no direct record that the British and the Tories consciously held some people as hostages, the indirect evidence is strong. Samuel Adams' son was also detained.

By May 10 it became painfully evident that Gage was not honoring his agreement. He still refused to see Warren or any other representative of the Provincial Congress. That day Warren wrote him a letter which was almost a cry of despair.

"May it please your Excellency, I am very sensible of the formalities which gentlemen in your situation generally think yourselves obliged to observe, but the present state of public affairs renders it necessary that you should seriously consider whether you are to sacrifice the interest of Great Britain and the peace of the Colonies to mere forms. Great complaints are made respecting the delays in removing the inhabitants of Boston. I assure you, Sir, that this people, irritated as they have been, will not with any tolerable degree of patience suffer the agreement made between you and the inhabitants of Boston to be violated. If you still retain those sentiments of humanity which I ever supposed had a very great influence upon your conduct, I for the last time request that you would without hearkening to the mad advice of men who I know have deceived you, and I believe care not if they ruin you, and the Empire, punctually comply with your agreement with the inhabitants of the town of Boston. I am, with sincere respect for your person and hearty wishes that you may take such steps as upon reflection your own conscience may approve.

"Your Excellency's most obedient
servant,

Jos. Warren.

"As no person living knows, or ever will know from me of my writing this I hope you will excuse a freedom which I very well know would be improper in a letter which was to be exposed to general view."

Gage never answered this letter.

The deepening crisis forced Warren to accept more and more responsibilities. Toward the middle of May he replaced the suspect Dr. Church as Chairman of the Committee of Safety in a bloodless and even noiseless coup. Now another, totally unexpected problem arose. A delegation of citizens from the Connecticut Assembly appeared on the scene as a peace mission prepared to mediate between Gage and Massachusetts. Warren was aghast. The one hope England had of forcing the Americans to their knees was to split the colonies. This, as the colonists saw it, was the basic idea behind Lord North's Conciliatory Resolution. It was also Massachusetts' basic peril. They had led the way in colonial resistance, always at the risk of being condemned as troublemakers, independence-seekers. Now, when they had the continent—or at least New England—united behind them, was not the time to allow one colony to talk peace. Warren met the challenge by writing directly to John Trumbull, the Governor of Connecticut, who was elected by popular vote and was therefore a sympathetic Whig.

"We fear that our brethren in Connecticut are not even yet convinced of the cruel designs of Administration against America, nor thoroughly sensible of the miseries to which General Gage's army have reduced this wretched colony." He then described the situation—seaports deserted because the people were living in fear of a naval attack—Boston occupied and its people held as hostages by the treacherous, Tory-dominated Gage. Finally Warren wrote the most violent words he had used yet: "No business but that of war is either done or thought of in this colony. . . . Our relief now must arise from driving General Gage with his troops out of the country, which by the blessing of God, we are determined to accomplish or perish in the attempt."

Four days later Trumbull wrote a reply to "Hon Joseph Warren, Esq. chairman of the committee of Safety," putting Connecticut totally behind Warren's policy and promising immediate armed support. The following day Warren conferred with the Connecticut embassy which had seen Gage the day before. Whatever terms Gage offered for a settlement were immediately nullified when Warren presented the gentlemen with a letter from their governor, cutting the ground from beneath their mission.

In the midst of this complicated and feverish diplomacy, Warren also found time to confer with a young Connecticut captain named Benedict Arnold who arrived in Cambridge with an ambitious plan to capture the key British fortress of Ticonderoga on Lake Champlain. Warren was enthusiastically in favor of it. The fort was a storehouse full of gunpowder, muskets and ammunition and its cannon were desperately needed to reinforce the scanty American armaments now in the siege lines. But Ticonderoga was, unfortunately, on New York territory and rather than risk alienating that colony which was not yet committed to the cause, Warren restrained the impatient Arnold and sent a letter to New York asking permission to launch an attack. This was, however, only a politic gesture on Warren's part. Three days later when the letter had barely arrived in New York, he persuaded his fellow members of the Committee of Safety to give Arnold a colonel's commission and authority to enlist not over 400 men in western Massachusetts for a "secret service." When Arnold arrived in Stockbridge, Massachusetts, on the western border, he learned to his chagrin that a band of New Hampshire and Connecticut men, locally called "Green Mountain Boys" under the leadership of one Ethan Allen, were already marching on the fort. Arnold was only twenty miles from Ticonderoga when he caught up with these rugged backwoodsmen who had been fighting New York authority with words and bullets for over five years in a dispute about the land rights of New Hampshire citizens. Arnold persuaded Allen to share the command with him, by virtue of his commission from the Committee of Safety, and the next morning the two colonels led their band of eighty-three irregulars in a dawn assault which caught the forty-five-man garrison asleep in their beds; the mighty fort, which General James Abercromby had failed to take in 1758 with an army of 11,000 men, fell without a shot being fired. The "gateway to North America," as it was then considered, was in American hands, and Massachusetts' rear was protected from an attack from Canada. More important, no fewer than seventy-eight cannon, from four-pounders to twenty-four-pounders, went with the prize, plus six mortars, three howitzers, thousands of cannon balls, nine tons of musket bullets and 30,000 flints.

Arnold meanwhile was determined to outdo Allen, and when the Green Mountain Boys got riotously drunk on Ticonderoga's rum, "committing," in Arnold's words, "every enormity and paying no attention to publick service," he marshaled about 150 of the men he had recruited under his Committee of Safety enlisting order, sailed north along the lakes and captured Fort St. Johns on the Canadian frontier. Other men, acting under orders from Allen and Arnold, captured two more lightly manned forts along Lake Champlain. The grandiose Allen was carried away by this string of victories and he was soon planning to conquer all of Canada. "I will lay my life on it," he wrote to the New York Congress, "that with 1,500 men and a proper train of artillery, I will take Montreal . . . it would be no insuperable difficulty to take Quebeck." Arnold, no less ambitious, was in full agreement. But the warriors got a rude shock when an order from the Continental Congress arrived instructing them to abandon all the forts, even Ticonderoga, and remove all the guns and stores to the south end of Lake George. They were also ordered to keep an exact inventory of what they took "in order that they may be safely returned when the restoration of the former harmony between Great Britain and these colonies, so ardently wished for by the latter, shall render it prudent."

Warren's fiery phrase, "no business but war" was hardly the motto of the Continental Congress in the month of May,

1775. The moderates were still in control and while they grudgingly admitted the justice of Massachusetts' cause, they were still convinced that a peaceful solution was possible. George Washington attended in the blue and buff coat of a colonel in the Virginia militia. But he was an exception. On the lips of most men outside New England negotiation was still the watchword. John Adams, never hesitant to speak bluntly, wrote to Warren: "We find a great many Bundles of weak nerves. We are obliged to be as delicate and soft and modest and humble as possible." The capture of Ticonderoga and the other lake forts embarrassed the negotiators extremely. It made the colonies appear to be on the offensive—the last thing they wanted after spending three full days listening to depositions and drawing up an elaborate brief to prove that the British had fired first at Lexington. The brief of the Massachusetts Provincial Congress was already on the high seas to London but the moderates thought their effort required official confirmation by the Continental Congress. When word was received that 5,000 British troops were expected momentarily in New York, the congress resolved that the city should receive them without resistance and even give them barrack room, as required under the Quartering Act, at provincial expense. In the last weeks of May and early June, the congress devoted itself to composing An Humble and Dutiful Petition to his Majesty, vowing Americans wanted nothing but immediate negotiation and "accommodation of the unhappy disputes."

Up in Massachusetts, Joseph Warren was trying to accommodate disputes too. But they were not between Britain and America; they were between the unruly soldiers collected around Cambridge and the government of the province. Trained in disputation by their town meetings, and with little or nothing to do except man the siege lines, the men fell to discussing the authority of the Provincial Congress and the Committee of Safety. What right did they have to make laws, collect public money and regulate the conduct of the army? Where did they derive their authority? Not from King George III. Did they suppose they could control the army merely because they had had something to do with forming it? Who was more important to the survival of the colony now, the army or the congress? Rapidly this thinking swept the camp; in regiment after regiment men squatted around their campfires and argued about it day and night. Any attempt to discipline a lawbreaker was strenuously resisted by his fellow soldiers. More alarming, the men began to look around them at the large farms and herds of cattle owned by some men and compare them to their own more modest possessions. Some of these estates belonged to Tories but the Provincial Congress was scrupulously protecting their property. Even those who were not Tories but owned what seemed like an unjust proportion of this world's goods came under severe scrutiny.

On May 16 Warren and the entire Provincial Congress had become sufficiently alarmed by the situation to dispatch an urgent request to the Continental Congress to adopt the army before Boston as a national force and help Massachusetts form a legal civil government. On May 26, with the petition still unanswered, he wrote again to Samuel Adams:

"The continent must strengthen and support with all its weight the civil authority here; otherwise our soldiery will lose all ideas of right and wrong, and will plunder, instead of protecting the inhabitants. This is but too evident already . . . the least hint from the most unprincipled fellow who has perhaps been reproved for some criminal behavior is quite sufficient to expose the fairest character to insult and abuse. . . ."

Then Warren, with a generosity which explains in itself his enormous popularity with the people of Massachusetts, abruptly changed his tone:

"You may possibly think I am a little angry with my countrymen, or have not so good an opinion of them as I formerly had; but that is not the case. I love—I admire them. The errors they have fallen into are natural and easily accounted for. It is not easy for men, especially when interest and the gratification of appetite are considered, to know how far they may continue to tread in the path where there are no landmarks to direct them. I hope care will be taken by the Continental Congress to apply an immediate remedy as the infection is caught by every new corps that arrives . . . For the honor of my country, I wish the disease may be cured before it is known to exist."

In forwarding these alarming messages to the Continental Congress, Warren was doing much more than serving as the local reporter for Massachusetts; he was exerting shrewd and much needed pressure to swing the congress—the rest of America—behind New England. He was also taking the most unprecedented and boldest step yet made toward American unity. Here was the great province of Massachusetts voluntarily putting itself under the control of the Continental Congress. Only a year ago, in the first session of the congress, some delegates were heard saying Massachusetts had a secret plan to conquer the other colonies by military force as soon as they pushed the British off the continent.

But the caution of the moderates still prevailed. The committee which considered Warren's letter replied that Massachusetts might order an election of representatives to a new Provincial Congress in June of 1776—a full year away. From these representatives a council or upper house could be chosen—"which assembly and council shall exercise the powers of Government until a Governor of his Majesty's appointment will consent to govern the colony according to its charter."

Between Warren in Massachusetts and the continental leaders in Philadelphia there was, for the time being, a gulf

almost as wide as the one which separated America from
George III. There was no royal army a half mile away from
the Continental Congress with authority to hang, draw and
quarter rebels. Friends and relatives were not held hostage
in a city from which many other friends and relatives had
fled as refugees. Fifteen thousand armed men were not on
their doorstep with ideas about governing at the point of a
gun. The congressmen needed a shock to jolt them out of
their complacency.

The shock was coming their way with the inexorable
movement of a great wave building up in the open sea or
the slow accumulation of an avalanche.

6

ONE of the prime movers of the avalanche was the man who stood now on the dark crest of Breed's Hill studying the almost completed American fort. Once, twice, William Prescott strode around it with Richard Gridley, checking the solidity of the walls, and then pronounced himself satisfied. Gridley promptly put the men to work on the firing platforms inside the fort and on a deep ditch around the outside into which they threw bushes, logs and any other likely looking obstructions they found in the vicinity.

With a grim interior smile, Prescott looked once more across the harbor at sleeping Boston. His former British brothers in arms would be more than a little surprised, Prescott was certain, when they awoke in the morning and found out how much their supposedly amateur American opponents could accomplish in a single night. What the British would do about it was, of course, the great question. If the colonel had any qualms, he suppressed them with a soldier's logic: what was the purpose of collecting an American army unless they were given a chance to fight—and incidentally to prove the conviction that possessed Prescott with religious fervor—that Americans could stand up to British regulars.

This military logic, which Prescott shared with many others, had become a more and more powerful influence in American thinking as the siege of Boston—and the existence of the Provincial Army—acquired permanence. It appeared for the first time less than a week after Lexington.

Israel Putnam, brigadier general of the independent army of Connecticut, which was cooperating with the army of Massachusetts and the army of Rhode Island in the siege, was on horseback directing his men at work on a fortification they were building along the Cambridge road. Colonel Prescott and Colonel Thomas Gardner of Massachusetts appeared on the scene and watched the operation for a few minutes. Putnam gave them a friendly greeting and Prescott, in his austere way, returned it. "I wish, General," he said, "your men were digging closer to Boston."

"I wish so too," Putnam replied. "I hope we shall all be of one mind before long."

Prescott was already a tower of strength in the Massachusetts corps. His regiment had been maintained at full strength since the day after Lexington; it was well organized and—compared to other American units—well disciplined. But the tall colonel was not the sort of man who enjoyed the cautious war of blockade and attrition Artemas Ward was waging against the British. Colonel Gardner had another, equally urgent reason for hungering after action. He had led his regiment into the fight along the Lexington road just as Lord Percy opened up with his two cannon. His minutemen were utterly panicked by the blast and ran like rabbits. The mortified colonel never did re-form them into a coherent fighting force, and though his men were by no means the only Americans who ran from the cannon that day, Gardner considered it a stain on his reputation which he was burning to erase.

Neither Prescott nor Gardner could approach the influence which Putnam had already achieved in the "Grand

American Army," as the local newspapers liked to call it. Gage himself was sufficiently impressed by his reputation to offer him the rank of major general in the British army if he was willing to desert to the King's service. (Putnam declined the bribe but remained on friendly terms with his former comrade in arms. When the siege made fresh meat scarce in Boston, he sent Mrs. Gage a side of beef for her large family in Province House.) Putnam had acquired his reputation largely through feats of personal courage; he had never commanded a large army; most of his experience was with guerilla detachments of 200 or 300 rangers. But he knew the business of soldiering and was not shy about expressing his opinions. He also had become a warm friend of Joseph Warren's.

When Putnam had led his sheep to the relief of beleaguered Boston, Warren had invited him to stay several days in his house, and the old warrior took an instantaneous liking to the young doctor. It was, on the surface, an incongruous friendship. The fifty-three-year-old veteran was a rough and ready soldier who dressed like the farmer he was and stuttered in private conversation. The eloquent Warren was a dandy who often spent more on his clothes than he could afford. But Putnam's mind was not as simple as he looked or talked. He had a keen grasp of the political issues in the struggle between colonies and mother country. He was also a sensitive man; in spite of the baker's dozen battles in which he had distinguished himself, he could, so it was said, still faint at the sight of blood. As far as Putnam was concerned, moreover, there was only one denominator for friendship: courage. He found more than enough to satisfy him in Warren.

On his side, Warren must have been delighted by the way Putnam gave it right back to his soldiering friends in the British regiments. The younger American was probably just a little awed by these tough veterans. Putnam had ducked the same bullets, marched the same miles. One day his old comrade, Major John Small of the Forty-seventh Regiment, began joshing him about American fighting ability. Did Putnam think it was true, as some members of Parliament said, that four regiments could march from one end of the continent to the other without opposition?

"Oh, probably true enough," said Putnam with a very solemn face. "They would meet no opposition if they let the womenfolk alone. But if they annoyed the women, a few brigades of females with broomsticks would chase them right into the ocean."

During the sixty days Putnam and Warren were together in the Cambridge camp, Warren somehow found time to spend hours with Putnam in his quarters, discussing military problems. The young physician was becoming more and more convinced that he would have to become a soldier in order to lead his people properly. He listened to Putnam's stories of his experiences against the French and particularly asked him his opinion of the quality of the provincial troops in comparison to the British regulars. Putnam insisted that when the provincial regiments were well officered, they were not inferior to the British. "Our men," he said, "would always follow wherever their officers led."

Constantly on everyone's mind was the fear that the British would attempt to break through the Boston siege ring. How many men would Putnam need to meet an attack of 10,000 British regulars?

"Let me pick my officers," Putnam answered, "and I would not fear to meet them with half the number— Not in a pitched battle, to stop them at once, for no troops are better than the British, but I would fight on the retreat, and every stone wall we passed should be lined with their dead. Our men are lighter of foot, they understand our grounds and how to take advantage of them; and besides, we should only fall back on our reserve, while every step they advanced, the country would close on their flanks and rear."

Warren also listened attentively to that frequently reiterated Putnam opinion which was largely responsible for the extensive fortifications thrown up by the army before Cambridge. "Americans are not afraid of their heads," he said again and again, "but they are very much afraid of their legs. Cover them and they will fight until doomsday." Another good reason for digging with which Warren was in thorough agreement was Putnam's conviction that the raw and undisciplined troops must be employed some way or they would soon become vicious and unmanageable. "It is better to dig a ditch every morning and fill it up at evening," Putnam told him, "than to have the men idle." Putnam was particularly vehement on this point; undoubtedly he offended more than a few Massachusetts men who did not agree with his fortification program because they did not have enough authority over their men to make them work regularly. One day Putnam rode up to a fatigue party which was doing more sitting than digging and angrily asked them the name of their regiment.

"Doolittle," drawled one prone soldier insolently.

"Doolittle? Do nothing at all," Putnam snapped.

He could insult them but he had no authority over these Massachusetts soldiers. Artemas Ward, who had the authority, in theory, wisely did not attempt to exercise it too strictly. The men were in no mood for authoritative government, either military or civil. This thoroughly unsoldierlike tendency was, ultimately, to be an argument in favor of desperate measures.

In the meantime, Putnam decided the men could use a bold gesture to give them confidence. On May 13 he marched all the troops except those on guard in the lines before Cambridge onto Charlestown peninsula. Over Bunker

Hill they marched and over the lesser, variously named hill, which we are calling Breed's, and down through the village of Charlestown, already deserted, and back along the south road which ran the length of the peninsula by the waterside. The line of march stretched for a mile and a half, and the guns of the British fleet, many of them less than 100 yards away, were trained on them, every step. The sailors stood by their loaded cannon, lighted matches poised above the touchholes; the first shot from the American line would have brought a murderous salvo. But the shot was not fired and the British guns remained silent. Both sides were still determined not to fire first.

Next came the "battle" of Noddle Island. The British, desperate for fresh meat for the troops and hay for their horses, began stripping the islands in Boston Harbor of livestock and fodder. The Americans decided to stop them. On May 27 a party of militiamen waded through the shallow channel to Hog Island (now East Boston) and began driving off its livestock. Admiral Graves had cached a substantial amount of naval stores on nearby Noddle Island and he sent forty marines in the armed schooner *Diana*, captained by his nephew, Lieutenant Thomas Graves, to protect his property. The Americans dove into a ditch on the Noddle marsh when the British opened fire from the schooner and they met the debarking marines with a volley which killed two and wounded two. The Americans then retreated to Hog Island and the outnumbered British watched helplessly while between 300 and 400 sheep, lambs, cows and horses were driven through the shallow water to provincial pastures.

General Gage sent eighty marines and two twelve-pounders to assist the admiral's men. Before they arrived, however, the *Diana* got into trouble in the treacherous channel and, with the wind and tide against her, began drifting toward the American shore. The admiral sent the armed sloop *Britannia* and a dozen barges from the fleet to tow her out. The Americans sent to Cambridge for reinforcements.

Within the hour Israel Putnam arrived with 1,000 men and two cannon. Joseph Warren, unable to resist the lure of battle, was with him. Nothing the British did could cure the drift of the *Diana,* and when the schooner was within musket range, Putnam called on its crew to surrender. They answered with a blast from their swivel cannon and four-pounders. Gage's men, meanwhile, set up their twelve-pounders on Noddle Island and began bombarding the Americans while the marines blazed away with their muskets. A ferocious fire-fight followed in which few men on either side were hit. The range was too great—Putnam at one point led his men into waist-deep water to get a closer shot. As darkness fell, the *Diana* went aground and the crew abandoned her. The Americans stood guard over the schooner for the rest of the night and at dawn they stole aboard the battered ship, stripped her of guns and sails and everything else they could pry loose, which included British uniforms and money, then burned her to the water line in full view of the enraged and frustrated British fleet. About an hour later, the sloop *Britannia* returned for another round and was soon so badly riddled by cannon and musket shot that she had to be towed off by seamen in rowboats.

Not a man was killed on the American side and the British casualties did not exceed a dozen but the skirmish received vast publicity throughout the colonies. In the Cambridge camp the raw soldiers, eager to prove their equality to the British regulars, magnified it into a major battle. Putnam's prestige, already great, rose even higher because of his leadership in the fight. To the optimists it began to look as if the "Grand American Army" was taking on a semblance of fighting form. But it was only a semblance. The Provincial Congress dragged its feet on handing out commissions to field officers above the rank of colonel. One reason was the hope that the Continental Congress would, any day now, adopt the army and hand out its own commissions. The temporary result, however, was a lack of brigadiers and an unbrigaded army. An army without brigades—Gage's small force was divided into three brigades of four regiments each—was nothing but an unwieldy mob.

As for the colonels, their regimental commissions were worth considerably less than their paper value of 590 men. The May 10 decision to summon all available officers and men without giving the recruiting officers a chance to complete their regiments and companies was absolutely necessary. But it gave the army's organization a blow from which it almost never recovered. Companies ranged from twenty-three to the official fifty-nine, and regiments varied from barely 200 to over 900. Ward and Warren had to cope with countless disputes in jurisdiction and charges of unfair competition among officers who began to recruit men from each other in the Cambridge camp. Colonel Jonathan Brewer was accused of luring men to his standard by advertising for "rangers"— irregular troops who would be sure to lead a more exciting life and have no worries about army displine. Warren summoned Brewer to the Provincial Congress and gently suggested that he stop; the army did not want rangers. The muster list for Brewer's regiment when he finally scraped together enough men was typical: instead of 598, he had 397, of whom only 302 had guns.

Equally typical was the petition which Warren received on May 25 from a group of Essex County captains. It was addressed to "the Honorable Committee of Safety for the Colony of Massachusetts Bay:

"Gentlemen:
"We the subscribers being captains of the companies now enlisted in the service of the government have made choice of Captain Moses Little to be our chief colonel and Major Isaac Smith to be our lieutenant colonel. We beg that your

honors will be pleased to direct or recommend that the aforesaid persons may be commissioned as officers over us.

Captains	The Number of Men
Joseph Gerish	59
Ezrah Lunt	61
Nath L. Warner	59
Abraham Dodge	70
Nathl Wade	59
Benjn Perkins	75
John Baker	59
Total	422

N. B. Captain Collins, Chairman of this meeting of choice has now a company of 59 men."

These captains were not only poor in arithmetic; six of the seven had been returned by Colonel Samuel Gerrish of Newbury as belonging to his regiment. Gerrish was a corpulent indecisive man and the younger officers had obviously decided they preferred to serve under the more vigorous Little who had commanded a company of soldiers from Newbury in the expedition against Louisburg and was now in camp as a captain.

The Provincial Congress appointed a committee to consider the matter. A week later, after meeting with Colonel Gerrish and his recalcitrant officers, they decided to allow them to send their petition to the Committee of Safety, to whom it was addressed in the first place. For two weeks no decision was made. In desperation the bewildered company commanders again petitioned the committee and on June 13 —only four days before Bunker Hill—the committee issued an order which gives a graphic picture of the army's appalling disorganization. Colonel Little and seven other colonels were told "to make a true return to the Committee of the claims and pretentions of the several gentlemen claiming to be commissioned as colonels; of the number of captains with their

respective companies who choose to serve under the above
named gentlemen as colonels; and of the number of efficient
firearms in each company, and of the place or places where
said companies are; at pain of forfeiting all pretentions to a
commission as colonel, in case of making a false return."

Two days later the committee granted Little's claims,
reporting: "the said Little has raised eight companies . . .
amounting inclusive of officers to the number of 509 men
who choose to serve under him as their chief colonel; and
all the said men are armed with good effective firelocks and
382 of them with good bayonnets, fitted to their firelocks."
This meant that Gerrish, deprived of seven-eighths of his
regiment, had to scrape up men where he could to form another one if he wanted to retain his commission. He managed it, but with disastrous results.

Another problem which occupied the seemingly sleepless
Warren was the British wounded. At his urging, General
Ward made scrupulously sure that the officers and men
taken prisoner along the Lexington road received the best
available medical care. Ward sent word to Gage in Boston
that if he "chose to have any surgeons of his own appointment attend them, he was at liberty to nominate them."
In his general orders he warned the "officers of the guards
who have the care of the prisoners to take the best care of
them and treat them in the kindest manner." In another
letter Ward urged Colonel James Barrett in Concord, where
many of the wounded were sent, "Pray keep them from any
infection that may arise from putting too many in one room
. . . provide everything needful for their comfortable subsistence."

By the early days of June many of these prisoners were
well enough to walk and Warren, at Putnam's suggestion,
arranged with Gage to exchange them for several Americans
the British had captured on April 19 and in later skirmishes
between the lines. On June 6 Putnam and Warren accom-

panied their prisoners to Charlestown escorted by an honor guard of the Wethersfield, Connecticut company under Captain John Chester. There were three British officers and five privates to be traded for eight American privates. The British exchange party was led by Majors Moncrieff and Small. They debarked from the *Lively* and met the Americans at the Charlestown ferry.

The moment Moncrieff and Putnam saw each other, they let out whoops of joy and in the words of an eyewitness "ran into each other's arms and kissed each other, to the great diversion and astonishment of the country people of the army." Moncrieff was an old friend who had campaigned with Putnam in the British-American capture of Havana in 1761. The wounded privates were sent on board the *Lively* and the officers, Putnam and Warren, adjourned to the house of Dr. Foster where they had lunch. At three o'clock the *Lively* delivered the American prisoners to the dock and they were fed at the Foster house and sent back to Cambridge. Moncrieff and the other officers were enjoying themselves so much with Warren and Putnam that they stayed for another two hours and did not go on board the *Lively* again until six o'clock.

Back in camp, Putnam told his sixteen-year-old son, Daniel, how gratified he was by the exchange. "Gage may call us rebels now if he will but why don't he hang his prisoners instead of exchanging them? By this act he has virtually placed us on an equality and acknowledged our right of resistance."

The next day, June 7, Colonel Prescott and a number of other officers visited Putnam's quarters to get a firsthand report of the exchange. Putnam gave them a lively story and then turned to Prescott: "Colonel, I saw ground yesterday that may suit your purpose. I suppose you have not forgotten your remark of the other day about digging; but more of this another time."

That evening, Daniel Putnam recalled, Prescott visited Putnam again and they "walked out together." For the next three or four days the Masachusetts colonel was a frequent visitor, and he and Putnam were constantly in "private conversation." On June 10, Putnam led the Cambridge garrison on another march across the Charlestown peninsula. Thereafter, he was, in his son's words, "thoughtful and absent in his mind."

"Broken sentences escaped his lips: 'We must go there . . . Think they will come out . . . Yes, yes, they must . . . I'll go with my regiment anyhow . . . We must go in the night . . . Says he will go if they let him . . . He's a good fellow—lay still—lay still I say till they come close—they won't hurt you—I know 'em of old, they fire without aim.' These and such like burstings of his mind continued for several days which left no doubt but he was contemplating some important military operation."

As early as May 13, Putnam had urged Warren and the Committee of Safety to fortify Bunker Hill and Prospect Hill, on the mainland directly behind Charlestown Neck. But the committee had decided it would be an aggressive move and declined his advice. Earlier, General Ward had contemplated occupying Dorchester peninsula to the south of Boston. But they had no heavy cannon and Boston was full of their friends. It seemed pointless to occupy a post which was not tactically useful when the Roxbury fortifications were more than ample to pen the British inside Boston. Besides, General Thomas, who was in charge at Roxbury, was adamant against the idea.

Now, on June 13, the news that Gage was planning to seize both peninsulas and, according to Howe's plan, strike finally at Cambridge, made all these deliberations and hesitations meaningless. The American policy of nonaggression suddenly became a policy of immobility. The incontrovertible fact that they had an army in their possession—and the British considered this rather than diplomatic negotiations, the first consideration—made them realize they were behaving like sitting ducks. The council of war met with Warren; Putnam promptly suggested his redoubt on Bunker Hill again. Colonels Prescott and Gardner vehemently seconded the motion. Artemas Ward, Joseph Warren and many others did not agree. "We have no powder to spare and no battering cannon," Ward pointed out. "It would be idle to make approaches on the town."

Putnam protested that he had no desire to make approaches on the town. What he wanted was a chance to draw the enemy out of town on ground where they could be met on equal terms; ground that could be fortified and had natural advantages as well. Fighting from behind cover with the ground in their favor Putnam was convinced that the Americans could inflict enough casualties on the attacking British to permanently cripple their small army and cut the legs off Howe's plan before it got under way. Thanks to their excellent spy system the colonials knew exactly how many regulars were in Boston: just under 5,000. Subtracting about 1,500 as an absolute minimum needed to guard their rear in the rebellious town, this meant Howe had a field force of little more than 3,500 men. It would not take particularly heavy casualties to cripple an army of this size.

"We will only risk 2,000 men," Putnam said. "And defend ourselves as long and as well as we can. If they drive us back, every wall will be lined with their dead."

His opponents argued that it could bring on a general engagement, for which they had barely nine rounds of powder per man. There was also the risk of committing raw troops against the regulars. To the shortage of powder, gray-haired, sixty-eight-year-old Seth Pomeroy, hero of wars against the French while Putnam was still a boy, had an answer. Americans could go hunting in the woods with only three charges and bring home a deer. They did not need as much powder as a regular soldier.

This was sheer imagination on Pomeroy's part but it made an impression. Putnam welcomed his support and came back with a more realistic argument of his own. Which was better, a general engagement fought on their terms or on General Howe's terms? As for the raw troops, action was what they needed. The army was "rotting away with idleness."

But suppose the retreat should be intercepted?

"We will guard against that," Putnam said, "and run when we can contend no longer with advantage; we can outrun them and behind every wall rally . . . till we join our friends again. But suppose the worst, suppose us hemmed in and no retreat; we know what we are contending for; we will set our country an example of which it shall not be ashamed and show those who seek to oppress us what men can do who are determined to live free or not live at all."

Warren's face came aglow at this declaration. He was the final authority in the conference room. President of the Provincial Congress and head of the Committee of Safety, he could stop the gamble with a word. It was an aggressive move. Their policy had been to do nothing aggressive, to let the British strike the first blow. But this obviously was now inviting disaster. Putnam was right too about the army rotting away. Some fighting was what the men needed to remind them that they were soldiers, not politicians. God knows, he wanted a chance to fight himself, to show England they meant business.

He had no doubt whatsoever about the forthcoming British attack. Only last night, with typical daring, he had slipped into Boston by canoe to check with members of the American spy ring. General Burgoyne, for one, had been telling everyone in town about the operation for over a week. Many junior officers were equally talkative. (Warren had recklessly doubled his risk by arranging to meet a young fellow doctor named John Jeffries who had not yet committed himself to either side. Warren offered him the surgeon generalship of the American army if Jeffries would get in the canoe and come with him. Jeffries thanked him, but refused.)

Slowly, his head down, the young doctor-turned-statesman paced up and down the room and leaned for a thoughtful moment over the back of a chair. Then, smiling at his good friend, he said: "Almost thou persuadest me, General Putnam. But I must still think the project a rash one. Nevertheless, if it should be adopted and the strife becomes hard, you must not be surprised to find me in the midst of it."

"I hope not," Putnam said. "You are yet but a young man and our country has much to hope from you both in council and in war. It is only a little brush we have been contemplating; let some of us who are older and can well enough be spared begin the fray; there will be time enough for you hereafter; for it will not soon be ended."

Warren's semi-acquiescence was enough. On June 15 the Committee of Safety passed the following resolution: "Whereas it appears of importance to the Safety of this Colony that possession of the hill called Bunker's Hill in Charlestown be securely kept and defended; and also some one hill or hills on Dorchester be likewise secured. Therefore resolved unanimously that it be recommended to the Council of War that the above mentioned Bunker's Hill be maintained by sufficient force being posted there and as the particular situation of Dorchester Neck is unknown to this Committee they advise that the Council of War take and pursue such steps respective to same, as to them shall appear to be for the security of this colony."

The council of war promptly resolved to "take immediate possession of Bunker's Hill and Dorchester Neck." But in order to launch a foray on this southern peninsula (in 1775 the words "neck" and "peninsula" were used interchangeably) the council had to secure the agreement of General John Thomas, at Roxbury, who had over 7,000 men under him. Because he occupied the "post of danger" where everyone thought the British assault would come, he guarded his forces jealously and gradually acquired a semi-independent command. When Putnam and two Massachusetts colonels, Samuel Gerrish and Jonathan Ward, a cousin of the commander in chief, visited Thomas to get his cooperation, he in turn called his own council of war; it was an army operated by committee. The Roxbury council vetoed their share of the operation. They still wanted no part of occupying the peninsula. The hope of a combined operation on both British flanks, which might have divided and confused Gage's small army, thus went glimmering, but Putnam returned to Cambridge still determined to launch his foray on Charlestown Heights as soon as possible. With Prescott's backing he persuaded the council of war to put the project into movement immediately.

Orders went out to the regiments of Frye, Bridge and Prescott, Samuel Gridley's artillery company and 200 of Putnam's Connecticut men. Prescott was in command. The Connecticut troops were led by Thomas Knowlton. The young captain was like his general when it came to speaking his mind. He told Putnam he "wholly disapproved of the project. It would probably prove fatal to the American troops for the British by landing at Charlestown Neck under the protection of the floating batteries and ships of war could cut off from the hill all supplies of provision and ammunition, besides rendering retreat extremely hazardous if not impossible."

Putnam did not argue with him. He simply said: "I am going. Will you come with me?"

"Yes," Knowlton said. "And every one of my men."

A little after sunset that night, Putnam called his son Daniel aside and told him to go to Mrs. Inman's farmhouse where he and the Connecticut officers had their quarters. It was about a quarter of a mile from the Connecticut camp, which was in another post of danger about two miles forward of the Cambridge lines not far from where the British troops had landed for their march to Concord. "You need not return here in the morning, but stay there tomorrow; the family may want you and if they find it necessary to leave the house, you must go with them . . . and try to be as serviceable to them as you can."

The youngster knew what was happening. He had watched his father's abstraction and self-communings for over a week. "My imagination pictured him mangled with wounds and none to help him," he said later. "I asked leave to accompany him."

"You may need my assistance much more than Mrs. Inman," the boy said. "Let me go where you are going."

"No, no, Daniel, do as I have told you," the gray-haired veteran said. It was intended to be stern but his voice suddenly broke and his eyes filled with tears. With an effort he regained his soldier's self-control. "You can do little, my son, where I am going, and besides there will be enough to take care of me."

It is only a little brush we are contemplating. Putnam's farewell to his son resembled much more the words of a man who was embarking on the most desperate gamble of his life. But it was a gamble born of much more than his pugnacious spirit. There was the bitterness caused by British and Tory threats of hanging and taunts of cowardice, which so rankled fighting men like Prescott. There was Gage's breach of trust with Boston. There was the idealistic courage of Joseph Warren which impelled him to regard the challenge of danger as a personal test. There was the growing menace of a political rather than a fighting army. There was the maddening tendency of the Continental Congress to talk peace while Massachusetts stared into the cannon's mouth. There was the menace of Howe's plan to break the siege.

There was, above all, the endless indecision of the King's ministers. On June 16, while Prescott was assembling his men on Cambridge common, the *Evening Post* in London reported: "The cabinet it is said is much agitated with contrary opinions since the last dispatches from America. Lord North is for conciliatory measures; the Bedford Party against it; while Lord R. is for withdrawing the troops from Boston." On the same day *The Morning Post and Daily Advertiser* declared: "If the ministry were desirous of covering their present confusion it were impossible, since the repeated councils and embassies from the various ministers so plainly declare it; but Lord North is too candid to attempt a denial of a fact so evident."

Down in Philadelphia, a new delegate to the Continental Congress sat with the Pennsylvania men. Benjamin Franklin had come home after eight years in England. Even after Chatham's humiliating defeat, the philosopher had refused to allow his temporary bitterness to blight his hopes for peace; for two more frustrating months he had continued to conduct secret negotiations with the ministry, mainly through William Howe's brother, Admiral Lord Richard Howe, who was a good friend of Lord Dartmouth's, the colonial secretary. At one point in these talks Franklin offered to pay for the Boston Tea Party out of his own pocket —a move which would have ruined him politically in America. The ministry, on its side, discreetly offered to give him any government sinecure he wanted if he would yield a little on the American terms for settlement. Negotiations broke down finally and completely when Franklin was told that the government might waive payment for the tea but was absolutely determined that the changes in the Massachusetts charter would stand. This was a question of liberty, not money, and Franklin's reply was a scathing negative. He began packing to go home.

His last day in England Franklin spent alone with his scientist friend Joseph Priestley. As they read newspapers from America, and Franklin marked out stories which Priestley was to extract for the English papers, again and again the philosopher was forced to stop because tears filled his eyes and ran down his cheeks. When he landed in Philadelphia on May 10, Franklin found almost all his fears come true. The "mad business of mixing soldiers and citizens" had spilled blood along the Lexington road. An American army confronted the British outside Boston. Yet Franklin made no attempt to impose his personal despair on the men in the Continental Congress who still talked desperately of conciliation. In private he advised his son, William Franklin, to resign as royal governor of New Jersey. But when William refused Franklin did not attempt to press the point. He knew perhaps better than any other man that the issue had now passed the realm of individual decision or parliamentary debate. If someone had come to him on the night of June 16, 1775, and told him that American soldiers were entrenching on Charlestown Heights, he would not have been surprised. But we can be certain that he would have wept at the prospect of the day to come.

7

ABOUT an hour before sunrise the first gray streaks of dawn began to lighten the sky above Boston Harbor. Slowly, from the damp quarterdeck of the *Lively,* the village of Charlestown took ghostly shape. The marine on the morning watch stared idly shoreward through the haze. His predecessor on the middle watch had reported hearing some sort of movement coming from the heights during the night. Perhaps the rebels were cutting the unmown hay in the pastures that checkered the hills behind the town. He chuckled to himself. Another frustration for poor old Tommy Gage and the soldiers on the shore. The men in the fleet had little sympathy for the army's problems. The dawn came on steadily now, and with it the houses in the back end of Charlestown became distinct and then the mass of the hill above them. There was something on top of the hill. The marine stared, aghast. Something was hardly the word.

Captain Thomas Bishop of the *Lively* tumbled from his bunk and rushed to the quarterdeck. Through the gray light his eyes followed the marine's excited finger. Dreamlike though it seemed in the predawn, it was definitely a part of the real world—this unbelievable fortification which had appeared on Breed's Hill during the night. It was not the work of amateurs. That much was evident at a glance. Confronting them on the southeast side was a redan jutting out like an arrowhead in the center of the south wall. Only professional military engineers added that kind of touch to their forts. Now men could be seen digging a ditch around the outside—another professional touch. Measuring against the working men, the captain estimated the walls were at least six feet high and solidly built.

Bishop wheeled and barked orders to the watch. The ship throbbed with the sound of bare feet on planking as the *Lively*'s crew of 130 rushed to their stations. A boatswain's mate put a spring on the cable to steady the ship for gunnery and slowly swung the sloop broadside to Charlestown. "Commence firing," Captain Bishop roared. With an ear-shattering crash the *Lively*'s ten starboard guns opened up on the American fort.

The booming cannon tumbled all of Boston from their beds. Admiral Samuel Graves, commander of the flotilla in the harbor, petulantly sent an aide to find out what in blazes the captain of the *Lively* was shooting at. Admiral Graves had had nothing but trouble since he arrived in Boston a year ago. His ships were undermanned and too few in number to blockade efficiently the vast coastline he was supposed to patrol. It was moreover his first experience with a large command. He fumbled furiously with his uniform while another broadside from the *Lively* boomed across the harbor. His aide returned to inform him that the captain of the *Lively* was firing upon some American troops "who were entrenching on the heights above Charlestown."

"He has no such orders," Admiral Graves snapped. "Tell him to cease fire immediately."

Admiral Graves had a low opinion of the Americans as soldiers. For him the words "Americans entrenching" carried the image of a few farmers with picks and shovels throwing up haphazard mounds of dirt. A good broadside from the battleship *Somerset* would send them flying like geese. Fifteen minutes later Admiral Graves was ready to descend for breakfast when his aide returned with a message from General Gage. "His Excellency would appreciate your examining the rebel fortifications on Charlestown Heights. They are reported to be substantial."

The admiral grunted unenthusiastically. Relations between Graves and Gage had been strained since the admiral's arrival. Gage had no authority over him; Graves received all his orders from the admiralty in far-off London. He frequently reminded the general of this fact and in his letters home reiterated that he had no responsibility for the army's problems and blunders, brought on, he invariably hinted, by Gage's incompetence. The interservice rivalry had a personal edge in it, the result of an argument Graves had had with Gage's father years before.

More than a few officers and civilians accused the admiral of profiting from the fresh meat that was sold under Boston counters at a guinea a pound. His ships were the only way this essential commodity could reach the town and they regularly scoured the harbor islands and seacoast towns in search of cattle. There is no doubt that Graves spent as much time trying to procure such niceties of his office as gilt-edged letter paper as he did preparing his ships for war. Also close to his heart were the fortunes of his three nephews who were serving as junior officers in his fleet. He was constantly wrangling with his captains because they would not give the lads the promotions Uncle Samuel felt they deserved.

Immediately after Lexington, Graves was advising Gage to burn Roxbury and Charlestown, seize Dorchester Neck and threaten the colonists with the destruction of every seaport in Massachusetts if they did not lay down their arms. From this posture of all-out war, he retreated in less than a month to the point where he was telling Gage that the navy was not at war with the rebels as far as he was concerned and he would not fire so much as one hostile shot until he had explicit permission from the First Lord of the Admiralty.

The Noddle Island fight rudely awoke him from this illusion. Not only had he had the discomforture of seeing one of his sloops captured, stripped of its cannon and burned to the waterline by these insolent Americans within cannon shot of his heavy warships, his nephew Thomas had been the officer in command. Graves irately blamed Gage and the rest of the army for the debacle. No matter if the skirmish had been fought on an island in the heart of Boston Harbor, it wasn't his job to protect these islands and their provisions from raiding parties. The raiders came from land and what came from land was an army problem. Thus reasoned Admiral Samuel Graves with sound nautical logic. No doubt he was turning similar thoughts over in his head as he trudged to the flat roof of his house and trained his glass on Charlestown Heights. What he saw made him gasp almost as unbelievingly as Captain Bishop aboard the *Lively* three-quarters of an hour earlier. "Order all ships to commence firing immediately," he said.

Ten minutes later with a roar that shook every window in Boston, the fleet in the harbor opened up on the rebel fort with 168 guns. At first they did nothing but tear chunks out of the earth a hundred yards below the crest of the hill. But they soon were coming closer. Again and again Graves saw shots smash against the side of the American fort. But they bounced harmlessly back. How could the rebels build something so solid in a single night? Graves watched while another broadside sent a shower of solid shot against the fort. No sign of panic, of disorganized rabble fleeting for their lives. They had taken cover inside the walls, but they were standing their ground against a bombardment that would have given regular troops some anxious thoughts. Admiral Graves was amazed.

Up in Province House, Thomas Gage was studying the Americans under fire and thinking different thoughts. Unlike Admiral Graves he had no illusions about American courage. No one who had marched and fought with men like Israel Putnam and George Washington could be so obtuse. But courage and training were not synonymous. That was why Gage found cause for hope in this new colonial challenge. The Americans were at their best in a running skirmish such as the foray to Lexington and Concord had become. They were at their worst in the kind of battle they were now choosing to fight—a clash of massed troops on a relatively open field. This was the kind of fighting in which British infantry had won again and again, almost always against superior numbers. Yes, Gage thought, it was possible, it was thoroughly possible, that colonial courage would be their undoing. It took more than courage to stand up to artillery and a thousand leveled bayonets. Perhaps they were giving him a chance to deliver a smashing blow that would enable him to regain the initiative.

If anything gave him second thoughts, it was the words of Prescott's brother-in-law, Abijah Willard, who was one of the loyalist councilors whom Gage had appointed under the new act of Parliament. When the guns began, Willard had hurried to Province House to see if there was anything he could do. Under the pretense of royal government Gage still maintained in Boston, the councilors were the governor's official advisers. Willard found Gage in an upper room, studying the American works through his field glass. The Governor General called him to his side and said: "Do you recognize the tall man walking on the parapet?"

Willard squinted through the glass and did indeed recognize him.

He handed the glass back to General Gage. "That is Colonel William Prescott, my brother-in-law," he said.

"Will he fight?" Gage said.

"I cannot answer for his men, but he will fight you to the gates of hell," Willard said.

"The works must be carried," Gage said.

The Governor General had called a council of war. Now his officers began to arrive. First came Henry Clinton with an "I told you so" look on his schoolmaster's face. Immediately behind came John Burgoyne, the third major general who had arrived with Clinton and Howe on May 25. He was a stranger to the New World but he had seen extensive duty on the Continent during the Seven Years' War. In 1759 he had commanded a combined British-Portuguese army which routed Spain's attempt to take over its peninsular neighbor.

Tall, florid John Burgoyne was fifty-three years old. He and Gage had been schoolmates at Westminster. But his personality was radically different. Burgoyne was a man about town and a member of Parliament with excellent connections gained through marriage, friendship and intrigue. He was ambitious and the moment he landed in Boston he began writing letters home to a half dozen lords in the cabinet and out giving them his estimate of the situation. Invariably, he damned Gage with faint praise and suggested that he, John Burgoyne, should be given more responsibility to cope with the crisis.

Thus far, however, all Burgoyne had contributed to the situation was an epigram and a proclamation. When they sailed in April, the generals had assumed peace still persisted in Massachusetts. On board ship in Boston Harbor they were informed that the city was under seige. Burgoyne demanded to know how many men were in the besieging army. About 10,000 he was told. "What!" he roared. "Ten thousand peasants penning up 5,000 of the King's troops? Let us in, we'll soon have elbow room!" Several wits in Boston immediately seized on the phrase. Soon children were shouting "elbow room" after Burgoyne in the streets.

The proclamation was by order of Lord Dartmouth as a last desperate try for peace. It was to offer amnesty to all Americans who would lay down their arms—except Samuel Adams and John Hancock. Burgoyne volunteered to write the pronouncement for Gage. The governor, undoubtedly awed by Gentleman Johnny's literary reputation, gave his consent. Though he is now relegated to the lower ranks of minor English playwrights, Burgoyne was considered a writer of talent in 1775. David Garrick, the greatest actor of the day, had appeared in his play, *Maid of the Oaks,* only a few months before the three generals left London. But like most minor authors the general was a victim of the prevailing literary vices. His peace proclamation, issued in Gage's name, was a masterpiece of eighteenth-century bombast.

"Whereas the infatuated multitudes who have long suffered themselves to be conducted by certain well known incendiaries and traitors in a fatal progression of crimes against the constitutional authority of the state have at length proceeded to avow rebellion and the good effects which were expected to arise from the patience and lenity of the King's Government have been often frustrated and are now rendered hopeless by the influence of the same evil councils, it only remains for those who are intrusted with the supreme rule as well for the punishment of the guilty as for the protection of the well affected, to prove that they do not bear the sword in vain." The message went on to declare martial law, condemn those in arms, "to be rebels and traitors," and then offered pardon to those who would lay down their arms or "stand distinct and separate from the parricides of the constitution." Samuel Adams and John

Hancock—"whose offenses are of too flagitious a nature to admit any other consideration than that of condign punishment." If Burgoyne had been searching for one final alienation of American hopes for a peaceful settlement he could not have found a better instrument than this proclamation. To begin by calling the free men of Massachusetts "infatuated multitudes" was enough in itself to send a wave of rage from one end of the province to the other.

Abigail Adams, who was convinced with her husband, John, that hope of peace was lost for good, sent the proclamation to her husband in Philadelphia with the following note. "Gage's proclamation you will receive by this conveyance. Satan when driven from the regions of bliss exhibited not more malice. Surely the father of lies is superceded. Yet we think it the best proclamation he could have issued."

Next to come through the doorway of the oak-paneled council chamber of Province House was a grim and worried William Howe. Gage mustered his manners to greet him but his words must have concealed mixed feelings. He understood army politics thoroughly and when Howe led his brother major generals ashore on May 25 to present their commissions to him, Gage must have known his days as commander-in-chief in North America were numbered.

After Howe came Brigadier General Earl Percy, the cocky son of the Duke of Northumberland. His soldierly command of the retreat from Lexington had done a great deal to rescue that situation from total disaster and had also considerably altered his opinion of the provincial soldiers. The day after the fight, he had written to Adjutant General Harvey in the London war office: "Whoever looks on these people as an irregular mob will find himself much mistaken. They have men amongst them who know very well what they are about. Nor are several of them void of a spirit of enthusiasm for many . . . advanced to within 10 yds to fire at me and other officers tho' they were morally certain of being put to death themselves in an instant."

Next came Brigadier General Robert Pigot. Of a well-born family, though not as high in the peerage as Northumberland, Pigot was a small, stocky man who had seen some hard fighting on the Continent and reputedly made up in courage what he lacked in size. He was to demonstrate this reputation amply before the day was over.

Finally, there was Timothy Ruggles, the tall, gray-haired loyalist who had a paper title as general of the Loyal American Associators. He was an ironic symbol of Gage's forlorn hope that a substantial portion of Massachusetts was loyal to the government. Ruggles was not even able to muster a full regiment in the King's cause. It is doubtful that Gage invited him to the council of war. Like Willard, he probably came as a volunteer, and the Governor tactfully permitted him to stay.

It was not a happy council. Of the four generals present, Howe had been an outspoken defender of the American cause in Parliament and Burgoyne had argued that conciliation was preferable to armed force. Clinton had declared, before departing, that he was not a volunteer but a soldier obeying orders. Percy's father had become so violently opposed to the idea of making war on the Americans that he had arranged to have his son recalled. But the gallant young brigadier refused the chance to depart because it would have meant leaving his regiment behind him. To complicate matters a little more, Howe had privately confessed to Burgoyne that he was reluctant to come to America not only because of his family's tradition of friendship but because he had an extremely low opinion of Gage as a general. Burgoyne, in his letters home, made amply clear what he thought of Gage's military talents.

To this muddle of hesitation and negation must be added the knowledge, which every man there shared, that many of their fellow officers in the army had, at considerable personal sacrifice, refused to serve against the Americans. The great Jeffrey Amherst, the master mind of the North American conquest in the Seven Years' War, had turned down a peerage and any job in the King's list of lucrative sinecures, "because he did not wish to fight his friends the Americans to whom he was so much obliged." Young Lord Effingham of the Twenty-second Regiment had resigned his commission when he was ordered to America. Chatham's son, a captain stationed in Quebec, had also resigned his commission. There were many others.

Finally, these were leaders of a peacetime army, suddenly involved in a major battle. At their head was a peacetime general, a man who had risen largely through his considerable talents as an administrator and a diplomat. Never had Thomas Gage displayed anything beyond the most average military ability. He had very little experience in leading more than a regiment in the field, and his record, through no fault of his own, included two of the most disastrous British defeats in North America—Braddock's rout and the bloody repulse at Fort Ticonderoga in 1758. One of the few times he had commanded an army his extreme caution had aroused the wrath of Amherst who was sometimes criticized for this defect himself.

Servants moved about the council chamber now, lighting candles. Burgoyne and Howe both looked sleepy. Only Clinton was full of bustling energy. He was for an immediate attack before the rebels had a chance to bring up more reinforcements or do more fortifying. He argued that the Americans had put themselves in a bag and "all we have to do is squeeze it." He wanted to land 500 men under the guns of the fleet near the narrow neck that separated Charlestown from the mainland. This would cut off the American retreat and the defenders of Charlestown Heights would have two choices—starvation or surrender. If they

attempted to break out of the trap or if the rest of the
army at Cambridge tried to reinforce them, again the fleet
guns would be on the British side.

Gage pondered for a moment, then slowly shook his head.
"We must remember, gentlemen," he said, "the enemy has
troops stationed at the Neck. How many we do not know. To
put 500 men between two enemy forces, each of which may
outnumber them, seems very dangerous tactics to me. It vio-
lates a fundamental military principle."

Gage had been ridiculed for this objection and accused of
trying to make war out of a manual. But he was not talking
abstractions. There was a regiment of New Hampshire
troops under James Reed stationed at Charlestown Neck,
and John Stark was at Medford, little more than a mile away,
with another 800 Hampshire men. As Stark was to demonstrate later in the day, he was not in the least afraid of the
guns of the fleet and he and his tough frontiersmen could
have made Clinton's landing a shambles. Moreover, neither
Gage nor Clinton knew how many men the Americans had
on Charlestown peninsula. Another thousand could be out of
sight on the far side of Bunker Hill.

Clinton had never commanded troops in an amphibious
operation. Howe had been with Wolfe when he led the
troops ashore at Louisburg and Quebec and had led his
own men ashore under the guns of his brother's ships at
Belle Isle off the French coast. Now he raised another objection to Clinton's plan. "General Clinton may not be
aware but we have very little equipment for the kind of
operation he suggests, and from the knowledge we have of
the shoreline at Charlestown Neck, it might be impossible
to land near the Neck even if we had a sufficient number of
flat boats."

He took out a map of Boston showing the city jutting out
into the sea on its own peninsula with Charlestown peninsula on the north and Dorchester on the left, each connected

to the mainland by a tiny neck of land like the string of an inflated balloon. There was, Howe pointed out to his fellow generals, a milldam some 500 yards forward of Charlestown Neck which ran across the narrowing bay to form a small inlet. For 100 yards in front of the milldam the mud flats made a landing impracticable. To go around the peninsula and attempt a landing on the north side, where the Mystic River met the sea, was even more difficult. Here there were several hundred yards of mud flats through which troops would have to flounder to shore. Getting men ashore in an amphibious operation, dry and as ready to fight as possible, is considered of prime importance even today; in 1775 when dampness could turn a soldier's powder into mush, it was even more vital. The only practical place to make a landing to secure the Neck was the mouth of Willis Creek, across the Charles River from Boston. This was where the troops had landed for their march to Lexington and where they had planned to land Clinton's division in tomorrow's offensive operation. But a landing here would be a full half mile from Charlestown Neck and they would probably have to fight their way through the entire American army, since the American generals would logically assume an attack here was aimed at Cambridge, the heart of their position, only two miles away.

Reluctantly Clinton was forced to defer to Howe, the acknowledged expert in amphibious operations. But he still protested vehemently against a frontal assault on the American positions. In this protest Timothy Ruggles joined him vigorously. An army as small as theirs could not afford heavy casualties and hope to remain an effective fighting force. Now Clinton suggested landing near Charlestown and marching through the town to the Neck. This met with even more vigorous objections from Gage and the other officers. Percy was there to testify to the American habit of hiding seven or eight men to a house and opening up on a British column as it marched by. It had cost him dozens of men on the way back from Lexington. Charlestown might well contain three or four hidden regiments right now. Some troops were definitely in the town; they had been seen in the streets by British sentries in Boston.

Gage admitted Clinton's major point. It was certainly important to hold their casualties down. But he also felt strongly that from a political point of view, the Americans should be met on the battlefield they chose. The reputation of the regular troops had been badly tarnished at Concord. What better way to restore it than to meet the rebels on the field of their choice and thoroughly thrash them?

Again, Howe agreed with Gage. His psychology was certainly sound. Moreover, the swarthy general had a compromise plan which he hoped would satisfy the basic principle of Clinton's operation, rout the Americans from their chosen fort and possibly even enable them to carry out the essence of their operation planned for tomorrow.

Quickly Howe sketched the American position on the map. As seen from Boston, the Charlestown peninsula resembled a huge swimming animal with three parts of its anatomy showing above water. The long rectangular line of Bunker Hill corresponded to its back; the more rounded summit of Breed's Hill might have been its head, which was turned slightly to the left; Morton's Hill, the third and lowest protuberance, might have been the nub of its nose; it stood on Morton's Point, the outermost tip of the peninsula.

Here on this point was the ideal place to land troops. For almost a half mile from the water's edge up to the American fort on Breed's Hill there was not a scrap of cover in which an ambushing force could defend the beach. The guns of the fleet could slaughter any foray from the rebel fort. They were also comfortably distant from whatever troops the Americans were maintaining on the peninsula's neck or even in the Charlestown houses.

Once landed, which way to go? The town of Charlestown, with its houses offering so much cover to American guerilla fighters, blocked any movement down the south shore. But along the shore of the Mystic, on the other, northern side of the peninsula, there was an uninterrupted field which led directly to the key to the entire American position—a crossroad midway down Bunker Hill which effectively sealed off the Breed's Hill redoubt both from reinforcement and retreat. There was, of course, the south road running directly from Charlestown to the neck, but this ran along the shore and the fleet guns would make any attempt to retreat or reinforce along that pathway a suicidal operation.

Now it was Howe, the master of light infantry tactics, who was speaking. Send a flying column of light infantry up that flank out of musket shot of the Americans on the hill and knife across the American line of retreat at the crossroads directly behind the redoubt. Nothing demoralizes raw troops—or even professional soldiers—as much as seeing the enemy in their rear. With the crossroads secured, the entire brigade would now launch a four-sided attack upon the American redoubt. Meanwhile, men from General Clinton's brigade would stand ready to board boats and make a landing on the shores of Willis Creek, just across Boston's Back Bay. For support they would have the armed transport *Symmetry*, which took very little water and could move close enough to Lechmere Point (which the creek bisected) to deliver excellent artillery support. If the battle on the hilltop became a rout, as Howe felt sure it would, Clinton would receive a signal to launch his attack and Howe would pursue the remnants of the rebel force on Charlestown peninsula down across the neck and join him for a general advance on Cambridge. In many ways their position would be superior to the one they would have had under their plan of attack for the following day. With one victory secure and the defeated stragglers streaming helter-skelter into Cambridge to sow seeds of panic up and down the American line, the chances of annihilating the American army and the whole rebellion were exceptionally good.

Almost as if they were underscoring Howe's argument, the guns from the army battery on Copp's Hill opened up on the American fort. They were the heaviest artillery the British had, eighteen- and twenty-four-pounders, and their thunder rattled the windows and shook the floors of Province House and every other building in Boston. Beneath them, in a grim counterpoint, the fleet guns continued to roar their more distant salvos.

Clinton was still not completely satisfied. What if the Americans chose to fight inside their redoubt, even though surrounded? "Unlikely," Howe said. "Anyway, I do not see how the works could be more than a redan." By this he meant a one- or two-sided structure which could easily be taken on the flank or rear. "Never in my experience," Howe went on, "have I heard or seen even regular troops capable of building a complete redoubt in a single night's work." With this Burgoyne, Pigot, Gage and Percy agreed. Lieutenant Thomas Page of the engineers and Howe's naval aide, Jourdain, who were present, also concurred. Clinton stubbornly stood his ground. "My opinion was," he said later, "and I gave it to General Howe and his aides-de-camp Mr. Jourdain and Mr. Page, that it was a complete redoubt, that behind this redoubt I feared there was a double stone wall with a lane between by which they could retire safely."

Gage, Howe and the other officers doubted the stone wall. Amazingly, they had no detailed topographical map which would have settled the argument. Nor did they try to find someone in Boston who knew the Charlestown peninsula well and could have told them. It was a minor point, in their opinion. They told Clinton that the hill was "open and easy of ascent" and could "easily be carried."

Gage had sent officers out to sketch the Massachusetts countryside in anticipation of his march to Concord. But he evidently regarded Dorchester and Charlestown Heights as home ground and never bothered to map them. They were, after all, fairly visible. But the telescopes of those days were crude instruments if at a half mile they made Breed's Hill look open and easy of ascent.

For the moment, Clinton had used up all his arguments. But Timothy Ruggles was by no means inclined to be silent. He was still warmly in favor of Clinton's ideas, agreed with him that it was a complete redoubt and bluntly told his British friends that the rebels would, even if cornered on four sides, fight to the death. He knew, better than they, the depths of bitterness which the conflict had aroused. Up there on Breed's Hill were desperate men who expected, if captured, nothing but the hangman's noose. They would never surrender. He was in favor of landing in their rear and not attacking them at all. Simply seal off the peninsula and starve them out. Everyone knew that the regulars were superior to the raw American farmers. Why throw away good British soldiers unnecessarily to prove a needless point? But Ruggles was a general without an army and a political leader without a following. We can be sure that the surrounding circle of professional soldiers was not inclined to pay much attention to him. Howe assured him that he had no desire to throw men away. The whole maneuver was designed to capture the fort and possibly the whole rebel detachment with a minimum of bloodshed.

Perhaps there was a certain lack of civility in the treatment Ruggles received from the regular officers. As an American he would be morbidly sensitive to any hint that he was being treated as an inferior. At any rate he is largely responsible for the myth that General Gage, with Howe's concurrence, decided arrogantly to "take the bull by the horns" and launch a carelessly conceived frontal attack on the American barricades. As Ruggles left Province House a loyalist friend hailed him across the lawn to find out what the generals were going to do. "They don't think the Americans will fight," Ruggles said angrily. "They're going to attack them up there." He shook his head and stamped off muttering, "A waste of good officers and men."

The myth of the arrogant frontal attack here begun by Ruggles was augmented by later events on the battlefield. The idea would have appalled any military man in 1775, and Gage who had labored so long to avoid bloodshed would hardly have decided to spill it in large quantities now at the first opportunity. Generals of the time were used to dealing with small professional armies in which it was essential to hold casualties to a minimum; never was this maxim more apparent to the leader of the minuscule British expeditonary force in Boston. Though a frontal assault was an accepted tactic, it was never carelessly or casually executed. Flanking movements, diversionary tactics and expert use of artillery were considered essentials in giving the assaulting columns a minimum of exposure.

The fundamental plan of battle decided, the conference had no difficulty assigning the generals to the tasks. Howe, as second in command, would lead the field force in the attack. General Pigot would serve under him as brigadier. Percy would be in charge of the lines at Boston Neck. Clinton would stand by in Boston, ready to launch his 600 men toward Cambridge the instant Howe gave the signal. General Burgoyne, to his chagrin, found himself assigned to the battery of artillery on Copp's Hill. It was an age when men were keenly conscious of reputation and hated to miss a chance to distinguish themselves. But Burgoyne was a professional soldier and took his orders without protest. He could not know, of course, that this vantage point and his skill as a letter writer (infinitely superior to his proclamation-writing talents) were to give future generations one of the most vivid battle descriptions in the history of warfare.

Outside Province House the town of Boston was in a vast turmoil. Everywhere people were climbing out on their flat roofs and pouring up to Beacon and Copp's Hill (then almost bare of houses), to watch the cannonade rip gashes in the green height on which the Americans still toiled. The sun climbed slowly up into the clear blue sky. Women went looking for bonnets and fans and men began complaining about the heat.

They were a mixed group, those civilian spectators of the bloody drama which was taking shape across the harbor. On one roof was the Lovell family—a grim illustration of how politics had divided Americans. The father was the headmaster of the Boston Latin School and a firm loyalist. His son James, also a teacher in the school, was a burning patriot and good friend of Joseph Warren's.

Over his father's violent protests, James Lovell had given the first oration on Massacre Day, four years ago. James and his family had a chance to leave Boston but the young teacher had refused to go. "I shall tarry if 10 sieges take place," he told a friend. "I have determined it to be a Duty which I owe the Cause and the friends in it and am perfectly fearless of the consequences." He longed to get into the fight, but delicate health and concern for his wife and six children prevented him. "An ill turn, of a most violent diarhea, from being too long in a damp place has confirmed Doctor Gardner's advice to me not to go into the trenches where my whole Soul lodges nightly." He contented himself with spying industriously for the American cause.

British officers were welcomed in the Lovell house. Colonel Samuel Cleveland of the artillery was a frequent visitor, largely to see the Lovell daughter. The colonel was close to his own age but the elder Lovell tolerated his at-

tentions in a spirit of loyalty, though we may be sure that
the stern old schoolmaster was careful of the young girl's
virtue. Still the colonel was enthusiastic enough about his
amatory progress to appoint another Lovell brother, Benjamin, as his clerk in the artillery office.

On Beacon Hill was Ann Hulton, the sister of the British
commissioner of customs in Boston. Though she had been a
resident of the New World for some seven years, she was not
a convert to American society. "They are," she confided to
a friend in England, "a rude, depraved, degenerate race,
amongst whom there is not one that has the least pretension
to be called a gentleman and it is a mortification to us that
they speak English and can trace themselves from that
stock." Part of her disenchantment is understandable; her
brother was the most unpopular British official in Massachusetts. Most of the bitterness in the quarrel revolved around
his job, to collect the parliamentary duties on imports and
exports. Several times in his career he had had to flee to Castle William when the Boston mob got out of hand.

Up on Copp's Hill, beside the booming battery, nineteen-year-old Peter Edes shared the view with General Burgoyne. Edes's father, publisher of the Boston *Gazette,* was
now in Roxbury, still printing patriotic blasts at the ministerial army with a few scraps of worn-out type which he
had managed to smuggle out of Boston. Peter was not a discreet young man. He loudly proclaimed within earshot of
the general and his artillerymen that he had come up there
to see the Americans "kick the British a—— off."

Another spectator, neither loyalist nor revolutionary, but
merely an unhappy victim of the quarrel, was Dr. Andrew
Eliot, pastor of New North Church. A peace-loving, God-
fearing man, deeply loyal to his king, Eliot could only la-
ment the bitterness raging around him and the misery it
brought both to him and his congregation. Not long after

Lexington he wrote to an English friend, "Last week I thought myself in comfortable circumstances, had a convenient dwelling, well furnished, a fine library, a large, affectionate and generous congregation, surrounded by a large number of desirable children. Now I am by a cruel necessity turned out of my house, must leave my books and all I possess, perhaps to be destroyed by a licentious soldiery; my beloved congregation dispersed, my dear wife retreating to a distant part of the country, my children wandering, perhaps left to perish for want. What doth Great Britain hope to gain from this unnatural contest? Must millions be sacrificed to a mere punctilio, to a mere point of honor? Forgive, dear sir, these severe reflections on the parent country. My heart is wounded, almost to death." Though he longed for his family, who were living with friends and relations in Massachusetts and Connecticut, Eliot's sense of responsibility to his congregation persuaded him to stay in Boston. For a man who had spent his life preaching the gospel of brotherly love, there would be no winner on Charlestown Heights. The sight of "Englishmen destroying one another" could only make him weep.

But no one, not even Dr. Eliot, could approach in intensity the division and confusion in the mind of Margaret Gage. She remained in her room throughout the day, unable to look upon the spectacle of war between her countrymen and her husband's soldiers. One part of her heart clung to those Americans, stubborn and proud in their makeshift fort, challenging the might of empire. Another, more personal part of her emotions went with those British officers and men who were soon to be bleeding and dying before these American entrenchments. She had entertained them in her home, knew their wives and children. Later, she told a friend that her feelings were well described in the lines spoken by Blanche of Spain, in Shakespeare's *King John:*

"The Sun's o'ercast with blood; fair day, adieu!
Which is the side that I must go withal?
I am with both; each army hath a hand,
And in their rage—I having hold of both—
They whirl assunder, and dismember me."

Elsewhere in Boston, the professional soldiers were getting ready for the fight. In the four or five pages usually given to Bunker Hill in the history textbooks, these men have been lost in a monolithic monotony, designated as the redcoats, or the regulars, or the British. Seen individually, they emerge as remarkably interesting human beings, as different in their attitudes toward the struggle into which they were moving as the civilians on the housetops and hills.

In his quarters on North Square, fifty-three-year-old John Pitcairn, major of the First Marine Battalion, was finishing a hurried breakfast. A portly, genial man, he was a veteran soldier, and the situation in Charlestown meant only one thing as far as he could see: action for the marines. His men were the toughest, best-trained troops in Gage's little army. They also had by far the best morale. In an age when soldiers were considered more insensitive and less intelligent than cattle, Pitcairn distinguished himself for the time and attention he gave his junior officers and enlisted men. He was a strict disciplinarian, but he was also absolutely fair. His men worshiped him. Even the townspeople of Boston respected the major's integrity. Gage passed on to him many of the disputes between the citizens and the troops, and Pitcairn often found himself sitting as a kind of police court judge. He quickly acquired a reputation for complete fairness and honesty. His letters show he was no intellectual; the justice or injustice of the quarrel between England and Massachusetts did not particularly interest him. His approach to the subject had the simplicity and the limitations of the professional soldier. Writing to his superior, the Earl of Sandwich, before Lexington, he said: "the deluded people here believe they are invincible. When this army is ordered to act against them they will soon be convinced that they are very insignificant when opposed to regular troops. . . . I am satisfied one active campaign, a smart action and burning two or three towns will set everything to rights. Nothing now, I am afraid, but this will ever convince these foolish bad people that England is in earnest."

But face to face and man to man, Pitcairn's fundamental humanity invariably came through, along with a good soldier's abhorrence of senseless bloodshed. He shared his quarters, which were in the home of Samuel Shaw, with several of his lieutenants. Shaw's son, Francis, was a violent patriot and never missed a chance to defend the American side. One night, a Lieutenant Wragg made a particularly insulting remark about the "rebels" during dinner, and young Shaw in a blaze of fury challenged him to a duel. Wragg promptly accepted and someone almost certainly would have been killed if it were not for Pitcairn. He calmed the two antagonists and convinced them that shooting was not the answer to their argument.

Ironically, only a few weeks later Pitcairn was being reviled by Americans as a monster who had ordered his bloodthirsty regulars to slaughter the defenseless minutemen on Lexington Common.

Many of his fellow officers lamented Gage's decision to send the light infantry to Concord under Pitcairn. If he had been commanding his own marines, men who knew and respected him, they avowed, Lexington would never have happened. Pitcairn himself always maintained that the British troops had not fired the first shot, though he freely admitted he lost all control of them a moment after the firing started. His story was very carefully recorded by Ezra Stiles, later president of Yale. "Pitcairn, a good man in a bad cause, saw a gun in a peasant's hand from behind a wall flash in the

pan without going off; and instantly or very soon 2 or 3 guns
went off by which he found his horse wounded and also a
man near him wounded. These Guns he did not see, but
believed they could not come from his own people. The im-
petuosity of the Kings' troops were such that a promiscuous,
uncommanded but general Fire took place, which Pitcairn
could not prevent; tho' he struck his staff or Sword down-
wards with all earnestness as the signal to forbear or cease
firing. This account Major Pitcairn himself gave Mr. Brown
of Providence a few days after the battle."

American accounts of the time painted Pitcairn as a glee-
ful butcher. Yet those who knew him were somewhat disturbed by the incongruity between their partisan versions of
the event and the major's character. William Gordon, one of
the most violent American writers, said: "To what I have
wrote respecting Major Pitcairn, I am sensible his general
character may be objected."

Though we have no record of it, sometime in the morning Pitcairn undoubtedly found time to see his son, Thomas,
who was a lieutenant in the Major's own Marine battalion.
Like Putnam and his son, they probably exchanged the halt-
ing phrases of a soldier's guarded emotions. Pitcairn had
nine children. Another son had discovered Pitcairn's Island
in the central Pacific which a group of rebellious English
seamen aboard His Majesty's ship *Bounty* were to make
famous fifty years later. For Pitcairn, the story already had
a tragic ending; the boy had been lost in a typhoon on the
voyage home. In many ways Pitcairn resembled Putnam;
he was a hearty man, who loved a good drink, a good meal
or a good fight. Both were famous for their profanity which
reached the high art of the professional soldier.

In his tent on Boston's Fort Hill, twenty-nine-year-old
George Harris, Captain of the Grenadiers of the Fifth Regi-
ment, was also preparing for action. He had marched under
Pitcairn on the expedition to Concord and had commanded

the rear guard on the way back along that bullet-swept road. Harris was somewhat unusual among the officers in the army. The son of a curate, he was neither a gambler nor a hard drinker. He had become a cadet at the Royal Military Academy at Woolwich through the influence of Lord George Sackville. His father had saved the nobleman in a brawl with a miller when they were classmates at Cambridge.

A letter he wrote home, shortly before the battle, gives a good indication of Harris' qualities as an officer. He tells of working with his men on one of a series of small fortifications which Gage had ordered for the seaward side of Boston common. "This letter will be finished by the side of my fortification," he writes, "mine I may safely call it, as I am not only planner and director, but partly executor—as often taking the spade as telling others when to employ it, which is attended with these good effects—exercise to myself and encouragement to the men who, you will be pleased to hear, fly to execute that for me which for others would be done with a very bad grace, because I set them a good example in not being afraid of work." This was an extraordinary gesture for a young British officer in 1775; in fact, it would be an extraordinary gesture for a young British—or American —officer in 1960. On the retreat from Lexington Harris had won Lord Percy's warm approval for the consideration he showed his wounded men. He even filled his grenadier's helmet with water during a lull in the fight and let them drink out of it.

The young captain was far from the bloodthirsty oppressor pictured by American propagandists for the officers of the "ministerial army." In the same letter he writes an affectionate postcard of New England: "I have now before me one of the finest prospects your warm imagination can picture. My tent-door, about twenty yards from a piece of water, nearly a mile broad, with the country beyond most beautifully tumbled about in hills and valleys, rocks and woods, interspersed with straggling villages, with here and there a spire peeping over the trees and the country of the most charming green that delighted eye ever gazed on. Pity these infatuated people cannot be content to enjoy such a country in peace. But alas! this moment their advanced sentinels are in sight."

Harris had lost his lieutenant in the Concord-Lexington skirmish and as a replacement had received a man who was in many ways the diametric opposite of the kindly, thoughtful captain. Francis Lord Rawdon was every inch the young British officer and knew it. Tall and athletic (but decidedly not handsome), the twenty-six-year-old Irish noble was a martinet with his men and an ambitious soldier. He was looking forward to the day with vast excitement. It was his first action and after a year of garrison duty he was unashamedly eager for a chance to distinguish himself. He had little interest in the politics of the situation and no sympathy for the American cause. The prospect of a good fight was all the fort on Breed's Hill meant to him.

Also eager in his preparations for battle was Captain William Glanville Evelyn of the King's Own Regiment. A handsome Irishman, Evelyn was thirty-three years old and had seen some service as a young ensign in the Seven Years' War. He was totally contemptuous of the Americans. In a letter to his father not long after he landed, he said, "Though upon paper they are the bravest fellows in the world, yet in reality I believe there does not exist so great a set of rascals and poltroons." Seeing them in action along the Lexington road did not change his mind. On April 23 he wrote to his father: "It is impossible but you must hear an account, and probably a most exaggerated one, of the little fracas that happened here a few days ago between us and the Yankey scoundrels. Our bickerings and heartburnings as might naturally be expected, came at length to blows and both sides have lost some men. . . . The rebels are the most absolute cowards on the face of the earth, yet they are just now worked up to such a degree of enthusiasm and madness that they are easily persuaded . . . that they are invincible."

In contrast to both the fire-eater Evelyn and the glory-hunter Rawdon was seventeen-year-old Martin Hunter of the Fifty-second Regiment. Hunter was an ensign (which corresponds to a second lieutenant in modern armies) and was the very model of the inexperienced shavetail. Only fifteen when he joined the regiment at Quebec, he was so short he tripped over his sword when he walked down the street. The French used to call out in astonishment when they saw him: *"Violà le petit officier!"* Hunter was taller now but he was still painfully green. In Boston he found a thoughtful, considerate superior in Major Pitcairn. When appointing him officer of the day, Pitcairn was always careful to provide Hunter with an experienced sergeant so he would not make a fool of himself as he went the rounds. The stocky lonely youngster grew deeply attached to the fatherly major and, like many other soldiers in Boston, was soon telling him all his troubles. He did not get along with his own regulation minded superior, Major Williams. Young Hunter had no political interest in the contest between colony and Parliament and the journal he kept is mostly concerned with ice-skating expeditions to Jamaica Pond and personal problems such as buying a pony and being abruptly ordered by Major Williams to sell it.

In his quarters on Bennet Street, Lieutenant John Dutton of the Thirty-eighth Regiment kissed his wife and two children goodbye. The lieutenant had not expected a war; he had brought his family with him to Boston expecting nothing more than a year or two of garrison duty. But he was ready to fight in spite of a bad attack of gout, from which he was not quite recovered. Did his wife beg him to report sick and escape the danger as many wives might? We do not know. We only know that he marched with his men.

This was Boston, military and civilian, on that hot Saturday morning in 1775 when the generals in Province House reached their decision, and William Howe sat down to write the morning orders, summoning Thomas Gage's army of pacification to war.

8

WHEN the guns crashed aboard the *Lively* and the first cannon balls hissed up through the gray dawn, Prescott's young farmers were still toiling furiously inside the hilltop fort. Like men shocked from a hypnotic trance, they dropped their picks and shovels and rushed to the walls to peer cautiously around them. Few had any familiarity with Charlestown and in the night they had marched where their officers commanded them. Now, they suddenly wondered just how wise those officers were. Before them the pastures ran down to the open harbor. Behind them the Charlestown peninsula stretched for a mile and a half, almost bare of trees, houses or any other kind of cover.

Peter Brown, the twenty-year-old company clerk in Prescott's regiment, recalled the moment vividly later. "Then we saw our danger being against eight ships of the line and all Boston fortified against us. The danger we were in made us think that there was treachery and that we were brought there to be all slain. And I must and will venture to say there was treachery, oversight or presumption in the conduct of the officers."

Prescott sensed their uneasiness and brusquely drove

them back to work. "All right, they know where we are now. All the more reason to finish the job we are doing. If we're going to fight behind these walls, we'll need firing platforms to stand on. The stronger the works, the less chance they'll dare to attack us. Come on, Brown! Come on, Farnsworth. Stop trying to see all the way to Cambridge. There's more work to be done."

Another broadside from the *Lively* went whistling over their heads.

"Let them waste their powder," Prescott said. "They can't touch us as long as we stay inside these walls. If you have to go outside, keep to the north where there's shelter."

Silently the men resumed their digging. Colonel Gridley moved among them, making sure that the firing platforms were the correct height and firmly built, worrying over the lack of carpenters and materials to build platforms for the cannon. Once more Gridley urged on Prescott the importance of completing the breastwork down the northeast slope of the hill to the swamp at the bottom; without it the fort could be flanked with ridiculous ease. On the south, or Charlestown side, the slope was much steeper and the scattering of houses on the back streets of Charlestown would provide a ready-made defense line. Once more Prescott assured him that he would put every available man on the breastwork the moment the main redoubt was finished.

The lean, wiry colonel from Pepperell did not show a trace of fatigue, but Engineer Gridley, older by some ten years, was looking more and more spent. Colonel Bridge and Lieutenant Colonel Bricket and the other field officers were also showing signs of weariness. Among the men the digging had slowed and lost its methodical rhythm. More than a few had given up and were slumped against the sides of the fort.

Grimly Prescott drove them back to work and his other officers joined him. Husky Major John Brooks, the twenty-three-year-old doctor from Reading, stood over his men and kept a sharp eye and a sharp tongue on laggards. Other officers, such as strapping, six-foot Ebenezer Bancroft of the same regiment, still worked beside their men. Captain Bancroft's gun, his pride and joy, stood nearby him; it was a French musket which he had taken from a dead enemy more than a decade ago. He was no longer that ardent youngster who went out to fight the French for his King. Since his last battle, he had become a substantial farmer and the father of nine children.

For all his complaints of heat and fatigue and his suspicion of treachery, young Peter Brown kept on working. He was a thoroughly likable youngster who said what he thought but did not let his doubts interfere with his duty. Working nearby him was his friend, Corporal Amos Farnsworth. Undoubtedly, Amos was working harder because he was the fresher of the two. He was in Nutting's company and had spent the night, as he later said, "on our centres by the waterside." He was a more reflective and sober young man than Peter Brown. Often he was filled with "anchous desires after holiness" and more than once lamented when he could not arouse his soul with prayers but found himself "ded in duty." He was also one of the few young men who had seen action. In the fight on Noddle Island, he told how "fifteen of us squatted down in a ditch on the marsh and stood our ground. And we had a hot fiar untill the Regulars retreeted. But notwithstanding the bullets flue very thicth there was not a Man of us kild. Suerly God has a faver towards us."

Another man who toiled with grim methodical persistence and needed no urging to hold his pace was Peter Salem, one of the free Negroes in Prescott's regiment. Nearby him were two other Negroes, Caesar Bason and Cuffee Whittemore. In the other two regiments were four more: Caleb Howe of Plymouth and Titus Colburn, Alexander Ames and Basilai Lew of Andover. Free Negroes were common in Massachusetts; some were escaped slaves, some had been freed by white masters in Pennsylvania, and even in states farther south. Already slavery was a burden on the conscience of many Americans.

Another good man whose presence intimated that this was more than an argument between a colony and a home government was James Dodge, who was born in Edinburgh, and spoke with a Scottish burr. He lived in Groton and, like many of his countrymen at home, believed the Americans were fighting for a principle which justified rebellion—not that a Scot needed too much justification for it, with memories of their own smashed revolts still fresh. Beyond his ancestry and his birthplace, we know very little about Dodge —except his bravery.

The bombardment from the *Lively* abruptly ceased. Many of the men took it as an excuse to stop working and stroll out of the redoubt to survey the scene. The rising sun filled the sky with its fire. In a moment the flat roofs and crooked streets of Boston were visible and on the green common the orderly rows of tents into which the regulars had moved for the summer. A few tiny figures could be seen hurrying around the common and along the streets; others were visible on the rooftops. Below them men were moving briskly along the decks of the *Lively* and the other men-of-war. It was an utterly peaceful scene—the ships nodding at anchor in a light breeze, the deserted town, the sea and sky full of rich color.

Suddenly, with an enormous crash, the entire fleet opened up on them. Cannon balls hissed around them like buckshot. With a wild cry they dove back into the fort. Now the bombardment was thunderous; the flat crash of the *Lively*'s ten guns seemed like a toy in retrospect. Cannon balls crunched against the earthen walls and whined through the air over their heads. Again the men showed

signs of panic and Prescott quelled it with brutal demands
for more work.

The ships of the line were firing solid shot. The day of
the explosive artillery shell had not yet dawned. When the
army battery on Copp's Hill went into action they would
occasionally use an eighteenth-century version of a shell
filled with gunpowder which exploded sometime after it was
fired. It was strictly an antipersonnel weapon, however; it
had no penetrating power. Against walls as sturdy as those
on Breed's Hill, solid shot was the standard recipe. Moreover, the exploding shell was an undependable weapon with
a fuse which either failed to work or blew up in mid-air before it reached the target. But whether the projectiles were
solid or explosive meant little to the Americans crouched
inside their fort; both varieties frightened them badly. Again
Prescott tried to quell the panic with demands for more
work.

Someone shouted sullenly from the rear of the ranks:
"Where's our cannon? Why haven't they sent us so much as
a gun?"

"We'll have cannon soon enough, won't we, Colonel?"
Prescott said, turning to Gridley. The chief engineer was
also head of the lone American artillery regiment.

"I will go myself, this very minute, to bring it on," Gridley said.

Later, Prescott in his curt soldier's language was to make
Gridley's departure sound like desertion. "The engineer
left me," he said. But his animosity was born when the woe-
ful officers and soldiers of Gridley's artillery came on the
field. Now he undoubtedly welcomed the decision of the
chief engineer to depart. There was nothing left for him to
do in the redoubt which Prescott or one of the other officers
could not supervise. More important, the mood of the men
made it imperative to get cannon on the field as soon as possible.

From the day of its appearance on the fields of war, untrained soldiers have had an inordinate respect for cannon, and the Americans were no exception. On the Lexington road, many officers felt certain that the entire British brigade could have been annihilated, except for Lord Percy's expert use of his two small cannon. At the first blast, the enthusiasm went out of the American attack, and for over an hour, while Percy prepared his weary men for a fighting retreat, the militiamen were afraid to venture forward in any substantial numbers. When Percy began his march they returned to the assault, but every time the pressure became severe, the Earl would wheel his cannon into position and again the American attack would wilt.

Even though they were surviving nicely under the shower of shot the British were sending at them now, the respect for big guns was obviously still a powerful lever in the men's morale. Prescott could see what they were thinking: how can we stand against the British without cannon of our own? These young Americans were willing to take on the regulars. But they wanted it to be a fair fight. They were sensible enough to hesitate about giving the British any more odds than they already possessed.

About a half hour after Gridley departed, Israel Putnam came galloping up the hill to roar his congratulations for the progress they had made. His appearance helped morale a little. He utterly ignored the cannon fire that was bouncing around him. But he was more important as a tangible link with the rest of the army in Cambridge.

"Are we going to be reinforced, General?" someone called from the ranks.

"You can be sure of it," Putnam said. "We are not building this fort to fill it with redcoats."

"What about cannon?"

"We'll have cannon enough within the hour."

"We will probably need more provisions before the day is

out," Prescott said. "Please ask General Ward to send us bread and meat."

"And rum," someone shouted.

"I think we have enough rum," Prescott said, ignoring the anonymous adviser. "Some beer would help, however."

"We will get everything we need," Putnam said. "Never worry about it. I am going straight to General Ward now. I have already seen him for a moment and reminded him to send on the reinforcements."

As he looked down upon the weary sweat-drenched faces of the men in the fort, even Putnam with his natural optimism must have had some doubts about the wisdom of the battle he had chosen to fight. Never did they look more like farmers and less like soldiers. With every crash of the cannon some ducked, or twitched, or trembled. Would they hold their ground when regular troops came at them with their cannon and massive volleys of musket fire? More than any other man in the Cambridge camp, Putnam had exerted himself to give them confidence and courage. But two months of disorganized camp life were not enough to create that esprit which gave men power to rise above their individual fears and draw courage from pride of regiment or army. This was the secret of the British infantry and Putnam understood it perfectly. He could only hope that another kind of courage—the courage of men fighting for a cause—would hold these young farmers together. Wordlessly, as he sat there emanating hearty optimism, Putnam must have cursed the grim fact that every man in this fort had been brought up to believe that British regulars were the finest soldiers in the world.

Putnam shouted a few more words of encouragement above the roar of the cannons and then spurred his horse down Breed's Hill toward Cambridge. The redoubt was almost completed now. The firing platforms of wood and earth were firm. The men obviously thought their job was done. Everywhere they were asking their officers about relief, and complaining mightily about hunger and thirst. Prescott was irritated to discover that many had not obeyed their marching orders, which specified that they were to bring a day's provisions in their knapsacks. "Listen to me, men," Prescott shouted above the cannonade. He stepped up on a firing platform and looked down at them. "We're not marching back to Cambridge just yet. There's more work to be done. We're going to build a breastwork out from this fort and down the north side of the hill."

By now it was eight o'clock. The sun was climbing slowly up into the cloudless blue sky. Already it was hot in the redoubt and as the summer earth dried out a fine dust began to fill the air, parching every throat and making many men cough and sneeze.

The men groaned audibly and a wave of murmured discontent passed through the ranks. "I thought we were going to be relieved," said one surly young private from Bridge's regiment.

"You'll be relieved when I give you an order," Prescott snapped. "Now, let's get to work!"

Tools in hand, the men streamed out of the fort and followed Prescott down the hill, watching while he marked out the line the breastwork must take. There were fewer cannon balls on this side of the hill and this made them feel a little more comfortable. In the fort Prescott left only the squad of men working on firing platforms for the expected cannon and a sprinkling of men to man the walls and keep a sharp lookout for the "enemy."

He took another detachment off pick-and-shovel labor at the breastwork and ordered them to move the garrison's small supply of liquids out of the line of fire. The refreshments consisted of several kegs of rum and a keg of water, which had been dumped from the wagons and lay exposed to the cannonade on the south side of the hill. Before anyone could obey the order, a cannon ball struck the water keg and smashed it. Ducking out between salvos, the men rolled the rum safely inside the redoubt where they sampled a round of it. It was good provincial rum but hardly a drink for men working in the blazing sun. It only made them more thirsty. They thought wistfully of the smashed hogshead of water and someone suggested that they dash down to Charlestown and draw some water from one of the town's wells. This struck everyone as a good idea and they started down the hill. At the head of the thirsty column was Asa Pollard of Billerica.

A cannon roared in the harbor and everyone froze. For a moment Asa Pollard was still on his feet before them but he was no longer the brawny cheerful young farm boy they all knew. He was a monstrous thing, gushing blood. A cannon ball had smashed off his head. Men near him found bits of blood and flesh clinging to their dusty, sweat-stained clothes. With a sickened cry they scrambled back over the hill to spread the word to their fellow soldiers, toiling on the breastwork. More than half the men instantly dropped their tools and raced to see the corpse. They stared horror-stricken while Prescott shoved his way through them. "What is it? What is it?" he was barking. He stared down at the headless corpse. "Who is it?"

"Asa Pollard of Captain Stickney's company in Colonel Bridge's regiment," a sergeant said. "What should we do, sir?"

Prescott looked around him at the circle of fear-stricken faces. A new kind of panic was sweeping his raw soldiers now. Not nerves, caused by the roar of cannon, but that basic stomach-twisting fear which the first sight of death creates.

"What shall we do, sir?" the sergeant said again in an utterly bewildered voice. The question hinted at a hundred things: retreat, rebellion, panic.

Prescott answered them all in two crisp words: "Bury him."

He turned to the men. "There's a whole breastwork waiting to be finished down there on the other side of the hill. In one minute I want to see every man here working on it."

The words broke the spell. Almost gladly the men turned their backs on Pollard's dead body and rushed once more to their tools. The sergeant proved to be more stubborn. "Bury him, sir?" he said following Prescott. "Bury him without prayers?"

"Without prayers," Prescott said.

"Yes sir."

Then Prescott with the intuition of a born leader saw that his men needed more than this matter-of-fact attitude toward death to brace them. Drawing his sword he sprang up on the parapet of the fort and strolled back and forth, magnificently demonstrating his contempt for the cannonade. "It was a one in a million shot, men," he roared. "See how close they come to hitting me!"

Up and down he strolled while the men watched in awed admiration. The ships seemed to redouble the pace of their broadsides as if they sensed the insult of Prescott's courage. Cannon balls crunched into the earth six feet beneath him and against the solid wall only a few feet behind him but he never flinched. The men burst into a spontaneous cheer and went back to work with new energy. It was getting hotter. Prescott himself threw aside his wig and cocked hat, revealing a head that was more than a little bald. For ten or fifteen minutes the work went well. Then Prescott saw a clump of men surrounding a regimental chaplain and the sergeant who had been so worried about prayers for the unlucky Pollard. The colonel sprang off the parapet and rushed over to disperse the group.

"I said I want to see every man working until I give the order to stop," he stormed.

"We cannot bury this brave soldier without prayers, Colonel," the chaplain said stiffly.

Prescott ignored him. "Get back to your work!" he said to the men.

Cowed, they drifted back to the breastwork and picked up their shovels. Prescott remounted the parapet. When he looked again, there were more men around the chaplain and he was persistently conducting a service over Pollard's corpse. Prescott swore mightily under his breath. But this time he did nothing.

About nine o'clock Colonel Bridge and his Lieutenant Colonel, Moses Parker, Lieutenant Colonel Bricket, Lieutenant Colonel Robinson, Prescott's second in command, and several other officers detached themselves from supervising the breastwork and approached Prescott. Like everyone else in the Provincial Army they had no hesitation about speaking their minds. The men were exhausted. They had been working all night with little food and water and it was obviously going to be one of the hottest days of the summer. When were they going to be relieved?

Major John Brooks, who was among the officers, recalled Prescott's reply vividly. He would not under any circumstances consent to being relieved if there was the slightest chance of a battle. "The men who raised these works are the best able to defend them," he said. "They have learned to despise the fire of the enemy." He was determined that "since they had the merit of the labor, they would have the honor of the victory." At the moment, however, he did not believe that the British would make an attack. The position they held was simply too formidable.

That Prescott believed the British would not attack is extremely doubtful. That he was forced to say it, to lie to his own officers, is grim evidence of how shaky the command structure was in the American army. The decision to allow captains and colonels to handle the enlisting and form companies and regiments had turned recruitment into a popularity contest. The average soldier was shrewd enough to see that his captain's rank depended on his continuing support and the same situation applied to a colonel, when confronted by a congress of his captains. The habit of forming committees and councils, which tormented Governor Gage, was by no means abandoned by these New Englanders once they became soldiers. Already several captains and one or two colonels had been voted out of office. It was a tribute to Prescott's determination—and to the power of his personality—that he was able to overcome this anarchic spirit when the common sense of the situation was almost totally against him.

The officers looked frankly dissatisfied but they returned to their posts. The sun beat down relentlessly and still the weary men sweated and toiled. The breastwork was taking shape rapidly—not quite as thick and formidable as the walls of the fort, but solidly built of earth and logs; no musket ball could penetrate it. Prescott strolled his parapet again, calling out encouragement to the grimy soldiers. "Just a few more swings of that pick, Salem. Come on, Brown, a little more dirt might mean the difference between a musket ball hitting that wall and you!"

About ten o'clock, with a rattle and a clatter, the American artillery came on the field. To a soldier with any experience they were a display not of American strength, but of weakness. There were only four guns and they were pitifully small—four-pounders which had been taken off the *Diana* after the skirmish at Noddle Island and fitted with carriages. There were larger guns in Cambridge, but General Ward obviously hesitated to commit them since they would be more difficult to withdraw in case of a retreat. There were two guns to a "train," drawn by a horse and commanded by a captain. The first captain was twenty-seven-year-old Samuel Gridley, son of the just departed colonel. The second was commanded by Captain John Callender. Each had a company of men under his command.

The artillery regiment had been in a state of total disorganization since the army came together. Experienced officers were few and most of the enlisted men had to be recruited from the infantry. Colonel Gridley did not help matters by making his son Samuel a captain and his son Scarborough a major. Not until the fourteenth of June— three days prior to this day—was the regiment pronounced ready to receive official commissions from the Provincial Congress; but the Committee of Safety was apparently still dissatisfied with its military quality, and the question was footballed back and forth between the two groups. Not an officer of the regiment had received his commission when the four cannon appeared on Charlestown Heights.

Over Bunker Hill they came, and up Breed's, past the line of weary men still sweating on the breastwork. They were greeted with a cheer, and a circle of eager admirers formed around them as they unlimbered the guns and wheeled them into the redoubt.

There they discovered the firing platforms were not yet ready. Ward had neglected to send carpenters along with the expedition, and the young farmers who were assigned to the construction job had, at best, only amateur talent in this direction.

A scream of anguish outside the redoubt made everyone forget the cannon. Aaron Barr of Prescott's regiment had voluntarily gone out to do some more digging in the ditch in front of the breastwork. He had apparently decided to imitate his commander's example and fearlessly expose himself to the British artillery. Most of the British shots were falling short and bounding up the hill. An eighteen-pound cannon ball can do terrible damage to a human being, even when it is rolling along the ground at the very end of its velocity. Early in the siege men were offered small rewards to bring in any balls the British fired toward the American lines, but the policy was quickly discontinued because too many of the militiamen tried to stop the rolling balls with their feet and ended up in the hospital as amputees. The ball that struck Aaron Barr was not rolling. It came bounding up the green hill like a live thing and as with Asa Pollard, before anyone could move, Barr was writhing on the ground with his leg beside him, a piece of smashed, bloody flesh.

This time there was no panic. Barr was carried to shelter behind the redoubt and Lieutenant Colonel Bricket and Major John Brooks used their medical skill to stop the flow of blood. Prescott detailed four men to carry the wounded boy back to Cambridge—although it was obvious that Barr would not live.

As the bearers trudged down Breed Hill with Barr in a crude stretcher made of blankets, one of the sentries Prescott had posted in the fort rushed up to him. "Colonel. There's troops mustering in Boston. Artillery too."

The man was right. Cannon were rolling through the streets toward the waterfront. A troop of cavalry, about forty strong, had formed up on the common. A mounted officer before them barked orders and they went galloping off in precise squads. Elsewhere on the common and at the other British encampments on Boston's hills, lines of brilliant redcoats could be seen mustering in front of their tents. It meant only one thing. They were coming over.

Prescott made no attempt to deceive his officers once the truth became evident. He instantly called a council of war. Once more he was told that the men were exhausted, dissatisfied and in no condition for action. And again he told them he was absolutely opposed to requesting relief. However, he did agree to send Major John Brooks to General Ward to ask for reinforcements and fresh supplies. It was four and a half hot miles to Cambridge and even Prescott felt that time was precious. He therefore sent Brooks to borrow

a horse from the artillery. Captain Samuel Gridley flatly refused him and proceeded to give Prescott a lecture on the
independence of the artillery. The guns were his responsibility. How could he draw them off without horses if there was
a general retreat? With a mighty effort Prescott restrained
his temper and told Brooks to walk.

Brooks trudged off down the hot dusty road which Barr's
stretcher-bearers had taken. The sun was mounting steadily
into the blue sky and the heat mounted inexorably with it.
In the fort, Prescott posted a guard over the rum with orders
to ration it strictly. He did not want any drunks on his hands.
Restlessly, he prowled around the hill and down the slope
past the growing breastwork, his body and mind full of
electric tension. He had taken off his blue officers coat. Now
he wore a light linen coat, called a banyan, and a wide-
brimmed farm hat which gave him some protection from
the sun.

One after the other Prescott mentally ticked off the possible British alternatives and what he could do to counter
them. If they attempted a landing on the Charlestown
wharves he could rush a regiment into the town—no, two
regiments—and make their progress through the streets a
bloody one—if they even got ashore. But they knew better
than to try that. Prescott had been at Louisburg and he
knew the agonizing and hesitation which had held up that
expedition while they debated the choice of a proper beach.
There had to be room to land in force and little or no cover
in which the defenders could take shelter from the covering
bombardment.

Behind the town, in his rear, was more probable. Should
he attack such a landing or stand his ground and hope the
New Hampshire regiment stationed on the Neck would
come to his support? Unlikely. They had no orders. Perhaps he could commit a regiment, with two cannon, to see
what damage they could do. Certainly they would never

have the regulars in a more vulnerable position. Sitting red ducks in their boats. His men could fall back through the town to the fort. Or should he oppose the landing at all? Let them make the attack. That had been the province's policy.

Suddenly, all Prescott's plans for dispatching regiments and commanding beachheads around his isolated peninsula evaporated. His two fellow regimental commanders, Colonels Bricket and Bridge, abruptly told him they were exhausted. They planned to retire to some houses on the northwest slope of Bunker Hill where they would at least be out of the sun. Prescott apparently did not make the slightest attempt to stop them, although he was technically in command and could have forbidden what he must have known was a mistake. Later, he simply said, "Colonel Bridge and Bricket, being indisposed, could render me but little service." The effect of their indisposition was all but disastrous. To use Prescott's terse language again "the most of the men under them deserted the party." Once more Prescott did not seem to feel he could legitimately stop them. They were not in his regiment and in this volunteer army men obeyed only the officers they elected. Israel Putnam had told Warren American soldiers were as good as their officers. They were now demonstrating that this maxim was a dangerously two-edged sword.

If Putnam had been on the field all day, there would have been fewer desertions. He was, as we have already seen, not so careful about telling soldiers not directly under his command what to do. Not that timidity prevented Prescott from asserting himself. He was more than capable of anger when the occasion demanded it. When he was a lieutenant at the siege of Louisburg he had contracted one of the epidemic fevers which swept that swampy encampment, and his men thought he was on the point of death. The regimental surgeon was called to examine him and he said, curtly: "There's nothing for me to do here," implying the patient was already too far gone. Prescott sprang out of bed, seized his sword and chased the terrified medical man out of his tent. A few days later he was well again.

On Breed's Hill, Prescott could have used his sword and his authority with similar effect. As the day wore on and it began to look more and more like they were going to fight the battle alone, a kind of mystique of honor seemed to possess him. None but the truly brave deserved to man this post of danger and he let the others, who skulked away, go with nothing but a stare of silent contempt. Beneath this stern code there was also a hardheaded practicality. He knew it was better to let the cowards go now than to try to hold them until the battle started. If they bolted then, their panic could spread through the ranks like an electric current and start a mass flight.

About ten o'clock Putnam's bulky figure appeared again spurring his horse along the crest of Bunker Hill. The daylight view of their position had alarmed him more than he cared to admit, but he had been unable to communicate his excitement to anyone in Cambridge.

The headquarters of the Grand American Army had been dozing in the morning sun when he galloped furiously through its empty streets to Artemas Ward's headquarters at Hastings House. He found the stocky, slow-moving Ward in his office studying a map of the American siege lines. "General," Putnam roared, "are the reinforcements ready to march?"

Ward gave him nothing but a long solemn stare. He had done a masterful job of holding the patchwork American army together for the last two months and he did not intend to let Israel Putnam annihilate it in a day. He told Putnam that he had issued orders to the regiments of Colonels John Nixon, Moses Little and John Mansfield and 200 Connecticut troops—but they were not scheduled to march until

5 P.M. Ward was a stubborn man. Governor Hutchinson had
found that out over ten years ago when he tried to bribe him
to join the loyalist party. The General's ardent support of
the patriot cause earned him his nomination as commander
in chief; his military experience was slight. In 1758 he had
served a campaign with the American militia which accompanied the British army led by Lord George Howe. The campaign had been a disaster and the militia had done little or
no fighting. He was elected colonel of the local regiment
after it returned to Worcester.

Unfortunately, in the campaign Ward's health broke down
and he became permanently afflicted with calculus, or
"bladder stone." This was a disabling, though not a fatal
illness, extremely painful when he was having an attack. Today he was having a severe attack. So Putnam confronted a
commanding officer who was in constant and often agonizing
pain—not a recommended situation for a man who needed
to keep his head clear and his judgment acute. He was also
the commanding officer Putnam had overruled in the council
of war by sheer force of his prestige and personality. It was
only human nature for Ward to remind him, now, that he
was still in command.

But Ward was also a deeply religious man with a stern
sense of responsibility inherited from his Puritan ancestors.
He would never for a moment sacrifice three regiments of
brave men out there on Charlestown peninsula just to
prove Israel Putnam was wrong. From where he sat, on that
humid Saturday morning, his refusal to reinforce Prescott
was based on sound military judgment. Ponderously, but im-
pressively, he traced out on the map before him the argument for his decision. The American army was distributed
along a semicircle running from Roxbury on the south to
Medford on the north. On the right was General Thomas,
Ward's second in command, stationed at Roxbury covering
both Dorchester Neck and Boston Neck. He commanded

eight Massachusetts regiments of about 4,000 men and also had 3,000 troops from Connecticut and Rhode Island to reinforce him. In the center, Ward was in direct command with fifteen regiments of Massachusetts infantry and one regiment of artillery, a total of about 6,000 men. In an advanced position at Inman's Farm only about a half mile from the Boston shore were 1,000 Connecticut troops under General Putnam. On the far left, at Medford, to protect against a boat expedition up the Mystic River, lay Colonel John Stark with his outsized New Hampshire regiment of 800 men.

Ward had proved himself an able besieger. The disposition of his troops took into account every conceivable operation the British might attempt to break out of Boston. No less a talent than General Howe, in his letter of June 12 to Adjutant General Harvey of the war office in London, paid Ward the compliment of saying: "The situation which the enemy has taken in forming the blockade is judicious and strong being well entrenched where the situation requires it and with cannon."

Running his finger over the "Cambridge lines," as the colonials called the entrenchments the troops had built about a mile and a half southeast of Harvard College, Ward explained to Putnam that he needed an estimated 6,000 men to defend them properly. Even if there were only 1,000 men on Charlestown's hills, this left him only 5,000 troops in Cambridge, since the three regiments that had marched last night had been part of the center defense. This, too, he reminded Putnam, was a paper estimate. "God only knows how many troops are at home for haying."

Ward then drew a line down the road from the bridge over the Charles River at Cambridge to Charlestown Neck, a distance of three miles by the main highway. About halfway to the Neck, just beyond Willis Creek, there was a junction with the road which ran from Lechmere Point across the creek. These two roads were the only routes the British could take to attack Cambridge without crossing the Charles River. This vital crossroad was the key to the whole American position and if Ward committed a substantial portion of his army to Charlestown it could become his Achilles' heel. It was less than a mile from North Battery in Boston to the shores of Willis Creek.

With the Cambridge lines drained of men—they were 3,000 yards long—nothing could stop the British from making a diversionary attack on the American redoubt in Charlestown and then lunging with their main force up this Willis Creek road which they had traveled to Lexington and knew well. Throwing one or two regiments across this junction to cut off the American force at Charlestown they could hurl the rest of the army at the stores and ammunition in Cambridge. Recognizing the importance of this crossroads, Ward had built a redoubt nearby called Fort Number Three or the Red House Fort because there was a red brick house on one corner of the road. An entire regiment was posted in this fort permanently while Putnam's thousand men from Connecticut camped at Inman's Farm, a half mile away, to support them.

Ward's argument made sound military sense. But Putnam's heart and soul were with the men on Charlestown Heights. A friend summed him up admirably when he said: "He does not wear a large wig nor screw his countenance into a form that belies the sentiments of his generous soul; he is not adept at politics or religious canting . . . he is no shake-hand body; he therefore is totally unfit for everything but fighting." Putnam reminded Ward that they had originally planned to risk 2,000 men and there were less than 1,000 on Charlestown Heights now. Ward was unimpressed. He simple reiterated that he could not risk weakening his fortifications before Cambridge by another man. Nor could the lines in front of Roxbury where a British attack was equally possible, spare any men. Putnam was willing to admit that the British might march on Cambridge or Roxbury or Fort Ticonderoga. But he did not see why that prevented him from having another 1,000 men to march onto Bunker Hill. Where was the Committee of Safety? He would carry his plea to them.

The Committee of Safety was in session in a nearby room. Warren was there, looking pale and haggard. He had been up all night dealing with Provincial Congress problems in Watertown and had ridden into Cambridge at dawn. He confessed to a splitting headache and seemed to be running a fever. He was obviously close to caving in from his endless succession of sleepless nights and decision-crammed days. The rest of the committee was not in much better condition. There was scarcely an hour of the day when they had not been in session for the past two months. The two generals presented their arguments to this group of nervous, exhausted civilians. Putnam made an eloquent plea for reinforcement and Ward, vehement now, opposed him with all the authority and emotion he could command. The committee, not surprisingly, was baffled. They had no military experience and here were the two men with the best military reputations in their makeshift army at loggerheads about a decision that was purely military. They decided to take Ward's advice and play a waiting game but urged him to put every available regiment on orders to march at a moment's notice.

When the debate on reinforcements broke up and the disgusted Putnam stormed out to return to Charlestown, the committee found Major John Brooks, dusty and weary from his four-mile hike, waiting in the anteroom. He brought Prescott's message requesting reinforcements and an even more urgent request for fresh provisions. Ward agreed to send the provisions immediately and asked Richard Devens of the committee to take care of it. He also asked Major Brooks to remain with him for the rest of the day as his

aide. It was an order which Brooks obeyed with reluctance.
This young man who was later to become one of Massachusetts' most notable governors had no desire to avoid the
fight. Actually Ward needed Brooks far more as an aide
than Prescott needed him as a fighting man. Fat, twenty-
five-year-old Henry Knox, who knew as much about artillery
as any man on the North American continent but had yet to
be given a commission in the army because he had no previous service to recommend him, had volunteered to serve
the general in a similar capacity. In addition, Ward had his
miniscule regular staff of two: Samuel Osgood, his personal
aide, and a cousin, Joseph Ward, who acted as his secretary.

The General had already dispatched Knox to Lechmere
Point with orders to report immediately any sign of an attempted British landing along Willis Creek. He now conferred with Brooks on the condition of the men on Breed's
Hill and was pleased to hear that they were taking the cannonade well. As they talked the guns boomed softly in the
distance like summer thunder. Brooks told him that the British had moved two floating batteries in close to Charlestown
Neck with the rising tide. Assisted by the armed transport
Symmetry lying a little farther out, they were raking the bare
narrow road with a continuous barrage, some of it ringshot
and chainshot—an eighteenth-century equivalent of shrapnel. It would be difficult to march raw soldiers through such
fire.

The first American soldier to ride through that hail of
flying metal on Charlestown Neck was Israel Putnam. He
did not give it a thought, except to spur his horse a little
harder. On the summit of Bunker Hill he found to his
mortification that there was not a single soldier at work on
entrenchments. He had assumed that Gridley would detach
some men from the finished redoubt and send them to the
summit of Bunker as soon as possible. Putnam was convinced
that a defense in depth was vital to American chances in the

coming battle. If the British drove these volunteer soldiers from their first line of defense on Breed's Hill and they had no other fortifications to fall back on they would not stop running until they reached Cambridge. Angrily he spurred his horse down Bunker Hill and up the slope of the lower hill to the redoubt. There Prescott and the other officers told him of the British preparations in Boston. "We must begin entrenchments on Bunker Hill immediately," Putnam roared above the cannon. "Have the men carry the entrenching tools up there."

Prescott protested that he could not spare a man. He had already lost too many through desertions and exhaustion. Putnam shook his head and insisted every one of them would return.

Reluctantly Prescott gave the order.

"Never," said an ironic eye witness, "was an order obeyed with more readiness. From every part of the line within hearing volunteers ran and some picked up one and some two shovels, mattocks and gabions and hurried over the hill."

For the moment Putnam did not particularly care what motive inspired this response from men who had been digging all night and half the morning in the blazing sun. He assumed they shared his zeal and were prepared to dig for a week and fight for a month if the cause called for it. He put them to work on trenches across the top of Bunker Hill, then turned his horse and rode hard for Cambridge once more. He did not like what he saw on Breed's Hill. The grumbling exhausted men up there were in a state of semi-revolt. If they did not get some food and water soon and see some fresh troops coming to their assistance they were liable to quit in disgust before a shot was fired. Through the storm of chainshot and ringshot he rode once more to Cambridge.

On Breed's Hill Prescott looked with dismay on his

dwindling brigade. He had barely 500 men left from the original 900. Only his own regiment remained reasonably intact. Even on their faces he could see growing uneasiness. These young Americans were not Prussians who were ready to die at a given order like robots. They strongly believed in the philosophy of running away to fight another day. It had proved to be a sound tactic at Lexington where they melted into the woods every time the British charged them. Why should they die like trapped fools on this idiotic hilltop?

The amateur carpenters came out of the redoubt and informed Prescott that the firing platforms were finally ready for the cannon. The colonel seized on the chance to go into action. But when artillery Captains Gridley and Callender marched their cannoneers into the redoubt, they found a perplexing omission. Colonel Gridley had neglected to provide embrasures—rectangular openings in the top of the wall—through which the guns could be fired. Moreover, young Gridley complained that the firing platforms looked as if they would collapse with the first round. He was right about the platforms. The young farmers assigned by Prescott had simply whacked away as best they could. The embrasures were more important. Unless they were made, the guns would never be fired to test the platforms. Gridley and Callender flatly refused to put their men to work on making them. Again Prescott was reminded that he had no authority over them. The artillery was an entirely independent department. The colonel turned to Captain Ebenezer Bancroft who was standing nearby and said wearily: "Do you know anything about cannon?" Bancroft said he had a little experience with them. "Do what you can," Prescott said and stalked away. All the entrenching tools were now up on Bunker Hill, and Bancroft and his men at first tried to claw openings in the wall with their bare hands. But the soft earth had hardened under the baking sun and their fingers were soon torn and bleeding. They tried hacking with bayonets but they were almost as useless. Then Bancroft got a bright idea. "Hoist those damn guns up on the platforms," he said. The artillerymen hoisted the guns and Bancroft loaded them. He aimed them straight at the walls and lit the fuse. A blast of smoke and flame erupted and lo and behold—there was an opening. He did the same with the second gun. At last the Americans were ready to answer the British barrage. Or so they thought.

The American artillerymen were unbelievably inept. It took them minutes to load the gun, and they seemed more than a little afraid that it might go off while they were too close to it.

This was, to be sure, no reflection on them. Firing a cannon in 1775 was a highly specialized and somewhat dangerous business; there were barely two dozen experienced artillerymen in the New World. (Colonel Gridley had been able to drive a hard bargain with the Provincial Congress in return for his services. They agreed to pay him £170 a year while on active duty and £123 a year for the rest of his life, when the army was disbanded.) Unfortunately, the scarcity of powder in Cambridge had given Gridley little chance to train his men. It took a team of seven men to fire light fieldpieces such as the young captain was now aiming at Boston. The cartridge, a wool bag full of gunpowder, was the first to go down the bore, shoved by the long-handled rammer. But the man at the rammer shoved and shoved and turned beet red while Prescott's infantrymen laughed at him; he could not get the cartridge more than one-third of the way down. Only now did Captain Gridley make a discovery which was to have disastrous effects in the battle to come; the cartridges carried in the sideboxes were all too big for these captured guns. This meant they had to be cut open and the powder shoved down the barrels with a long-handled ladle. It made for slower, more nerve-wracking work;

not even a veteran would be enthusiastic about handling loose powder under fire.

Once the right amount of powder was in the bottom of the bore, then the wad, a loose knot of cotton rags, was shoved down to compress the explosion until it built up maximum pressure. Next came the ball or "shot." This was carefully inspected for dirt or any surface irregularity since the slightest defect could cause it to jam in the bore and blow gun and crew sky high. The loading was now complete and the "powder monkey" came forward. This man was entrusted with a "passing box" filled with fine grained powder which he sprinkled into the touchhole or vent at the rear of the gun. The powder monkey had to be a reliable anthropoid with a good set of nerves; priming powder was highly explosive and not under any circumstances to be spilled. Next came the man in charge of the pick, or priming wire, which was shoved down the vent to punch a hole in the cartridge so it would be more likely to ignite. The gun was now ready to fire. Everyone stood back at a respectful distance except Captain Gridley who struck a match and put it in his linstock—a long stick with a ring or clamp on one end which saved him from singed fingers when he inserted the match in the touchhole.

Gridley sprang back nervously as the priming powder caught; the gun quivered as the flame leaped down the vent into the cartridge. Then came the crash. Gridley's lieutenant, Woodward, fired the other gun at the same time. In the clear air everyone could see the two balls curve slowly out over the harbor and smack harmlessly into the face of Copp's Hill, about 100 yards below the British battery. The Americans in the fort gave a parched but hearty cheer. They were fighting back at last. They did not give a hoot whether they hit anything. It was just hugely comforting to give the British a blast of defiance.

Now the gunners had to clamber up on the swaying gun

platforms and clean out the guns. The wormer, a long-handled corkscrew, was inserted to pull out the old wad. Then came the sponge, a long-handled wooden plug covered with sheepskin, woolly side out, which was dipped in a nearby bucket of water and inserted to swab out the burned powder and kill any leftover sparks.

Slowly, and still nervously, Gridley's men reloaded and the captain fired another round. His aim was still short, but the effect of the guns' recoil on their firing platform was much more serious. The supports cracked and the whole structure swayed. Gridley looked anxiously at Prescott. He was obviously not eager to fire again. Prescott told him to stay at it. Twice more the balls soared across the harbor to plunk harmlessly against Copp's Hill, still at least 100 yards short of their target. On the fourth round, with a creaking crash, the artillery platform collapsed. Prescott stared at the wreckage and suggested that Gridley might take his four guns outside the redoubt and continue his duel from there. By now he could not have had the slightest confidence in these amateur cannoneers. He was obviously thinking once more about his men's morale.

Reluctantly Gridley obeyed the order and marched his neophyte gunners out to do battle with sixteen times as many guns, any one of which was heavier than his entire battery combined. After great difficulty they fired a salvo which the Copp's Hill gunners quickly accepted as a challenge. In a moment shots streamed over the Americans' heads and tore up chunks of earth around them. Most of the artillerymen promptly took to their heels leaving Gridley and his fellow captain, Callender, in a state of total frustration. It was now that young Peter Brown watched Gridley as he "swang his hat three times to the enemy" and retreated behind the redoubt. Badly shaken, young Gridley lost his head. "I'm not going to leave my guns on this hill to be destroyed," he said. "If Captain Callender wishes to stay, he has my permission but I'm going to retreat to Bunker Hill."

Prescott let him go without an argument. Callender looked like a better man and two cannon were almost as good as four; more precisely, they were almost as useless as four, since there was no platform from which to fire them.

By now it was about eleven o'clock. The British bombardment gradually slackened. The battleship *Somerset* fired a salvo every five or six minutes as did the battery on Copp's Hill, but the smaller ships were silent, no doubt to conserve their ammunition.

Wearily Prescott mounted the parapet of the fort and stared down the empty peninsula. Not a sign of a wagon with food or water. Not a sign of reinforcements, which he would gladly accept now. Up on Bunker Hill the men who had so eagerly carried off the entrenching tools were demonstrating that their motive was not an extraordinary fondness for digging. With Putnam gone, there was not one of them working on this second line of defense.

The sun beat down. Inside the redoubt the men lined up for the last of the rum. The few who remembered to bring food gnawed on their boiled beef and sometimes shared it with their friends. Peter Brown thought about the cool well just outside his farmhouse door. He could see his mother, fetching a dripping bucket to the top, at this very moment. He could feel the lovely, quiet shade of the kitchen. Suddenly he wanted to run, run all the way down the empty peninsula, through Cambridge and never stop until he was there in that kitchen, in his mother's arms. Abruptly he caught himself. He was twenty years old. He was a man. He looked up at Prescott and found strength in that stern, unsmiling face. Beside him, Corporal Amos Farnsworth said his prayers. He was still certain God had a "faver toward them."

Back in Cambridge, Israel Putnam again assaulted Ward and the Committee of Safety with a demand for more troops. Ward still insisted on waiting. And where were the supplies, Putnam roared. Did they think that men who were near collapse from hunger and thirst could fight a battle? What were they trying to do, betray those brave men who were risking their lives while they sat here in the cool shaded safety of Cambridge? As for the supplies, Richard Devens of Charlestown explained to Putnam that they were having the devil's own time trying to find horses and wagons. Everyone had heard about the British cannonade and no one seemed inclined to risk his property or his skin for the cause. "Get them at pistol point if you have to," Putnam roared.

Devens, a thorough patriot (he had supplied Paul Revere with his horse on April 18) vowed that he would take Putnam's advice. He then turned to his fellow committee members and Ward and launched into an impassioned speech in favor of reinforcements. Charlestown was his home, he declared, and he was well aware that General Gage had vowed he would burn the town if Americans attempted any military operations on the peninsula. He was aware of this and yet he had voted to send the troops to the heights. In fact, a few days before when the plan was being discussed a committee of refugees from Charlestown had called on General Ward and told him that he had their permission and approval for the expedition in spite of the fact that they knew their homes and property would probably be destroyed. If he and his fellow townsmen were willing to sacrifice so much, how could they sit here hesitating to take every step to guarantee success? Was his home to be burned for nothing? This would be the almost certain result of half measures and timidity.

Deven's oratory carried the day. The committee voted for reinforcements and Ward bowed to their command.

Nothing that happened on June 17 was stranger than this voted order from a group of unmilitary politicians forcing the commander in chief of the American army to make a military decision which he abhorred. Nevertheless, Ward obeyed with a sound eye on his tactical position. He was still convinced that it would be courting disaster to weaken his center around Cambridge by another man. He sent orders therefore to the New Hampshire regiment encamped near Medford on his extreme left flank. They were to detach 200 men to Breed's Hill as quickly as possible and keep the rest of the men on marching readiness. It was the best order Artemas Ward would give all day.

9

MAJOR GENERAL WILLIAM HOWE'S orders for the British army in Boston on Saturday morning, June 17, 1775, were thorough and precise.

"The ten eldest companies of grenadiers and the ten eldest companies of light infantry (exclusive of those of the regiments lately landed) the 5th and 38th Regiments to parade at half after eleven o'clock with their arms, ammunition, blankets and provisions ordered to be cooked this morning. They will march by files to the long wharf. The 43rd and 52nd Regiments with the remaining companies of light infantry and grenadiers to parade at the same time with the same directions and march to the North Battery. The 47th Regiment and the first battalion of Marines will also march as above directed to the North Battery after the rest are embarked and be ready to embark there when ordered.

"The rest of the troops will be kept in readiness to march at a moment's warning.

"One subaltern, one sergeant, one corporal, one drummer and twenty privates to be left by each corps for the security of their respective encampments.

"Any man who shall quit his rank on any pretense or shall dare to plunder or pillage will be executed without mercy."

With the methodical precision of professional soldiers the army came to life. Regimental cooks had been toiling feverishly since early morning to prepare the three days' supply of boiled beef and bread the men were to carry in their knapsacks. Regiments were mustered and every man accounted for. The names of those to be left behind on security duty were posted.

The orders themselves were graphic proof of the British intentions. Howe was not ferrying 2,300 crack troops to Charlestown peninsula merely to knock some rebellious Americans off a relatively insignificant hill. The blankets, the full knapsacks, the three days' cooked food, the two dozen officers and men left behind "for the security of the encampment" all meant only one thing: that night Howe hoped to sleep in Cambridge. Burgoyne confirms this in a letter written a few days after the battle. After describing the plan for raising the siege, he narrates the American appearance on Charlestown and says: "It became necessary to alter our plan and attack on that side." But the basic plan —to seize both Charlestown and Dorchester peninsulas, and then smash the American siege lines before Cambridge—remained unchanged.

Much unjust criticism has been heaped on Howe and Gage for overburdening the men with marching gear in a battle which as it developed made the blankets and three days' provisions painfully unnecessary. British conduct at Bunker Hill has often been held up as a tragic example of the regulation military mind at work. Their misfortunes were attributed to an inability to alter their routine thinking to cope with the military ingenuity of their American opponents.

The British made mistakes at Bunker Hill, but clinging to outmoded military routine was not one of them. Howe had learned his warfare under the brilliant Wolfe, one of the great improvisers of military history. He was partly responsible for the development of light infantry tactics which, adapted and modified by Napoleon, enabled him to sweep Europe. Gage was also an experienced light infantry commander.

Even the retreat from Lexington, which to the average American's mind is summed up in the image of a redcoated column scampering frantically down the road while sharpshooting farmers bang away at it from nearby rocks and trees, was by no means so simple. Lord Percy sent squads of flanking parties roaring through the woods on either side of the column and more than one unsuspecting minuteman, trapped between the column and the flankers, died with a bullet or a bayonet in his back.

If anyone could be accused of fighting in routine style on June 17, 1775, it was the Americans. The redoubt was built, their whole position was selected according to the best principles of "grand tactics" studied by every professional soldier in Europe. It was they, not the British, who deliberately chose a formal battle. But they chose it, like good professional soldiers, where the natural advantages were in their favor. The American leaders were no more military amateurs than their British opponents were blundering robots.

Some of the most violent criticism has also been heaped on Howe for moving so slowly. The redoubt was discovered at dawn. Many a hindsight specialist has pointed out that if the British had moved quickly and landed regiments on Charlestown by nine o'clock, the Americans would not have even begun their breastwork along their left flank and there was not at that time even a hope of reinforcements. Others have accused Howe of wasting the morning dallying with his mistress, one Mrs. Joshua Loring, the wife of a prominent American Tory. Some months later there is rather definite evidence that the general did take an interest in this lady. But at this point Howe had been in Boston exactly three weeks, and most of his time had been spent planning a major offensive. More important, Howe was too experienced a soldier to fling troops hastily on what amounted to enemy territory without a plan of battle or a chance to reconnoiter the situation and estimate enemy strength. The British were keenly aware that the Americans had 15,000 troops to their 5,000. How did they know there were not 3,000 or 4,000 additional troops waiting out of sight on the northern slopes of Bunker Hill or in the hills just beyond Charlestown Neck?

There was, moreover, a fundamental flaw in the equipment on hand for an amphibious landing. In the Seven Years' War with the French, the British had acquired a high degree of skill in this difficult military art and had even developed a crude but effective landing craft with planked-up sides to protect the troops from musket fire and a flat bottom which took practically no water. Not one of these boats was available to Howe. He had to depend on the navy's rowboats, which offered his men absolutely no protection while they landed, and drew more water. Because of these boats and the mud flats which ringed Charlestown peninsula, a landing could not be made before the flood tide, at two o'clock in the afternoon. Lack of flatboats also explains in part why Howe chose Morton's Point, which was as far away as possible from American troops. He was acutely aware that his men would be sitting ducks in the ships' boats. How much this was on Howe's mind can be seen from his correspondence. In three separate letters to England, between June 12 and June 22, he laments that "not one of our old accustomed flatboats" was in Boston.

Aside from this problem, Howe had plenty to occupy his time before embarkation. We have a fairly good record of his activities for the morning. After the council of war ended and the general orders were written he went on board the battleship *Somerset* with Admiral Samuel Graves to see what kind of cooperation he could get from the navy. The brother of a great admiral, Howe had a keen grasp of the basic principles of amphibious assault and he wanted the maximum amount of cooperation from the ships of the line at his disposal. There was no unified command in 1775. What unity was achieved had to be negotiated and Graves' record of cooperation thus far in the campaign was not good. The admiral proved to be consistent. Howe wanted Graves to warp the *Somerset* in as close to the beach as possible to give him maximum artillery support while landing, but after a lengthy conference Graves decided that it could not be done because there was not enough water off the beach to take a ship of the *Somerset*'s size. The admiral concluded that his large ships "could give no other assistance than that of lending boats, men, ammunition and other stores to the small." He therefore sent two officers and thirty-six seamen from the *Somerset* to the armed transport *Symmetry* and twenty seamen to the sloop *Falcon*. Sailors from the transport *Preston* manned the *Spitfire* sloop with six three-pounders.

In this conference, Howe undoubtedly made another request which Graves also refused. Since he was going to advance up the shore of the Mystic River, and there were already signs of activity on Bunker Hill, it was only logical for him to request the transfer of one ship of the line around the peninsula into the Mystic to support him. Graves said no, because he did not have the slightest knowledge of the river's shoals and mud flats. He had been admiral of the American station for over a year and they had been fighting a quasi-war for over two months, but Graves had failed to take soundings in a river which was less than a quarter of a mile from the anchorage of his flagship—a river, moreover, which might well have been used at any time for an offensive expedition aimed at flanking Cambridge. Such was the quality of the naval support which William Howe had to accept on this day of crisis.

Graves now proceeded to position his eight ships and two floating batteries (planked-up musketproof rowboats each mounting two twenty-four-pound cannon). The *Glasgow,* which had just come off the ways, joined the *Symmetry* and the floating batteries in the bombardment of Charlestown Neck to cut off American reinforcements. The small sloops *Lively, Falcon* and *Spitfire* were assigned the task of covering the landing and bombarding the redoubt while the *Somerset* lay out in the channel and joined them at a distance.

Howe was not terribly pleased with this arrangement. He was well aware that the lightly gunned sloops could not do any effective work against the solid American fortifications. But he could not give any orders to Graves (nor could General Gage) and they were suddenly fighting a war 3,000 miles from home. Like all soldiers, Howe was practical. He did his best with the men and materials that were available on the spot. There was hardly time to send for more ships or men—or a new admiral. Moreover, the *Glasgow* and the *Symmetry,* the two heaviest armed ships after the *Somerset,* were needed to cover Clinton's proposed encircling movement up Willis Creek—and for the time being to bombard the Neck across which American reinforcements must move.

Howe meant business. So did the other professionals who were getting ready to fight. On Fort Hill Gage's old friend Lieutenant Colonel James Abercromby inspected his companies of grenadiers. Abercromby had come over to Boston in advance of his regiment, which was slated to reinforce Gage, and had been given the grenadier command in the interim. He was, like Major John Small, a good friend of Putnam, Colonel John Stark and many other Americans. He had been one of the first British officers to throw away his parade-ground uniform and put on buckskins to march with the colonial irregulars against the French and Indians. By some accident of propaganda, a rumor had gone around Boston that Abercromby said the Americans were cowards. The best answer to the accusation is a letter which he wrote to Robert Rogers after a victory over the French years before: "The General . . . returns you and your men thanks for their behaviour and has recommended both you and them strongly. . . . You cannot imagine how all ranks of people here are pleased with your conduct and your men's behaviour; for my part it is no more than I expected."

Nearby Lieutenant Colonel Clarke was readying his light infantry. They and the grenadiers were crack troops, the cream of the regiments. The grenadiers were the tallest, strongest, toughest soldiers in the army, experts with the bayonet. They had been formed over 150 years ago to hurl the crude heavy explosive grenades then in use. Though the grenades proved impractical, the idea of marshaling the finest soldiers in the regiment into picked companies proved to be a good one. They were available for special missions requiring extra reserves of courage and strength. They quickly generated their own military tradition and distinct pride in their prowess. For the light infantry, endurance and agility were more important than strength. They fought on the flanks of the army as skirmishers. Ordinarily each regiment had a company of grenadiers and a company of light infantry. On June 4, probably at Howe's advice, Gage had formed all the grenadiers and light infantry in Boston into separate battalions and assigned them new encampments.

These grenadiers and light infantry were the troops who had marched out on April 19 to strike what General Gage hoped would be a decisive blow at the Americans in Concord. Every American schoolboy knows the story of the courage displayed by the untrained Yankee minutemen that day. The courage and endurance displayed by these same grenadiers and light infantrymen has been more or less lost to view. Yet their accomplishment, viewed objectively, is impressive. They had been up all night and had marched close to twenty miles when the fighting started. They then proceeded to fight their way back through a countryside ablaze with musketry. To march almost forty miles in twenty-four hours and fight almost every step of the way home is no small order. The memory of that running battle in which they had 273 men killed, wounded, or captured still galled them. They were eager for the chance to get sweet revenge across the harbor in Charlestown. When Abercromby and Clarke told them where they were going they were answered with cheers.

Down on Boston common the regular or "line" regiments were also getting ready to march. These regiments were considered the finest in the British army. Except for national pride in the U. S. Marines, Americans have little understanding or appreciation of the pride of corps which has stirred Englishmen for generations and provided English military history with so many feats of heroism. No matter how often a regiment changed its personnel it retained a distinct identity and its history was as well known as the exploits of any individual hero.

At the head of the list, both numerically and chronologically, was the Fourth or "King's Own" Regiment, still in service today as the Royal Lancasters. On its colors it carried "the lion of England" personally presented by William III in acknowledgment of their devotion to his royal person. In 1690 the Fourth fought magnificently at the Battle of Boyne in Ireland, where William's victory made him undisputed King of England, and they were one of the first units ashore in the 1704 capture of Gibraltar, which established British power in the Mediterranean. Thereafter the men of the Fourth had fought with distinction on Minorca and Sardinia, in Spain and Flanders and in 1746 bore the brunt of the Scottish assault at Culloden.

Lord Percy's regiment, the Fifth (still in British ranks today as the Northumberland Fusiliers) had seen over 100 years of service, going back to the days when the British Legion was the crack corps in the army of Holland's Prince of Orange. They had fought in Portugal and at Gibraltar, and during the Seven Years' War had carved a heroic record in a long list of now forgotten battles in Central Europe culminating in Wilhelmstahl, where they took twice their own number of prisoners and were henceforth permitted to wear special caps, modeled after those of the French Grenadiers whom they had so decisively shattered. In Ireland, where they were stationed for some years, their smart appearance earned them the nickname of "The Shiners."

Best known of all the regiments in Boston was the Twenty-third, or Royal Welch Fusiliers. These were the heroes of the sanguinary battle of Minden, in which a combined English-German army smashed a massive French attempt to conquer Germany in 1759. The Royal Welch were the backbone of the British brigade which was accidentally ordered to advance while the rest of the allied army remained motionless. In perfect formation they moved forward, alone—5,000 men against 56,000. Directly in front of them were three ranks of French cavalry and on either side was a crossfire of sixty French cannon which mauled them unmercifully. They stood their ground and the French cavalry charged. A massive British volley sent the horsemen fleeing. Still the rest of the army failed to come to their support. The French cavalry and infantry charged them again and again, but the Royal Welch and its brother regiments, standing without cover in an open plain, took them all on, and broke every attack. By the time the rest of the army came up, half the French were in retreat. The distraught French commander said of the nine British regiments: "I have seen what I never thought to be possible, a single line of infantry break through three lines of cavalry ranked in order of battle and tumble them to ruins." Many an Ameri-

can had drunk a toast, in 1759, to the Royal Welch, the
"heroes of Minden." So great was their reputation that one
colonial patriot complained, when they arrived in Boston,
that the ministry was unfair to send out such a regiment, the
mere sight of whose standards sent shivers of fear up American spines.

The Thirty-eighth, the Forty-third and the Fifty-second
Regiments were not as old as the Fifth or Royal Welch. But
they too had fought all over the world, with considerable
distinction. The Thirty-eighth had been stationed in the
West Indies, considered deadly duty because of the un-
healthy climate, for over sixty years. At Quebec Wolfe had
placed the Forty-third in the center of his line—a key position. The defeated French later said they "leveled and fired
like the single blast of a cannon. Never had they known
so fierce a fire or such perfect discipline." The regiment
went on to distinguish itself in the conquest of Cuba, where
more than half the British expeditionary force died of disease and wounds before Havana fell. Today, the Forty-third
and Fifty-second are combined, and are known as the Ox-
fordshire Light Infantry. Thirty years after Bunker Hill
they were part of Wellington's famous Light Division, which
fought Napoleon's generals to a standstill in Spain.

The Royal Marines were also a proud and traditionally
tough corps with a hundred-year history. They were the first
British conquerors of Gibraltar and had successfully defended the Rock against more than one Spanish and French
assault. In 1759, they made the Seven Years' War the first
truly world war by swarming ashore at Manila and adding
the Philippines to the empire, only to see George III
promptly give the islands back to Spain. Howe had fought
beside them in the siege of Belle Isle, the Seven Years' War's
somewhat more successful equivalent of the Dieppe raid,
and it was no accident that he now took with him the first
battalion of these rugged sea soldiers under Pitcairn.

Vital as these regimental traditions were, the men in the ranks of these regiments were more important. We have already met some of them. But we need to know more about the lives they led as soldiers if we are to completely appreciate the drama into which they were marching.

There is scarcely a soldier in any modern army in the world who would not mutiny if he were forced to endure what the enlisted men in the service of George III accepted as their lot. Enlistment was for life. A private was paid eight pence a day (about ten cents, American). Out of this pittance he had to pay for his food, clothing, medicine, repair of his weapons and a dozen other charges, called "off-reckonings." As a result, his take-home pay was usually zero. In 1775 an irate officer published in London an anonymous pamphlet complaining about the deplorable pay of the average soldier. "From the 8 pence per day which is issued for the pay of the soldier when all deductions are made for clothing, for necessaries, for washing, for the paymaster, for the surgeon, and for the multiplied articles of useless and unmilitary fopperies (introduced by many colonels to the oppression of the soldier for the credit and appearance of the regiment) there is not sufficient overplus for healthful subsistence; and as to the little enjoyments and recreations which even the meanest rank of men can call their own in any country, the brave, the honorable, the veteran soldier must not aspire to." Even the officers were hard pressed for cash. The author of the anonymous pamphlet pointed out that in 1775 the prices of bread and butcher's meat were four times higher than they were when the current rate of pay was established and a tailor, a weaver or a mechanic could live on his wages more respectably than an officer.

Discipline was harsh. Theft was punishable by death, and for a hundred other offenses the lash was the standard prescription. William Howe was considered a humane officer and was enormously popular with the men. Yet his orderly book is a grim picture of the standard disciplinary methods of the day. Here are a few cases selected at random. "Thomas Bailey, grenadier in His Majesty's Corps of Marines. Tried by the General Court Martial . . . for striking Lt. Russel of the Fourth or King's Own Regiment and of insolent mutinous behavior. The Court . . . have found him guilty of the latter and therefore sentence him to receive 800 lashes on his bare back with a cat-of-nine-tails. . . . Thomas MacMahan, Private Soldier in His Majesty's 43rd Regiment of foot, and Isabella MacMahan, his wife. Tried by . . . Court Martial for receiving sundry stolen goods, knowing them to be such are found guilty of the crime laid to their charge and therefore adjudge the said Thomas MacMahan to receive 1,000 lashes on his bare back with a cat-of-nine-tails . . . and the said Isabella MacMahan to receive 100 lashes on her bare back at the cart's tail in different portions and the most conspicuous parts of the town, and to be imprisoned three months. . . . Thomas Owen and Henry Johnson, Private Soldiers in His Majesty's 59th Regiment of foot, tried by the General Court Martial . . . for having broken into and robbed the store of Messrs. Coffin, storekeeper, of sundry goods, the Court having duly considered the whole matter before them is of the opinion that the prisoners are guilty of the crime laid to their charge and doth, therefore, by virtue of the power and authority to them given and granted by the 2nd Article of War, Section 20, adjudge that the said Thomas Owen and Henry Johnson do suffer death by being hanged by the neck until they are dead."

A thousand lashes could kill a man unless he were exceptionally strong or they were administered over the course of a week or two, a policy which many officers followed. Nothing revolted the Americans as much as this custom of flogging common soldiers. John Adams in his diary gives a graphic description of the horrified fascination with which the people of Boston watched their first flogging, a mass operation in which ten men were tied in a row and lashed until they fell to their knees, screaming, their backs laid open.

The time and attention a man was required to give to his uniform was almost preposterous. Few soldiers could prepare for parade in less than three hours. First, they had to dress their hair; stiff curls were worn on either side of the face, and a long tail behind, with a liberal use of pomatum (or the end of a tallow candle) to keep the hair plastered in place. Then came the familiar red greatcoat, which had at least a dozen brass buttons to shine and facings to whiten with pipe clay. Shoes had to be gleaming, and the gaiters clayed and put on moist to make sure they dried tight. The single shoulder belt (the crossed belts, so often shown in popular prints, did not become regulation until after the Revolutionary War) also had to be gleaming white with clay, and the cartridge box, waistbelt and every other item of clothing shined and spotless. The soldier's gun, though affectionately called "Brown Bess" soon lost this coloring, under regimental orders. The brown paint was literally rubbed off the weapon until the entire gun, down to the stock, was gleaming steel.

What could possibly prompt a man to choose such a way of life? Few of the enlisted men were volunteers. Every regiment in the army maintained its own recruiting squad in England and took what it could get by fair means or foul. It was customary for English judges to commute a prisoner's sentence if he agreed to enlist. Many another young man met a recruiter in a pub and woke up the next morning with a wicked hangover and a lifetime enlistment. Once a man accepting the "king's shilling," the standard bonus for signing enlistment papers, he was in for life and it did not matter whether he was drunk or sober when he took it in his hand. A popular ballad of the day gives a picture of standard recruiting practices and also a grim insight into the attitude of the average person toward the army.

JIMMY'S ENLISTED
or
THE RECRUITED COLLIER

Oh what's the matter w'you, my lass
An where's your darlin' Jimmy?
The sowdger boys have picked him up an
Sent him far, far frae me.

Last payday he set off to town
An them red-coated fellows
Enticed him in an made him drunk
An he's better gone to the gallows.

The officers in this army were of two distinct groups. First were the sons of upper class families such as Rawdon who pursued a military career for political power and personal prestige. Howe, Clinton and Burgoyne all had noble blood or noble connections and all held seats in the House of Commons. Thirty-two-year-old Lord Percy was elected in absentia shortly after he arrived in Boston with his regiment.

The second group of officers were those who came from middle-class families and lacked the necessary connections and money to rise beyond a modest rank. Money was vital to advancement. Although Parliament had tried repeatedly to stamp out the practice, commissions in every regiment were bought and sold like pieces of real estate. It cost £3,500 for a man to become a lieutenant colonel in a line regiment, a major £2,600, a captain £1,500, a lieutenant £550, and an ensign £400. So matter of fact was the purchase system that these prices along with slightly higher prices for commissions in the artillery and cavalry were published in the "Military Guide," a highly respected and much used manual for British officers.

The fact that commissions were for sale did not automatically lower the quality of the average officer. The nobles went into the army young—Howe was on active duty at the age of sixteen—and they learned the business of war not in a classroom but in the barracks and on the battlefield. The middle-class officers who formed the backbone of the regiments usually accepted without bitterness the fact that they had no chance for the higher ranks and came to regard "the regiment as their home." The efficiency and reputation of their unit became a matter of deep personal pride to them, and many like Pitcairn were considerate and even concerned about the welfare of their men. Typical of such career officers was Major Roger Spendlove of the Forty-third. He had spent over forty years in the regiment and had been wounded three times—once with Wolfe on the Plains of Abraham, again at the conquest of Martinique and a third time at the capture of Havana.

Most British regiments in Boston were commanded by lieutenant colonels or majors. The colonel was home in England keeping the regimental books and profiting handsomely by it. Every regiment was allowed, *sotto voce,* a certain number of invisible soldiers who were carried on the active list but whose pay went into the colonel's pocket. All purchases of food and equipment went through the colonel's hands, and he alone decided how sticky his fingers would be. The colonel sometimes, though not always, had a sincere interest in the regiment's welfare but he was, in the final analysis, in the business of "farming" his battalion, and everyone expected him to make a reasonable profit from his crop. Since colonels made the real money in this system, a general's title was purely an honorary goal. All the generals were also permanent colonels of regiments, the more famous the better, because they were less likely to be abolished in time of peace. William Howe, for instance, was colonel of the Welsh Fusiliers.

During the thirteen years of peacetime duty from which they were abruptly emerging, the turnover in personnel had been small and most of the regiments had become as intimately connected as the members of a family. Off parade, senior officers treated their juniors as equals, invited them to dinner and loaned them money. There were also bonds of deep affection between seniors like Spendlove or Pitcairn and the noncommissioned officers, many of whom had also been in their regiments for two and three decades. The upper class officers could also be considerate and even generous to their men. When Lord Percy's regiment sailed for America he paid almost £700 out of his own pocket to transport their wives and children with them.

There was in 1775 no provision for taking the families of enlisted men on foreign service. An enlisted man could not marry without the written permission of his commanding officer, who was usually disinclined to give it. But most commanders, though not as generous as Percy, were willing to look the other way and tolerate marriages without legal certificate. The Forty-third Regiment had 92 women and 71 children in Boston. The Fifty-second, 84 women and 100 children, the artillery brigade 121 women and 123 children; almost every regiment had close to 100. These dependents were granted rations out of the army stores and given quarters, though they were never mentioned on the official rolls. More than a few of the officers also brought their women along; most of these liaisons were legal, but not all. Captain Evelyn had as his companion one Peggie Wright, who had been a "servant" of his family in Ireland.

The women of the enlisted men served more than one useful purpose—they washed and mended and cooked for their soldier husbands, and they became army nurses when there were wounded in the hospitals. These quasi-wives also gave General Gage many disciplinary headaches. Rum selling was one of several ways they devised to raise a little extra cash for their wants, above the bare subsistence they received from army stores. Gage issued a steady barrage of orders against the practice, but got nowhere. On May 4, his warning had a note of desperation in it:

> "As there are many complaints of most scandalous drunkenness at this critical time among the troops, that the women of different Corps in defiance of all order sell rum and other spiritous liquors to the Soldiers; it is the Commander in Chief's positive orders the officers commanding regiments examine into those complaints; and those women who do not pay obedience to Order to be *immediately* seized and put on board ship."

Diarist Lieutenant John Barker noted that "there was an order of this kind some time before, but was taken little notice of notwithstanding the word immediately, which scarce a general Order has been without since we came to the Continent."

About this time Gage began organizing his medical service. Each regiment had its own hospital; he now planned to create a general hospital and ordered "A Discreet active Woman from each Corps" to serve as nurse. He had trouble getting this order obeyed also. On May 29 he issued another order: "Any women who may be wanted as nurses at the General Hospital, or to do any other business for the service of the garrison and shall refuse to do it will immediately be struck off the provision list."

Letting the enlisted men bring their women was the army's best answer to the problem of desertion, which was a constant plague to all armies in this period. Fully half the Prussian army, where discipline was the harshest in the world, was constantly employed in keeping the other half from deserting. The Austrian army lost one-fifth of its men through desertion in a single campaign. In Boston, the British problem, women notwithstanding, was more acute, because the Americans deliberately encouraged would-be deserters to come over. Anxious to win some professional military talent to their side, they offered money and farmland and bombarded the British camp with leaflets to remind the average regular how green the grass was across Back Bay. It was effective propaganda; Lord Percy in his letters home told of squads of officers scouring the countryside for deserters. Frederick MacKenzie, the Adjutant of the Welsh Fusiliers, tells in his diary of one man, Robert Vaughan of the Fifty-second Regiment, who was caught deserting on March 3 and ordered to be shot. Gage reprieved him the night before the execution. A few days later, Vaughan deserted again, this time successfully, and took several friends with him.

After Lexington and Concord, desertions dropped off sharply. Boston was ringed with sentries, making an escape much more hazardous, and the penalty, if caught, was now certain death, with no hope of a reprieve. Moreover, the army's professional pride was wounded by the mauling they received on the Lexington road; this, plus the accumulated resentments from a thousand scuffles with liberty boys in Boston streets brought the British fighting spirit to a boil. If the Americans were willing to stand and fight on Charlestown Heights, most of the soldiers marching under Howe's orders were eager to even the score.

Most—but not all. Certainly men like Abercromby and Small could have had little enthusiasm for killing old friends. They too must have been aware that back in England many of their fellow officers were resigning their commissions rather than fight Americans. In the English countryside, where the ministry was frantically trying to raise more troops, recruiting officers wearily reported almost total failure. In Ireland, usually a ready source of fresh troops, several recruiting parties were beaten up and chased out of town. The English middle and lower classes were almost unanimously opposed to the ministry's policy. That much of this disenchantment affected the enlisted men in Boston is doubtful. Americans' cries about taxation without representation meant nothing to them, since neither they nor anyone else in their class voted in eighteenth-century England.

Still, there were undoubtedly a few who wondered why they were about to risk their lives to make America safe for English customs officers. Back in England, if they were not in the army, they probably would have been smugglers themselves. Throughout the middle decades of the eighteenth century, there was scarcely an able-bodied man in the English lower class who did not practice the profession. Manufacturers complained that they could not get workers because the money they offered could not compare with the profits a man made as a smuggler.

There were mixed feelings, therefore, in more than one rank as the regiments formed up precisely at 11:30 and, with a swirl of fifes and a rattle of drums, swung through Boston's streets to their embarkation points at North Battery and Long Wharf.

Their fifers played the very same tune to which the Americans had mustered on Cambridge common at six o'clock the night before: "Yankee Doodle." The British had begun playing the song in derision and the Yankees had doodled it into a rallying cry. Twenty companies of grenadiers and light infantry and the Fifth and Thirty-eighth Regiment, a total of 1,056 men, marched to the Long Wharf, which jutted out into Boston Harbor far enough to see from its end the shorter Griffin's Wharf, where the fateful tea had been dumped. At North Battery the Forty-third and Fifty-second Regiments formed up with the grenadiers and light infantry from the Thirty-fifth Regiment, the Sixty-third Regiment and the Second Marine Battalion, a little over 500 men. It took time to embark these men in the fleet rowboats. A soldier with full pack does not climb

down a ladder and step into a bobbing small boat with
undue speed; one false step would send him like a rock to
the bottom of Boston Harbor. There was also the problem
of lowering four six-pounders, four twelve-pounders and
four five-and-a-half-inch howitzers into these same boats,
which were not built to handle artillery. After an hour of
sweating and cursing, twenty-eight boats were loaded and
six companies of grenadiers and light infantry were still on
the North Battery. Since it was absolutely essential to catch
the flood tide, Howe decided to leave them there. About one
o'clock his armada of rowboats set out in a long double line
for Charlestown peninsula. They had loaded on the south
side of Boston, out of sight of the Americans. Now, as they
rounded North Battery and headed across the mouth of the
Charles River, the artillery on Copp's Hill and the ships of
the line, all of whom had slacked off firing while the loading was in progress, opened up with every gun on the
American redoubt. The sloop *Spitfire,* which drew the least
amount of water, was less than fifty yards from shore, blazing
away with its six three-pounders. The *Lively* and the *Falcon,* with their twenty guns, sent broadside after broadside
over the sails of the smaller ship. Howe and other officers
must have instantly noticed their fire was falling far short.
Apparently they could not elevate their guns enough to zero
in on the redoubt. This gave Howe some anxious moments
and he must have cursed Admiral Graves for his refusal to
take a chance on bringing the *Somerset* in close enough to
effectively use its heavier and more numerous guns. His soldiers were like painted targets upright in these flimsy rowboats. A solid blast of musket fire or grapeshot from an
American cannon could wound or kill every man in a boat.
He knew the Americans had cannon and he was depending
on his naval support to keep them out of action. Again he
probably wondered why they didn't have their musketproof
flatboats which had served them so well against the French.

It must have been infuriating to a soldier of Howe's capacity to find that equipment he regarded as essential had been casually discarded by the accountants who ran the war office.

With methodical rhythm the British sailors stroked across the placid harbor, past the *Spitfire, Lively* and *Falcon* who were wreathed now in clouds of their own gunsmoke. They stayed well out in the middle, beyond musket shot of snipers along the shore. Then Howe, in the first boat with the light infantry of the Royal Welch Fusiliers, gave the signal and they changed course sharply and with all possible speed made for the point of land he had chosen. The ground between Morton's Point and the American redoubt was practically devoid of cover. The possibility of an ambush was therefore slight. But the Americans could have three regiments behind that hill or crouched in the breastwork ready to charge the moment his first boats turned toward the shore, revealing their beachhead. For the spectators in Boston, the moment was equally tense. Ann Hulton wrote: "Great was our trepidation less they should be attacked by superior numbers before they could be all assembled and properly prepared."

Howe depended on his light infantry to cancel the challenge of an immediate attack. The moment the boat grated on the sandy beach he was out of it and his tough agile Royal Welch Fusiliers poured after him. Beside them boats containing the light infantry of the Fourth, Tenth and Fifty-second Regiments touched and more men sprang out. Quickly Howe sent these 150 picked troops racing up the shore of the Mystic to form a skirmishing line in a hollow about 200 yards in front of Morton's Hill. The remaining companies of light infantry were ordered to the brow of Morton's Hill. The grenadiers came next. Howe drew them up on the top of the hill to the left of the light infantry. Now boats were touching all along the shore and the regular infantrymen were struggling out of them to form up on the slopes of the hill where they would be sheltered from American snipers. There was the inevitable confusion involved in getting men out of boats and into companies, connecting separated soldiers to companies and separated companies to regiments. But this was a well-officered army and the confusion was held at a minimum. Howe supervised the process with his usual vigor, elated that they had landed so neatly.

Grunting and sweating, the artillerymen unloaded their heavier weapons and dragged them up the shallow hill to form a line between the grenadiers and light infantry. In twenty minutes Howe could relax and joke with his officers. His beachhead was secure.

Suddenly there were shouts and a mixture of curses and cries over on the left, where General Pigot was forming up his brigade. In a few moments five frightened-looking men were led through the ranks at bayonet point and shoved in front of Howe.

"What is it?" Howe said impatiently.

"Deserters, sir," Pigot said sternly. "They broke out of ranks and ran for the American lines."

Howe stared at the white-faced men. "The morning orders said: 'any man who shall quit his rank on any pretense will be executed without mercy.' You knew this?"

The men nodded numbly.

"I would like to hang all five of you," Howe said. "But we need men. Hang those two," he said, selecting the two men in the center purely at random.

The men flung themselves on their knees, begging for mercy. Howe shook his head and they were dragged to some nearby trees. The hangman's knot was pulled taut at their necks and while their comrades watched in mournful silence, they were jerked aloft to struggle for a few minutes and then dangle motionlessly in the beating sun—an ominous reminder that this was not a game they were about to play.

William Howe valued and invariably won the affection of his men. But he was a professional soldier and he knew there were times which called for discipline rooted in terror. Yet for a moment, as those two condemned men twisted in their death agonies, he must have wondered about the ironies of war and politics which had shoved him onto this muddy beachhead. Up in that fort on the hilltop were men who would have followed him against a common enemy, such as France or Spain, far more willingly than those red-coated soldiers who were gasping their last breaths at the end of the biting rope. The truth of the matter was William Howe had no more appetite for fighting Americans than these nameless unfortunates (no record was made of their deaths; they were simply listed among the casualties). But he had an officer's pride and an Englishman's sense of duty to sustain him—and a dream of reputation to lure him.

10

For a man under fire moments become hours; for Prescott's men crouched in their fort on top of Breed's Hill the hours became centuries. The morning dragged to a close with the British bombardment now slacking off, then regaining vigor and then slacking off again, but never ceasing entirely. There were no more casualties. Asa Pollard and Aaron Barr had taught everyone the folly of reckless exposure. Heat and hunger were far more threatening than cannon to these citizen soldiers. Neither Major Brooks nor fresh provisions appeared from Cambridge.

On the crest of Bunker Hill, a half mile behind Breed's Hill, a few men toiled beneath the watchful eye of Israel Putnam. Most of the entrenchers had quit from sheer exhaustion. Along the grassy slopes all the way to Charlestown there was not another sign of a human being. As the sun rose toward the vertical in the noon sky the heat and dust inside the little fort seemed to double and redouble. "We began to be almost beat out," Peter Brown said, "having no victuals but a little salt pork and no drink but rum." Mutterings about treachery and irresponsibility rose to a new pitch.

Prescott moved quietly among his men, checking their ammunition. They had been issued fifteen rounds last night, but each soldier also had a personal supply which he had carried to camp with him. The quantity varied, but from testimony taken later most of the men had between thirty and forty rounds before the fight started. It was not enough for a prolonged battle, and Prescott looked anxiously toward Cambridge more than once, hoping to see a reserve supply of ammunition coming across the Neck.

The troops, with no previous experience, at least did not worry about this problem. They sprawled inside the baking hot fort, some of them dozing, some checking their guns, some discussing with their veteran officers the fighting qualities of the regulars.

Occasionally, when Prescott was drawn into a discussion, he would tell them that there was only one rule they needed to remember: reserve their fire until the order was given. This was the secret of Wolfe's great victory before Quebec. He had waited until the French were less than forty yards away, and then, with one ferocious volley, he had torn away their whole front line. They never recovered from this first massive blow.

About this time a Colonel Porter reported to the Committee of Safety that he had duly delivered two kegs of beer "through ye shot and shell of ye floating batteries to ye troops in Charlestown." Unfortunately there is no record of his reaching the redoubt. The colonel's courageous delivery was probably made to the diggers on Bunker Hill who were, to be sure, just as thirsty as their friends in the redoubt, if not as deserving.

By now the British bombardment had slacked off almost completely. Only the battery on Copp's Hill threw an occasional salvo in their direction and their aim was wildly erratic.

Suddenly with an enormous roar all the British guns

opened up again. Peering nervously over the wall of their fort the young farmers saw the three sloops, the *Lively,* the *Falcon* and the smaller *Spitfire,* move in close to shore and begin raking the hillside below them with repeated broadsides. Then around the outermost tip of North Battery came the British boats, a long shining double column of glittering steel and brilliant red. In the bows of the lead boats were brass cannon, polished to perfection. It was an awesome sight. To the hot, thirsty, exhausted men it must have seemed a calculated display of imperial magnificence.

With cannon ripping the ground in front of him, Prescott knew that he had no genuine hope of preventing the British landing. But he decided to make a gesture. He detached Captain Knowlton and his 200 Connecticut men with Captain Callender and his cannon "to oppose them," as he later said. Knowlton and his men filed out of the redoubt and down the steep hill into the open ground beyond the end of the breastwork. By now the first British boats were ashore and the light infantry companies were moving up to their advanced skirmish position. Knowlton and his men were totally perplexed. There was no hope of getting past the light infantry to harass the British landing. Even without these pickets, it would have been madness to send 200 men across a half mile of open ground, to assault that glittering array of scarlet and steel now rapidly pouring ashore and assembling on Morton's Point.

Knowlton heard a familiar voice roaring at him from the rear. It was Israel Putnam. The moment he saw Howe's landing point the old campaigner realized, in part at least, the British intentions. Putnam and everyone else must have expected Howe to land closer to Charlestown, in a more direct line from the Boston shore, and assault the redoubt from the south. It was here that they had posted their cannon platforms and their redan. But from his position on Morton's Point, Howe could ignore these strong points and move in either or both directions for an attack—north along the Mystic shore or south along the Charles.

"Here, here," Putnam roared at his favorite captain. "Man this fence. They are flanking us fast." He pointed to a low fence, with a base of stone, and two upper rails of wood. It was about 100 yards to the rear of Breed's Hill, almost on the base of Bunker.

The Connecticut men were groggy with fatigue. But they called on a last reserve of strength and began fortifying again. They ripped rails off nearby fences and jammed them in between the two rails already in position on their makeshift barricade "and made a slight fortification against musquet-ball." Before the fence there was a shallow ditch, the dry bed of a small creek which ran only in the spring. Except for this slight natural breastwork, the field before them was level ground, broken only by the many fences with which the citizens of Charlestown enclosed their grazing land. The fence was almost 200 yards long. Too much for Knowlton's 200 men to defend with any hope of success. "Stand fast men," Putnam roared. "There will be help on the way in a half hour, or I'll know the reason why." Wheeling his horse, he thundered down the peninsula toward Cambridge.

At the end of the breastwork the American artillery was trying, once more, to go into action. Young Gridley had rejoined Callender, probably on Putnam's orders, and the clumsy tragi-comedy of the untrained gunners and equally untrained officers began again. Up in the redoubt Prescott must have writhed in agony at their incompetence as the British boats deployed into line to beach simultaneously. Never was an army a better target for artillery. In fact, from the moment Howe's boats cautiously rounded the North Battery, they could have been massacred if the Americans had had enough cannon competently manned on Breed's Hill. Finally, Gridley's men began firing, but their aim was again deplorable. The four-pound balls sailed over the boats into the middle of the harbor. Only one shot came close, and here the British were lucky. One ball went down the whole length of a boat and stove out the stern without touching a man. A few minutes later the British field artillery landed and went into action from Morton's Hill, and six-pound shot began whistling past the amateur American gunners. Most of the enlisted artillery men promptly vanished again. A near miss cracked one of Gridley's cannon wheels and he decided the position was too precarious. The cartridges still did not fit the guns and every charge had to be broken open and ladled into the barrel. It was certainly not the best way to fight an artillery duel. Gridley hitched up his guns and once more departed for Bunker Hill. Callender stood his ground, but with growing disgust, unable to fire his guns or command his men.

Meanwhile Israel Putnam was arousing Cambridge in tempestuous fashion. At Inman's Farm where his 1,000 Connecticut troops were holding one of the key positions in the American center, he went pounding through the camp shouting: "To arms! To arms! The British are landing on Charlestown!" He left his oldest son, Captain Israel Putnam, Jr., to spread the word to all the companies. Captain John Chester, head of the crack Wethersfield company, vividly recalled receiving the alarm from the captain. "Just after dinner on Saturday, the 17th, I was walking out of my lodgings quite calm and composed, and all at once the drums beat to arms and the bells rang and a great noise in Cambridge. Captain Putnam came by on full gallop. 'What is the matter?' says I. 'Have you not heard?' 'No.' 'Why, the regulars are landing at Charlestown,' says he, 'and father says you must all meet and march immediately to Bunker Hill to oppose the enemy.'

"I waited not," says Chester, "but ran and got my arms and ammunition and hasted to my company who were in the church for barracks and found them nearly ready to march."

All around the town in Putnam's wake bells rang and soldiers rushed to join their regiments. In a matter of minutes the entire American army was ready to advance on Charlestown.

It was magnificent heroics, but it was hardly good tactics. If Putnam had his way the entire American center would have been denuded on the instant, leaving Ward, the Committee of Safety and the army's precious stores utterly defenseless. With admirable firmness in the face of such formidable enthusiasm, Ward again kept his head. He sent his own regiment, commanded by his cousin, Jonathan Ward, to reinforce Colonel Paul Dudley Sargent at Lechmere Point, where a British beachhead aimed at Cambridge was most likely to appear. Colonel Thomas Gardner's regiment was ordered to the redoubt on Prospect Hill, one of the main fortifications protecting the Cambridge road. Another regiment under Colonel John Patterson joined him there. Half of Putnam's Connecticut men were ordered to the Red House Fort, guarding the vital crossroads on the Cambridge to Charlestown road.

With his GHQ thus reasonably protected, Ward sent orders to nine other regiments of Massachusetts men and another company of artillery under Major Scarborough Gridley and Captain Samuel Trevett to advance to Charlestown. An express rider was sent galloping to Medford to order on Stark and the rest of his New Hampshire troops. What happened to Ward's orders for the Massachusetts regiments remains shrouded in mystery. These men were scattered over a three-mile area, and Ward's staff was minute. It took some time to send them orders. But the orders were apparently also badly mangled in the transmission or Ward, with his stubborn caution, sent them with reservations about advancing. At any rate, most of these men were soon under arms, but they spent the early hours of the afternoon marching vaguely about the countryside.

Only in the New Hampshire camp were the orders clearly understood and rapidly executed. But here there was another delay. When the first order, to send 200 men forward, arrived around eleven o'clock, Colonel John Stark immediately decided to prepare the entire regiment for a fight. Strange as it may seem, these 1,200 men who were guarding the left flank of the American army were almost entirely devoid of ammunition. New Hampshire, a frontier province, was short of cash, compared to the more established and prosperous communities of Connecticut, Rhode Island and Massachusetts. Soon after they arrived in camp, Stark was writing home to report that many of his men were without blankets or provisions, and more than a few lacked guns. Most of the men from the other colonies brought a personal supply of powder and ammunition with them. New Hampshire supplies were lean here, too.

Quickly Stark rushed a detachment to headquarters, and they brought back lead and powder. The lead came from the Cambridge Episcopal Church's organ which the American dissenters had melted down a few weeks ago. Each man was issued a gill of powder and molds to make bullets. The molds proved useless, because their guns were of a wild variety of calibers. They had to pound the bullets by hand to make them fit their highly individual weapons.

If they were poorly equipped, these New Hampshire men more than made up for it in enthusiasm and fighting know-how. Their commander, lean, taciturn John Stark, had a reputation as a soldier second only to Israel Putnam. He had been a captain in Rogers' Rangers during the French war and had survived dozens of bloody fights against forest-skilled Indians and French irregulars. His regiment was the largest in the army, almost 800 men. Half of them he recruited in the Cambridge camp, when they responded to the call of the minutemen; the other half he enlisted in New Hampshire within six hours; such was the magnetism of his name. Only a few weeks ago, the British had tried to bribe him with a full colonel's rank, which he contemptuously refused. His parents were Presbyterian Irish and he inherited their stern, uncompromising nature. His face, with its strong nose, high cheekbones and thin, set lips, was typical New England Yankee. But the Irish in New Hampshire honored his ancestry by rallying to him.

Almost as impressive was Stark's major, huge, six-foot-six Andrew McClary. This giant with a voice to match his size had led the New Hampshire militiamen into Fort William Henry, in Portsmouth, early in the previous December and seized the cannon and powder there—a revenge which helped to even Gage's seizure of Massachusetts' powder in September. He too had been an officer in Rogers' Rangers. Like Putnam, he had been plowing his fields when he heard the news of Lexington. He had rushed to his house, flung his saddlebags on his horse, promised his sons to "kill a redcoat" before he came back and rode for Cambridge.

The uniformless soldiers Stark and McClary led were, man for man, the best troops in the amorphous American army. For the other New England colonies, the frontier was relatively remote and there was little or no excuse to use a gun, especially in self-defense. Even hunting was difficult, since the woods were already thinned and powder was scarce and expensive. In New Hampshire, the frontier began at the end of the yard and the woods were still full of game. Stark's men were much more used to handling guns than the majority of the Grand American Army. They were also considerably tougher. One company of sixty New Hampshire men from Nottingham marched the moment they heard the news of Lexington, on the afternoon of April 20, and made the distance to Haverhill, twenty-seven miles, by dusk, "having run rather than marched" and were in Cambridge, fifty-five miles away, within 20 hours.

It was 1:30 before Stark's men swung out from Medford

and almost two o'clock before they picked up the companies
of Reed's regiment, who were camped just beyond Charlestown Neck. When they reached the Cambridge road and
headed for that narrow neck of land, they found the highway
blocked by a tangle of companies from at least two Massachusetts regiments, afraid to risk the ferocious fire from the
eighteen-gun *Symmetry,* and two floating batteries, which
had been rowed right up against the milldam, and were
blasting away with four twenty-four-pounders. Stark asked
for the road and the Massachusetts men were more than
willing to give it to him.

Without a glance to right or left, Stark led his rugged
woodsmen out onto the strip of land which was barely thirty
yards wide and without a tree or a shrub for cover. Captain
Henry Dearborn had the honor of commanding the lead
company, and he marched beside his colonel. It was the
young captain's first action, and he could not restrain a
quiver of nerves as the cannon balls screamed overhead and
chainshot and ringshot hissed around them. Men toppled
in the dust or cried out in anguish and stumbled out of the
ranks. But Stark did not increase his steady parade march
by so much as a pace. The jittery Dearborn abruptly asked
his colonel if they should think about "quickening the
march of the regiment, that it might sooner be relieved of
the galling crossfire of the enemy."

Years later Dearborn could still vividly recall the answer
he received: "With a look peculiar to himself, he fixed his
eyes upon me and observed with great composure: 'Dearborn, one fresh man in action is worth ten fatigued ones' and
continued to advance in the same cool and collected manner."

In perfect order, at the same regular pace, the New
Hampshire men strode up Bunker Hill to the crest, where
Israel Putnam was still trying to get some sort of secondary
fortification built. From Bunker one glance told Stark what

he should do, and undoubtedly Putnam urged the same conclusion on him. Knowlton's men, at the rail fence, held the key to the entire American defense, and they were pitifully few. Springing up on one of Putnam's unfinished earthworks, Stark gave his men a brief, pungent speech. They could see the British, drawn up there on Morton's Hill. For months these arrogant redcoats had been calling Americans cowards. Now was a chance to show them just how wrong they were. The New Hampshire men responded with a tremendous cheer and poured down the hill behind their colonel. Within minutes they were manning the 150 yards of fence which lay between Knowlton's detachment and the Mystic River and they were busily adding some improvements which their frontier instincts suggested. In front of the fence was a quantity of recently cut hay which one of Charlestown's residents never had the time or courage to collect. Stark ordered his men to take the hay and stuff it between the fence rails and hang it over the top. They also took pieces of earth, bushes and anything else they could find which might deflect a musket ball and filled every crack and gap. Stark's purpose was twofold; to give his men some protection, however inadequate, and persuade the British that the cover was a good deal more solid than it was.

It was now about 2:15 P.M. Portions of other Massachusetts regiments began to come on the field. Colonel Jonathan Brewer took up a position to the left of Knowlton, in the gap between the breastwork and the rail fence. Thirty-two-year-old Willard Moore, Major of Ephraim Doolittle's regiment, brought on about half his soldiers and helped Prescott's detachment man the breastwork. Portions of Bridge's regiment, and Bricket's men, who had followed their colonels into temporary retirement, returned to fight in the redoubt with them and at various other points along the line.

The crucial gap between the breastwork and the rail fence was filled, in part, by the swamp at the base of Breed's

Hill. But there was still a passage, around the head of the swamp, through which the breastwork could be flanked. Here, Colonel Gridley returned to add one final, important defense to his day's work. Under his direction, some Massachusetts men hastily ripped up rail fences and threw together three v-shaped little forts, or flèches, which covered this gap with an enfilading fire.

From their redoubt on Breed's Hill, Prescott and his men could only watch this furious activity on their flank. Certainly Prescott understood the tactical importance of what these New Hampshire and Massachusetts men were doing. But his inexperienced soldiers, must have been bewildered. Here they were, still unreinforced and unsupplied on their isolated hilltop, while over a thousand men were toiling on a defense line almost a hundred yards in their rear. It did not make sense to their weary, uncomprehending eyes, and it probably did nothing but increase the feeling that they were the forgotten legion. This suspicion was instantly and permanently banished by the appearance of a glittering figure in the entrance of their fort: Joseph Warren.

The doctor was well known for his fine clothes. But for his appearance on Breed's Hill, he surpassed himself. His waistcoat was pale blue, with silk fringes, and laced with silver; his breeches were white satin, with silver loops. Under his coat was an immaculate white ruffled shirt. The uniform may seem strange to us. But it was traditional, and expected, in 1775 for a general to wear his best clothes into battle.

Only three days before, at his personal request, Warren had been elected a major general in the Massachusetts Provincial Army, but his commission had not yet been issued. The Provincial Congress had asked him to become the surgeon general of the army, but he had refused. He was determined, he told them, to share the risks into which he had led his countrymen.

To the men on Breed's Hill, Warren was far more than a general. He was the president of the Provincial Congress, the chairman of the Committee of Safety, the confidante of Sam Adams and John Hancock. Even his expensive clothes played a part in banishing the suspicion and fear which had been weakening the resolution of these weary young farmers. They blended perfectly with Warren's insouciance; they were almost a taunt to the resplendent British brigades drawn up on Morton's Point. Suddenly Prescott's men felt immensely more sure of their position, more confident in the tactics which had led them out on this exposed peninsula. It was not the decision of fumbling subordinates, or even worse, traitors. The best, bravest, wisest men in Massachusetts must approve it or Warren would not be here in his stylish best to share their danger.

Many people have called Warren's decision to go to Bunker Hill that day rash and reckless, but he understood his fellow Americans better than his critics. He knew that more than anything else they needed confidence in this conflict. He also seemed to know instinctively one of the axioms of warfare in every age: men fight better for a leader who shares their risks. Theodore Roosevelt, Jr., on the eve of another battle, put it succinctly in a letter to his wife, explaining why he was going in with his men on the first wave on "D" Day. "It steadies the young men to know that I am with them; to see me plodding along with my cane . . ."

Early in the morning, just after Putnam's first visit to headquarters, Warren had surrendered to total exhaustion and excused himself from the Committee of Safety. He lay down in a nearby bedroom in Hastings House and dozed fitfully until noon. Then he arose and dressed and rejoined the committee, announcing his headache was gone. He conferred briefly with the committee about sending messages to the nearby towns to call out the militia for reinforcements, and they all agreed it should be done immediately. While they talked a post rider came pounding up on a dusty horse to deliver messages from the Continental Congress. Warren was enormously pleased to discover that the hesitant founding fathers had taken some of the advice he had urged on them in so many letters over the last weeks. Congress had ordered purchases of saltpeter, sulphur and powder and 5,000 barrels of flour for the army, to be paid for out of Continental funds; this meant they were edging a little closer to adopting the army as the official fighting force of the nation. Even more important was the second message, which recommended that the people of Massachusetts form a legal government; here, at last, was the answer to the danger of army control, against which Warren had struggled so anxiously over the last sixty days. The doctor forwarded the letters to the Provincial Congress and then began strapping on his sword and cartridge box.

Elbridge Gerry, fellow member of the Committee of Safety and one of Warren's oldest and closest friends—they had been roommates at Harvard—asked him where he was going. "To join the troops on the hill," he said quietly.

Gerry exploded. A good politician (he was to become our fourth Vice-President and along the way create the gerrymander) he was a slight, excitable, intellectual man who had no talent or appetite for soldiering. He simply could not understand Warren's compulsion to place himself in the front lines. "We need you here," he said. Then he voiced the feeling of dread which possessed more than one Massachusetts leader that day. "Besides, you know the project is absolutely mad. Every man on that hill is going to be killed or captured before evening."

Warren gave him a mournful look and said, "I hope not. Whatever happens, the men need encouragement."

A terrible presentiment must have swept over Gerry. His next words were harsh. "If you go, you will certainly be killed."

Warren answered him with a Latin epigram. "It is sweet and fitting to die for your country."

A few minutes later, Israel Putnam roared through Cambridge, the church bells rang and the drums beat to arms. Warren said goodbye to the committee. Now, en masse, they beseeched him not to go. For a few moments, it looked like they were ready to restrain him forcibly. Warren retreated slightly and said: "Perhaps I will ride over to Roxbury, and inspect the lines there, instead."

Artemas Ward had departed in this direction a few minutes earlier, and everyone said it was an excellent idea. Warren rode off to Roxbury, but he did not inspect the lines. He went to his family's farm, where he said goodbye to his four children and his mother. We have no record of what was said, in the few minutes the young doctor-turned-general could spare to these five people, who meant more to him than anyone else on earth. All his actions during the day suggest that a foreboding seemed to possess him, almost a knowledge of what was going to happen on Breed's Hill.

We can be sure, from what we know of him, that Warren never so much as hinted of a premonition to his two sons and two daughters. Danger always made him debonair, gay. He probably joked with them and promised them solemnly that he would somehow find time to see them more often. To his mother, a stern old Puritan lady, who shared her son's courage, he would be more frank. He undoubtedly told her where he was going and what little there was, in the way of money, if he did not come back. Almost certainly, he left a farewell message for Mercy Scollay, still in Boston. From Roxbury, the city's steeples and hills were visible in the burning sunlight. He had not seen his fiancée since April 19, sixty days ago, but he had met often with her father, who as one of the selectmen helped Warren conduct his secondhand negotiations with Gage. Warren and Mercy probably communicated in this same distant fashion.

For a moment, looking across the no-man's-land between Roxbury and his beloved Boston, Warren must have been swept by a vast, baffled sorrow. "Not fifty men in the province" had expected this quarrel between England and America to shed blood, he had said in a recent letter to a friend in New Hampshire. Warren was not one of those fifty.

He had fought for peace. Again and again he had restrained hotheads in the Provincial Congress who shouted for independence and armed revolt. Peace was a special, deeply personal value for Warren—it meant time for medicine, a new life with a woman who loved him deeply, a happy home for his children. But peace was now a lost cause. There was nothing left to do but share the terror and danger with his countrymen on Breed's Hill. Joseph Warren kissed his children goodbye and rode for Charlestown.

Warren crossed Charlestown Neck at full gallop, ignoring the British bombardment, and rode to the summit of Bunker Hill. There he met his student, Dr. William Eustis, who was setting up a field hospital on the north side of the hill. From the summit of Bunker the whole scene was spread out before them—the New Hampshire men on the left flank still toiling on their makeshift fortifications at the rail fence, the ranks of dusty farmers in the redoubt and behind the breastwork, the glittering red and white British files drawn up on Morton's Hill. In the harbor the booming ships of the line, their sails and decks wreathed in gunsmoke, and across the sparkling water the city of Boston, with its entire population, so it seemed, jammed on the rooftops, covering the hills and crowding the shore line.

Warren left his horse with Eustis on Bunker Hill; it might be useful for carrying the wounded back to Cambridge. He walked down the long slope of Bunker to the foot and found Israel Putnam surveying the men at the rail fence. More Connecticut men had come on, led by Putnam's old comrade in arms, Major Durkee. Putnam received the young doctor warmly. Since Warren was now a major general, the Connecticut veteran offered to receive orders from him. Warren shook his head. "I am here only as a volunteer. I know nothing of your dispositions, nor will I interfere with them. Tell me where I can be most useful."

Putnam pointed to the redoubt. "There you will be covered," he said.

A little angry, Warren said, "Don't think I came to seek a place of safety. Tell me where the onset will be most furious." Putnam again pointed to the redoubt. "That is the enemy's object, and if you can keep them from it, the day will be ours."

On his way up to the redoubt, Warren stopped to talk with Massachusetts Colonels Jonathan Brewer and John Nixon. "Do you mean to stay with us, General?" Brewer said.

"I mean to stay," Warren said.

Nixon said: "We have no officer to lead us. We ought to have some particular one for the orders to come from. Why can't you take command?"

The crusty Brewer was more blunt: "We must have a head and he ought to be a general. We are all colonels here and one colonel is only as good as another."

Flattered though he must have been, Warren was too honest to deny his inexperience. "If you will act as a council," he said, "I will give you my views as commander. If you approve of them, they can go as commands."

It was hardly a workable arrangement, especially for the battle they were about to fight. But the officers accepted it as better than nothing. Brewer recommended a young man from his regiment, Needham Maynard of Framingham, as an aide for Warren, to carry his orders around the field.

The conversation was the first sign of a flaw which was shortly to cause chaos among the green American troops. Putnam was, by reputation, the ranking officer on the field, and his actions throughout the battle show that he considered himself the commanding officer. But no one from Massachusetts or New Hampshire was inclined to take orders from him, a Connecticut man. For them he was just another colonel. They were about to find out that an army led by colonels was equivalent to an army led by no one.

In the redoubt Prescott saluted Warren and asked if he had any orders to give. Warren replied that he had none. "I shall take no command here," he said. "I have not yet received my commission. I came as a volunteer with my musket to serve under you and shall be happy to learn from a soldier of your experience." He then turned to the men and told them that he had come to encourage a good cause and that 2,000 reinforcements were on their way. They burst into an enthusiastic cheer.

About this time two other volunteers appeared on the field, each, in his own way, a symbol which strengthened those who were already in the lines. The first was Joseph Otis, the younger brother of James Otis, Boston's first great spokesman for colonial rights. For almost ten years James Otis had battled royal governors and commissioners of customs; they were years in which he had been the leader of a tiny minority, spat upon by the loyalists and ignored by the majority. Bitterness and the loneliness wrecked his law practice and his health. He began to drink heavily and display signs of what a modern psychiatrist would call manic depressive psychosis—periods of great depression followed by equally extreme periods of excitement. Finally he got into a brawl with a customs officer at the British Coffee House and was carried home with a deep wound in his head. Thereafter the James Otis Boston loved vanished into the mist of madness. For days and weeks he sat in his sister's parlor, staring mindlessly out the window at nothing. The excitement of Lexington and Concord had stirred him out of his lethargy, and he had gone with his brother Joseph and his brother-in-law, James Warren (no relation to Joseph Warren) to Watertown, where Warren was serving in the Provincial Congress. When young Joseph Otis heard about the impending fight on Breed's Hill, he had borrowed a musket and tramped ten miles to the lines, where he took a post at the rail fence.

The second volunteer was Seth Pomeroy, a more potent source of military encouragement. The old soldier had returned to his home in Northampton on June 15, just before the Committee of Safety voted to fortify Charlestown. Since he had been one of the most ardent supporters of the venture in the earlier council of war, Putnam had immediately dispatched a messenger to bring him back. The veteran, who was not in good health, had ridden all night and most of the day—it was 100 miles from Northampton—to get into the fight. When he reached Charlestown Neck, he dismounted and sent his horse back to Cambridge. It did not belong to him and rather than risk it in the artillery barrage he preferred to walk the last hot mile.

On his shoulder Pomeroy carried a gun he had made himself. He had been a noted gunsmith in his youth, and more than a few of the Massachusetts men he joined in the lines were carrying weapons that had come from his shop. Seeing him, the men with good military memories must have taken heart, because he was living proof that provincial troops could fight well from behind barricades. In 1755 he had been one of the commanding officers at the battle of Lake George, a fight which took place before most of these young farmers had been born. There several thousand provincials behind barricades had taken on about 1,400 tough French regulars, under a then famous European soldier, Baron Deskiau. The French had launched a frontal assault, confident of an easy victory. The fight had lasted all day, and in the words of the dying Deskiau, who was captured with three bullets in him, the Americans had, "in the morning fought like good boys, in the noon, like men, and in the afternoon like devils." Pomeroy had given the unlucky baron his third and fatal wound, and he went home with Deskiau's sword for a trophy. Now he strode into the lines and held up his musket. "You see this gun?" he shouted. "Thirty years ago, to this very day, I was carrying it at Louisburg when the French surrendered. We beat the French regulars without any help from the British that day. We'll do the same thing to the redcoats today."

Few men along the fence besides Pomeroy were able to remember that first of many sieges which the British and Americans laid against the great French fortress on Nova Scotia. But it, too, was a potent memory to revive. That year, 1745, the Americans had won the fight alone, with only a naval squadron and a few British field officers to advise them.

Behind the rail fence, John Stark was thinking about tactics, not encouragement. Heroics were not in his line. Up and down he paced, studying the American position. What would he do if he were William Howe, a general with a reputation as a light infantry leader? A frontal assault? Hardly. Howe would look for a way around, probe for a hole to get his light infantry into the American rear.

Suddenly Stark saw the hole. The rail fence extended to the edge of a bluff, eight or nine feet high, and below it was the beach of the Mystic River. At high tide it was barely a dozen feet wide—but that was more than enough room for a British light infantry column. "It was," Stark said later, "a way so clear that the enemy could not miss it." Quickly he ordered 200 of his best men to break up some stone fences nearby and build a breastwork on the beach, to the water's edge. He laid his men down behind this crude barrier in three ranks, and he himself took personal command of the position.

Prescott, meanwhile, had been keeping a keen eye on the

British movements, and when he saw two of Howe's regiments under Pigot move out from the beachhead and take up an advanced position about 200 yards closer to Charlestown, he immediately saw that he would have to protect his flank in force. He dispatched 150 men under his Lieutenant Colonel, John Robinson and Major Henry Woods to take what cover they could find in the town and prevent any attempt to advance through it to attack the redoubt in the rear. Putnam helped by sending three companies of Massachusetts men and a company of Reed's New Hampshire troops to join Prescott's detachment in the village. The Americans wasted no time. They scattered into the houses and barns on the outskirts of the town and busily loopholed them. One fresh company captained by Nathaniel Warner of Moses Little's regiment, Prescott stationed behind a stone fence to the right of the redoubt. It was not a full company —only twenty-two men. But Prescott could not spare a man to help them. He now had barely 150 left in his fort.

Up on Bunker Hill, Putnam was becoming more and more frantic for solid reinforcements from Cambridge. Help continued to arrive in a piecemeal trickle, sometimes a company, sometimes barely a squad. The Massachusetts captains and colonels were simply leaving behind the men who refused to cross the Neck; Putnam would have shot them.

Leaving the skeleton crew still working on his entrenchment, he spurred his horse to Charlestown Neck. The *Symmetry*, the *Glasgow* and the two floating batteries were still pouring a methodical fire up and down the narrow strip of land as Putnam rode across it for the fourth time that day. On the other side he found himself in the midst of chaos. There were regiments, or at least clumps of men, scattered along the road for a good half mile, intermixed with wagons and civilian onlookers. Richard Devens of the Committee of Safety was waving a pistol at the head of one wagon driver, but the man absolutely refused to risk his horses against the

British bombardment. Putnam ignored him as a hopeless civilian and concentrated his wrath on the troops. He called them cowards, traitors and many other names not printable here and then proceeded to ride his horse back and forth across the Neck a half dozen times to prove to them that the British gunners were not aiming at anything in particular. But the thirty-yard-wide stretch of road was simply too frightening to most of these raw troops. The cannon balls threw up great clouds of dust, until a haze hung in the air, making it all the more ominous looking. "They were convinced," one writer says, "of his [Putnam's] invulnerability but were not so convinced of their own." A few companies dashed across, single file, but no more.

Disgusted, Putnam spurred his horse for Bunker Hill again. As he stormed up the road who should be jogging toward him but Captain John Callender with his two cannon. He had given up trying to rally his men; they had either gone home or mingled with the infantry. Putnam asked Callender where he was going. The captain said he was retreating.

"On whose orders?" Putnam said.

"My own," Callender said. "I have no cartridges."

Putnam got down off his horse and opened the side boxes of the two cannon. They were practically full. He pointed his pistol at Callender's head and ordered him to turn around and take the cannon back into the lines. Callender obeyed with great reluctance while Putnam spurred his horse back to the Neck to encourage the companies that had come across and lead them up onto Bunker. When he reached the foot of the hill with these men the exasperated general found Callender's cannon but no sign of the captain.

Then, to his vast relief, Putnam saw a familiar face: Captain John Ford of Bridge's regiment who came marching up with his company. He was one of the heroes of April 19, with five British soldiers to his credit in the running fight.

Putnam ordered Ford and his men to drag the cannon into the lines once more. Ford protested that neither he nor his men knew anything about operating them. "Let that be my concern," Putnam roared. "Do as I tell you." Ford acquiesced and his company dragged the two four-pound pieces into the gap between the breastwork and the rail fence.

The American defense was now as complete as the combined efforts of Stark, Putnam, Prescott and Gridley could get it. Considering that they operated in almost complete independence of each other, except for some slight liaison supplied by Putnam, they did an amazingly good job. Since Thomas Gage had peered across Boston Harbor through his telescope in the early dawn the rebel challenge had grown far beyond the isolated fort on the exposed hill, where several hundred exhausted farmers crouched, praying for quick relief. It was now a solid line of over 2,000 men, more than half of them fresh and ready for battle, which stretched from one side of the peninsula to the other. In spite of the impromptu way some of the tactical decisions were made, it was by no means an amateur defense. It had evolved under the keen eyes of veteran soldiers who understood the fine points of military maneuver almost as thoroughly as William Howe.

Yet over the whole battle line there still lingered the question which could only be decided in blood. Could these untrained Americans stand up to regular troops, coming at them with bayonets leveled and cannons roaring? The difference between a professional and an amateur soldier, as every veteran on this field knew, was the professional's ability to stand his ground while men fell on his left and on his right. He was hardened to the grim facts of war. What would Peter Brown up there in the redoubt do if the man next to him toppled over, blood spurting from his shattered face? What would Thomas Boynton do if the man next to him suddenly dropped his gun and ran like a rabbit? How much could they depend on sixteen-year-old Corning Fairbanks of Jonathan Brewer's Regiment?

Down at the rail fence there were youngsters like twenty-year-old Ralph Farnum and nineteen-year-old Ashael Nims. Ralph Farnum's company had only arrived in camp the night before, after a long hungry march from Acton, Maine. They had answered the pealing church bells when Putnam roused Cambridge and came on the field as a unit. Putnam had sent them to the rail fence. Ralph's mother had wept bitterly when he enlisted. He didn't particularly want to be a soldier, nor was he enormously enthused about the patriot cause. A recruiting agent from Massachusetts had persuaded him and the other young men in town to join up, and Ralph had marched because everyone else was marching. Ashael Nims had shown even less interest in joining the volunteer company from his New Hampshire town of Keene. He was engaged to be married. But one man, who had already put his name on the list, lost his nerve, and Captain Stiles had called on Ashael to replace him, for the honor of the town. Impulsively, Ashael had said yes. What was he thinking about now? How many more of these nineteen- and twenty-year-olds were suddenly wondering if they had been sold a bill of goods? What would it mean, all this lofty oratory about freedom and rights, when the other side answered with bullets?

Would they fight or run?

They did not know the answer themselves, but they would know it in a very few minutes.

II

Down on Morton's Point, William Howe turned his back on the dangling corpses of the two deserters and assembled the twelve junior officers who were to serve as his staff. They included Howe's personal aide-de-camp, Captain Sherwin, Lieutenant Page of the engineers, the naval aide, Lieutenant Jourdain and Captain Nicholas Addison, a descendant of the essayist, Joseph Addison. The captain had arrived from London only the day before and had probably been invited to join the staff through his friendship with General Burgoyne.

Howe's thoroughly professional organization was a doleful contrast to Artemas Ward's staff, which at this moment consisted of four men, two of whom were not even members of the army. Napoleon considered his staff the key to military success. "To move a great army," he declared, "the commander must have a hundred tongues, eyes and ears. These tongues, eyes and ears are his staff officers. The staff is the great motor which makes the army move according to the combinations and sudden inspirations of its commander." Howe had twelve men to help him organize and operate a battle line which never exceeded a mile. Ward had four men to superintend a front of nine miles and keep him in touch with a battle which was being fought four miles away. Putnam, the quasi-commander on the field, had no aides whatsoever.

American staff problems did not concern Howe at the moment. He was much more interested in what the Americans had been doing along the slope of Breed's Hill since he examined their position from the *Somerset* in the morning. "Our friends have been hard at work, it would seem," he said. "I think we had better go forward, gentlemen, for a better look." Howe led his officers down the slope of Morton's Hill and did not stop until they reached the hollow where the advance guard of 150 light infantry waited for orders. Mounting the other side of the hollow, the general coolly ignored the rebel cannon which he could see being wheeled into position between the breastwork and the rail fence. The cannon troubled him only slightly. What was going on around and to the rear of the cannon was much more disturbing.

Men were streaming off Bunker Hill and working feverishly to throw up additional defenses along the whole American flank. The original plan of attack, which involved nothing more arduous than a brisk march around Breed's Hill to that key crossroads in its rear, was suddenly confronted with a bristling entrenchment. Even more alarming was the number of men the Americans were now prepared to commit. Through his glass Howe could see several hundred on Bunker Hill and, like any good general, he felt certain there were many more out of sight. At the rate they were moving up Howe estimated they would outnumber him two to one in the fortifications with perhaps another 1,000 men in reserve. He decided to send back to Boston for the Forty-seventh Regiment and the First Battalion of Marines plus the 216 light infantry and grenadiers which he had been forced to leave on North Battery.

Howe and his staff returned to Morton's Hill and the

general ordered the troops to eat lunch. The critics who later accused Howe of sluggishness and poor discipline at Bunker Hill have made much of this decision to dine. Howe supposedly took the whole affair so casually that he allowed his men to enjoy their lunch before attacking. The dangling corpses by the water's edge were a better indication of just how seriously Howe took the expedition. More important, if we remember that he hoped to march these men all the way to Cambridge before nightfall, and they had had no lunch as yet, feeding them becomes much more reasonable.

In good order the regiments opened ranks and the men slipped off their knapsacks and went to work on their rations of boiled beef and biscuit. A few officers may have dined more variously, depending on what their orderlies were able to find in the Boston shops. But with fresh meat selling for a guinea a pound, most of them probably ate the same boiled beef the enlisted men were eating. Howe and his staff did have the pleasure of good wine which the general's valet, Mr. Evans, had been careful to bring over in ample supply. More maddening to Prescott's thirsty men on Breed's Hill were the large tubs of rum from which generous portions were ladled to the men. All armies in 1775 were convinced that a soldier fought better with some liquor in him. Prescott's men had brought rum with them, and back in Cambridge Artemas Ward had a barrel set up in front of his headquarters and he issued a healthy slug to each man in the regiments he had ordered forward as reinforcements.

We know something about the backgrounds and regimental traditions of these redcoated soldiers of George III. While they sit before us, in full marching order, eating their lunch, let us take a closer look at their equipment and weapons. Both are basic to understanding why and how they fought at Bunker Hill. In histories of the Revolutionary War the British army has generally been pictured as a smooth-running fighting machine whose chief defect was inept leadership. The American soldier is depicted as ragged and poorly armed, the British as equipped with every modern weapon of the day and expert in their use of them. The truth is rather far from this generalization. The British army in the eighteenth century was not a particularly efficient organization and no one had yet made any equation between the value of a soldier's equipment and its usefulness to him in warfare. Appearance was considered more important than adaptability, and the uniform of the private soldier, particularly, was not designed either for comfort or speedy movement.

Summer or winter the men of the line regiments wore the same heavy greatcoats with sleeves "tight as stockings." The stock, or waistcoat, was equally tight and had a high stiff collar which forced the soldier to keep his head up, even when the sun was in his eyes. His pants were as tight as possible and the gaiters, put on wet, frequently shrank so that they hampered the circulation in his legs. From the belt around his waist hung his bayonet scabbard which knocked against his calves as he walked. On his right hip, supported by a broad, constricting belt which ran over his shoulder and across his chest, was his rectangular cartridge box, which interfered with his haversack if, as now, he was carrying his full equipment.

The standard pack contained extra clothing, a brush and blackball for his shoes, a blanket, provisions, a canteen and a fifth share of the general equipment belonging to his tent. Every man under Howe at Bunker Hill was carrying this quantity of gear, which weighed about 100 pounds. Add his fourteen-pound rifle, his one-pound bayonet and a pound or so of musket balls and cartridges, and you are close to a 120-pound load. The average soldier today goes into battle with less than sixty pounds, and he is not expected to fight with it on his back unless an emergency situation demands it.

The light infantry and grenadiers carried similar packs

and wore similar uniforms. The grenadier's uniform was identical with the line infantry except for extra braid, buttons and other frills; only his headgear was different. To enhance his supposedly fearful appearance, he wore a black bearskin cap which added almost a foot and a half to his height. The light infantry under Wolfe had worn short green jackets, with bearskin ruffs around their necks, and loose pantaloons, to give them maximum freedom of movement. But after the Seven Years' War British army policy was dominated by officers who had served with the Prussians in Europe and developed an extravagant admiration for things German. They argued that the empire would never again have to fight in the wilderness and persuaded the war office to discard these unmilitary-looking uniforms in favor of the chest-constricting, neck-garroting *Deutsches* style.

The uniforms of the officers were as unmilitary as the enlisted men's strait jackets, but they were more comfortable. There was no choking collar, and the coat was more loose and flowing. Up to a point they were allowed to decorate themselves with braid and style their coats and hats according to their individual tastes; those with money and the inclination did so. Lord Rawdon, for instance, was going into action wearing a "catskin cap," hardly a government issue. Around their waists the officers usually wore long, brilliant sashes which served as a kind of slung stretcher for carrying the owner off the field in case he was wounded. Generals usually felt it their duty to be best dressed, and Howe, something of a dandy, was resplendent in braided red coat and white satin breeches.

All the officers below the rank of major were armed with short swords and a light musket called the fusee. In battle the officers were used to firing their weapons along with the troops, although more progressive generals, such as Clinton, deplored the practice. In his journal, Clinton declared: "I reprobated the use of the fusee for officers, argued that an officer has enough to do to keep his platoon together and while he could command the fire of that he did not want his own for his defense, that if he fired with his men . . . he became instead of their chief the worst soldier in his platoon, that he would have no dependence on his men and they no confidence in him, but this had been too long an American custom to get the better of it . . ."

Around their necks the officers, including Howe, wore gorgets. Originally this was a large steel plate designed to protect the throat in medieval warfare, but when gunpowder made armor obsolete, it shrunk in size to a small, purely ornamental crescent, often of gold, and bearing the regimental device. Glittering in the bright sunlight they were to make the officers prime targets for the waiting Americans.

Being a target was not, however, considered a major problem in eighteenth-century warfare. The standard weapon was the musket, which the British soldier called "Brown Bess." This smooth-bore flintlock weapon was three feet eight inches long in the barrel and weighed fourteen pounds. It could kill at 300 yards, but its accuracy was totally unreliable at anything greater than 100. The soldier who could hit his man, even at that distance, was a rare exception.

Major George Hanger, one of the foremost authorities on arms at the time, declared: "a soldier's musket, if not exceedingly ill bored (as many of them are) will strike . . . a man at eighty yards; it may even at 100. But a soldier must be very unfortunate indeed who shall be wounded by a common musket at 150 yards; and as to firing at a man at two hundred yards, you might as well fire at the moon." The modern American army M-1 is a deadly weapon at 500 yards.

The musket's limitations made massed firing at close range the only effective technique. The bayonet, which was fourteen inches long, was considered a preferable weapon by most officers. You will understand why when you see what it took to load a Brown Bess. The bullet was a round leaden ball weighing about an ounce; it came wrapped in a strong paper cartridge containing the proper amount of powder. To load, the soldier first tore the end off the cartridge with his teeth, then sprinkled a few grains of powder from it into the musket's priming pan and finally rammed the cartridge and ball down the barrel with an iron ramrod.

Twelve separate motions were required to load the long, heavy gun, and firing it was even more formidable. When the soldier pulled the trigger, a hammer holding a flint was snapped forward against a steel lip, called the frizzen, from which it struck sparks. This lip was part of the cover of a "pan" holding the sprinkled pinches of powder. The blow of the flint forced open the pan, igniting the powder, which then (hopefully) flashed into the touchhole and into the barrel of the gun, where the rammed cartridge was waiting to be ignited. Often the gun would "flash in the pan"—the cartridge would fail to ignite—and more powder would have to be sprinkled into the pan. If the gun did not even flash in the pan, this meant the flint was worn and had to be replaced. A soldier always carried a spare, since the cheap quality flints he received from general issue wore out in fifty or sixty firings. How often the guns missed fire can be gleaned from Ensign Hunter's remark that early in the morning, before they were ordered to march to Bunker Hill, the Fifty-second Regiment had been issued new muskets and they had tried them out on Boston Common; the men were pleasantly astonished because not one had failed.

When the cartridge did explode, it was with a recoil powerful enough to dislocate a careless man's shoulder. Firing into the wind, the soldier also had to be wary of flame spurting back through the touchhole, which could easily blind him. Moreover, the bullet, round and subject to the slightest wind pressure, went out along a heavily dropping trajectory.

If he hoped to hit anything at a distance, a soldier had to hold his gun in an iron grip and keep it on target with ferocious concentration, take into account wind and the bullet's weight and any individual peculiarity in the bore of his weapon.

As for aiming, the British manuals of the day barely allude to it. Here is how they were told to fire in the drill manual Gage's soldiers used in Boston: At "Present!" the soldier was to "Step back about six inches with the right foot, bringing the left toe to the front"; at the same time "raise up the Butt so high upon the Right Shoulder, that you may not be obliged to stoop too much with the Head, the right cheek to be close to the Butt and the left Eye shut and look along the Barrel, with the right Eye from the Breech pin to the muzzle." Nothing was said about aiming at anything in particular, nor of using the gun's front sight. There was no rear sight.

Fast, not accurate firing was the object with such a weapon. Well-coordinated men were able to fire five shots a minute with a Brown Bess and three was considered a minimum for the regular soldier. This minimum was carefully worked out on a highly practical basis. If a regiment of 500 men were defending a line against an attacking force, they were expected to fire two volleys in the twenty or twenty-five seconds it would take the attackers to cover 100 yards on the dead run. The second volley would hopefully be delivered at less than thirty yards. This meant the closely packed charging mass would have to endure no less than 1,000 bullets before they got home with the bayonet.

At Concord Bridge the first three ranks of Captain Walter Laurie's company had fired, en masse, at over 100 American minutemen, who were less than fifty yards away. They hit two. Amos Barret, who was one of the untouched targets, later wrote: "It is straing that their warnt no more killed but they fir'd to high." Yet by the military expectations of the day, the British had done quite well. Marshal Saxe, the great French general, said in his memoirs: "I have seen whole volleys fired, without even killing four men." He was describing volleys along a regimental front, involving 400 or 500 soldiers. There was, undoubtedly, some accuracy in the saying of the time, that it "took a man's weight in bullets to kill him."

If the musket was an inaccurate weapon by modern standards, it did, when it sent its heavy bullet home, have terrible stopping power. The one-ounce balls were fearfully destructive. They smashed bones; they tore out entire muscles from arms and legs. There was a little ridge along the circumference of the ball which caused ragged wounds in the body wherever it struck. A man who was hit by one of these deadly black messengers, even in the arm, and stayed in the fight had exceptional courage and endurance.

The Americans crouched behind their entrenchments carried the same kind of guns. Many of them were of more ancient vintage than the "Brown Bess," going all the way back to Queen Anne's War, thirty years before, but they were all loaded and fired on the same principle. Though the Americans had a reputation among themselves, at least, as marksmen, there is some question as to what that term meant considering the weapons they were handling. One historian has pointed out that in the retreat from Concord and Lexington the British had 273 casualties out of 1,800 men engaged. Fairly accurate computations based on the reports from the various townships who sent men into the fight add up to a total of 3,763 Americans engaged at one time or another during the day. Each of these men was supposed to carry thirty-six rounds into the fight, and we know that many carried twice that number. If the average militiaman had fired only twenty rounds, this would come to 75,000 shots with only 273 hits. Only one bullet out of 300 found its mark. In the day's work, only one man out of fifteen hit anybody.

On the Pennsylvania and Virginia frontiers around this time another weapon was being manufactured which was to have a great deal to do with giving Americans a later reputation as marksmen. It was called the "rifle" and unlike the musket, which had a smooth bore, its barrel had spiral grooves which gave the bullet rotation and vastly increased accuracy. But there were no rifles at Bunker Hill. There was in fact not a single rifle in the entire State of Massachusetts on June 17, 1775.

The motley farmers waiting in solemn silence behind their various barricades had one advantage over their British opponents; they were trained to aim at their targets. Since the first of the year, the militia companies had been drilling with a manual which was written not by a British parade-ground martinet, but by one of their own officers. Timothy Pickering's *Easy Plan of Discipline for a Militia,* published in Salem in 1775, simplified the British method of loading and firing. The men primed and loaded in ten motions, from a single order. But most important, for the first time in any military drill book, the results of the American frontier experience appeared in print: the men were taught to aim: "Lean the cheek against the butt of the firelock, shut the left eye and look with the right along the barrel, from the breechpin to the sight near the muzzle, at the object you would hit; or in other words, to use the well known phrase, take good sight."

Unfortunately, because of the desperate scarcity of powder, the Americans had had practically no chance to practice firing. This, more than anything else, explains their ineptitude at Lexington. But the emphasis on aiming at a particular target, plus the memories of his father's frontier experiences, where Indian warfare made marksmanship essential, gave the American soldier a slight superiority over his British cousin, man for man, and weapon for weapon, as they confronted each other in battle array at Bunker Hill.

Under the booming guns of the fleet Howe's rowboat armada pulled slowly back across Boston Harbor once more and deposited the Forty-seventh Regiment, the First Battalion of Marines and the six flank companies of grenadiers and light infantry on shore a few hundred yards closer to Charlestown than the first landing. Lunch was over and Howe was now ready to move. He had with him a total of 2,600 officers and men. He strode to the top of Morton's Hill and looked over his well-rested and well-fed army.

"Gentlemen," he said, "I am very happy in having the honor of commanding so fine a body of men: I do not in the least doubt that you will behave like Englishmen and as becomes good soldiers.

"If the enemy will not come from their entrenchments, we must drive them out. At all events, the town of Boston will be set on fire by them.

"I shall not desire any one of you to go a step further than where I go myself at your head.

"Remember, gentlemen, we have no recourse to any resources if we lose Boston but to go on board our ships which will be very disagreeable to us all."

With the rattle of drums and the squeal of fifes Howe began to move out from his beachhead. He divided his little army into two brigades, the first consisting of the light infantry, grenadiers and the Fifth and Fifty-second Regiments under his command, and the second consisting of the Thirty-eighth, Forty-third and Forty-seventh Regiments, the First Battalion of Marines and the six newly landed flank companies under General Pigot. Howe's plan was to deploy Pigot's four regiments against the American redoubt and breastwork. The grenadiers and the Fifth and Fifty-second Regiments were to move against Stark's men at the rail fence. But none of these regiments was ordered to launch a frontal attack. They were to make a demonstration with musket fire supported by artillery, to freeze the Americans in their defensive positions all along the line. With their attention fixed on what looked like an imminent frontal attack, they would be totally unprepared for the appearance of the light infantry in their rear.

How were these picked troops going to reach the American rear? The original plan, to march blithely around the redoubt out of musket shot along the Mystic, was not possible now, thanks to the men at the rail fence. But Howe still thought the basic plan was workable. He simply modified it slightly to meet the new situation.

While the grenadiers and regular infantry began a slow advance across the fields, the light infantry would move in a flying column along the beach of the Mystic River. The bank was high enough to hide them completely from the troops behind the rail fence. There was some kind of slight stone wall manned by a few Americans on the beach, but at a half mile it hardly looked like a formidable obstacle. The beach was not wide enough at high tide to contain more than a few companies. It was, of course, a frontal assault— not the kind of tactics for which the light infantry was trained. But the American defense left Howe no alternative. To advance through Charlestown, if it contained a substantial number of rebels, would be a much bloodier job than brushing aside a few farmers on a narrow beach.

Basically, Howe—and everyone else in the British army —assumed that the Americans could not compare in firing proficiency to regular troops. This was why a limited frontal assault made sense to him. There would probably be one volley from behind the stone fence. With green troops it was not presuming too much to expect at least half the shots to go wild. Before the Americans could reload, the light infantry would be on top of them with their bayonets. They would cut through them as if they were made of paper. Then up the bank behind the rail fence the light infantry would come, and now they could use their mobile training with destructive effect, while the grenadiers and regular infantry stopped demonstrating and charged the demoralized Americans from the front. Certainly Howe's plan was sound, and there was not an officer in his command who would have changed it. Every one of these professional soldiers shared the basic assumption that the Americans would fire one wild volley, possibly two, and from there the bayonets would decide it.

On Pigot's side of the field, things were not going smoothly, even at this early hour. As he began to deploy his men into two long, well-ordered lines, in order to envelop the redoubt from the rear as well as the sides, the outermost regiment, Pitcairn's marines, ran into a hail of musket balls from the Americans firing from their loopholed houses in Charlestown.

By now there were at least 300 Americans in the village and they quickly drew the first blood at Bunker Hill. Again and again a marine toppled over with a groan or a cry of anguish and badly needed men had to be ordered out of line to take him back to the boats on the beach. Without orders, but simply from an instinct for self-preservation, other marines began firing wildly in reply, unnerving the nearby regiments. The entire line began to flounder into confusion. Pigot was forced to refuse his flank—shift Pitcairn's regiment to the left, facing Charlestown, rather than the redoubt.

The marine major, no man to take this kind of punishment without hitting back, sent his companies charging into the town, and a bloody house-to-house struggle began. The Americans did not attempt to make a stand. They fell back when they could and then drifted forward again when the infuriated marines turned to deal with another trouble spot. More than one sniper was cut off and died in bitter hand-to-hand struggles in the empty rooms from which he was firing, or fell with a bullet in his back as the marines sent volleys sweeping down the narrow streets after their fleeing tormentors. Prescott's officers, Lieutenant Colonel Robinson and Major Woods, were soon driven out of the town, but they stubbornly refused to quit the fight. Marshaling what men they could find, they made a fighting retreat down the back streets and rejoined Prescott in the redoubt.

But remnants of the other companies Putnam had sent down stubbornly refused to go away, no matter how often Pitcairn tried to flush them out. With hunter's stealth they flitted from house to house and with Indian cunning never stayed in one place long enough to be trapped. It was the kind of fighting Americans liked best, and the story of Captain Benjamin Walker is a good example of why Pitcairn and Pigot had so much trouble. Walker was driven out of Charlestown with Woods and Robinson, and most of his company scattered. He promptly roamed up and down the line, recruiting adventurous souls from other companies, to "hang on the flank," and within minutes was back in Charlestown fighting again. Pitcairn again drove him out, and once more Walker returned with new recruits for this deadly but exciting game. Finally, the exasperated Pigot sent word to Howe that he could not advance unless something was done about Charlestown. "It alone," Howe said later, describing the predicament of his second-in-command, "would have given him sufficient employment."

At this moment Admiral Graves stepped ashore from his barge, "to be near General Howe," as he later reported, "for the sake of seeing whether any further aid could be given." Howe must have given him a sour look. If he had put a ship in the Mystic River, as Howe requested, earlier in the morning, the British army would not be in its present predicament. From the Mystic a rain of shot could have been flung on the defenders of the rail fence, and Howe could have walked his army up the shore, unopposed. The general must have pointed this out, because the admiral now did his best to repair the damage. He ordered the floating batteries which were bombarding the Neck to cease fire and row for the Mystic. (Howe had not asked for these, earlier, because they were intended to support Clinton's proposed landing at Willis Creek, and they also carried the heaviest share of the responsibility for keeping Charlestown Neck closed to American reinforcements.) The admiral still stubbornly refused to commit one of his ships to the unknown river. He would also seem to have been discouraged by the almost complete absence of wind. At any rate it was the blunder of the day. The floating batteries took practically no water; they could be rowed in almost to the beach—but they were a mile and a half away, up against the milldam at the opposite end of the harbor. Worst of all, the tide was about to turn, and without sails the clumsy, heavy craft had to make their slow way down the Charles against the current and up the Mystic, also against the current.

As Clinton later complained, the guns, which were under the volunteer command of Lieutenant Colonel Thomas James of the army artillery, "quitted the first position, where he was doing great service and both tides being against him could not get to the second, his service therefore was wanting." If Graves had ordered the *Lively* or even the small sloop *Spitfire* to round Morton's Point and gamble on getting stuck on a mudflat to blast the rail fence, Bunker Hill would have been a rout from beginning to end. But the memory of Noddle Island, where he lost his sloop *Diana* and almost lost his beloved nephew Thomas, must have been still large in the admiral's mind. He was, to say the very least for him, not a gambler.

The admiral was, however, able to carry out another important request for Howe. Here is how he tells it in his memoirs, where he cultivates the quaint habit of speaking of himself in the third person. "The General, observing the mischief his left Wing sustained by the fire from Charles-Town, the Admiral asked him if he wished the place burned, and being answered Yes, he immediately sent to the Ships to fire red hot Balls (which had been prepared with that view) and also to Copp's Hill Battery to desire they would throw carcasses into the town."

In a moment Graves' gunners were pouring their glowing "hot shot" into Charlestown, and carcasses—hollow balls filled with burning pitch—were crashing down from Copp's Hill. The wooden homes and stores caught fire almost immediately. Just to make sure the job was thorough, Graves sent a party of marines from the *Somerset* to fire the docks and shipyard. In his memoirs the admiral said, smugly, that "the town was instantly set on fire in many places, and the Enemy quickly forced from that station." This is hardly true. At least a company of dogged Americans clung to their posts in the burning town throughout the entire battle. But many snipers were forced to flee as the village rapidly became one enormous conflagration.

A few moments later, Pigot reported himself satisfied that most of the snipers were flushed out, and Howe ordered the advance to resume. Why did he not wait for the floating batteries to arrive from the Neck, to clear the rail fence? Simply because time was running out. It was after three thirty, and if he had any hopes of driving the Americans all the way to Cambridge, he had to start immediately. Night fighting was not considered sensible in 1775—and for Howe, who would be moving through a hostile countryside, it would have been suicide. Howe must have also been encouraged by the spirit of his men. In rank after rank there were shouts of "push on, push on," and "let's get at the dogs."

Obviously they were burning to erase the embarrassment of Lexington and Concord. So the advance began, with Pigot moving slowly on the redoubt and Howe, though he had more distance to cover, moving out with equal deliberation across the broad, level field toward the rail fence, a half mile away.

At first the spectators in Boston thought Charlestown had been fired to throw a smoke screen across Breed's Hill for the advancing regulars. It certainly would have helped them, but luck was on the American side here. An almost imperceptible southwest breeze wafted the smoke out across the harbor toward the open sea.

The flames consuming Charlestown meant much more to those mute watchers in Boston than a military advantage. The twentieth century has become accustomed to destroying cities and scorching the earth. But in the warfare of 1775, only savages burned civilian houses and plundered private property. Many of the Bostonians, fearing their own city was slated for the flames, had moved their furniture and clothing into the cellars of Charlestown friends. Numbly now, they saw everything they owned vanish before their eyes. Others knew that priceless treasures, such as the 200-year-old Mather library, and furniture and ivory and silk brought home by Charlestown ship captains from all over the world were being senselessly destroyed. There were tears on both Whig and Tory cheeks as Boston watched Charlestown burn. Even more than the two confronting armies, it spelled war with all its futile horror and destruction.

Howe's light infantry was in his first line, his grenadiers in his second and the Fifth and Fifty-second Regiments in the rear. His field artillery was on his left maintaining a steady fire on the fence ahead of them. True to his word, Howe led the way; his tall figure in shining red and white and gold was clearly visible from the American lines. There were reasons for his pace. He had a half mile to march and the sun was burning. He was careful not to exhaust his men. It was also good psychology to let the Americans meditate for a while upon the impressive mass of steel and manpower bearing down on them, regimental pennants proudly flying, drums and fifes filling the intervals between the blasts of cannon.

Not until Howe reached the hollow where his 150 light infantry pickets were stationed did he reveal his intentions. There, about a quarter of a mile from the American lines, all his light infantry, the Welch Fusiliers of Howe's own regiment in the lead, filed off to the right and down onto the Mystic beach. They instantly quickened their pace and became the flying column on which William Howe was betting his reputation.

Pigot's men were within musket shot of the redoubt now and the guns of the fleet and the battery on Copp's Hill shifted their target from the Breed's Hill fort to the growing cloud of Americans on Bunker. To the British they were obviously an American reserve, and Burgoyne and Graves did their best to discourage them from advancing with a searing barrage of metal.

On the field, Howe had only his six-pounders to support him now. But the artillerymen were having trouble. The ground was marshy; a man's foot would sink into mud up to his ankles every few steps. The gunners struggled like beasts of burden but the guns bogged down again and again and fell farther and farther behind the advancing infantry. The four twelve-pound guns never got into action at all, bogging after the first few feet. The lighter six-pound pieces made better headway, but their gunners suddenly discovered they were embarrassingly short of ammunition. They had emptied their side boxes and called for more balls, which were promptly lugged forward from the beach. But when the boxes were opened they were found to contain nothing but twelve-pound balls. There was not a six-pound ball to be found in the entire supply. They stood there scratching their heads in perplexity when an enraged staff officer rushed up to find out why they had ceased fire. They told him and he rushed back to Howe who must have cursed the ineptitude of Lieutenant Colonel Cleveland, Gage's chief of artillery. "Tell them to fire grape," the general said disgustedly. A few minutes later the guns went into action firing another eighteenth-century version of shrapnel—small round pieces of metal about the size of a musket ball. Unfortunately, grapeshot was ineffectual at a range of a quarter of a mile or more, and Howe suddenly found himself all but devoid of artillery.

Cursing his luck and the heat, he quickened the pace of his advancing ranks. He was behind schedule already. According to plan, his grenadiers were to be in position to charge the demoralized rail fence defenders the moment the light infantry swept around the rebel flank. He soon found himself confronted by other unexpected difficulties. Most of the Charlestown peninsula was pasture land on which the citizens of the town grazed their cattle. Since they had fled two months ago and taken their cows and sheep with them, the grass had grown almost waist high. This had partially obscured the sturdy stone and rail fences with which, in true New England fashion, each citizen had carefully delineated his private property. Again and again Howe found his companies in chaotic disorder, as the heavily loaded men struggled over these obstructions. Then near the foot of Breed's Hill there were some brick kilns and two small ponds which disrupted his line completely. It took several minutes to re-form on the other side of the kilns.

"Forward, men! Forward!" Howe cried. With a cheer the red line surged after their general, only to find themselves involved with more sets of fences. Frantically, they smashed the wooden rails with their musket butts and swung themselves over the stone bases.

On the left, Pigot was having similar trouble with fences, and he was confronted by a hill which slanted away at a fifty-degree angle in some places. He was also still harassed by roving bands of Americans sniping at his flanks from behind walls and from windows of buildings on the outskirts of the blazing town.

To the men on the ground it was hot, breath-catching work. Their backs ached, their uniforms were drenched with sweat and curses from sergeants and officers rained down upon them as they were told again and again to straighten their lines, to stay in formation.

A comfortable half mile away in Boston the advance was a brilliant, awe-inspiring spectacle. The two scarlet lines moving slowly forward, their polished gun barrels and bayonets flashing in the sunlight, cannon booming behind them, and in the foreground the burning village of Charlestown. From Copp's Hill Burgoyne saw it all, and in his description of it he rose above the mediocrity of his literary talents.

"And now ensued one of the greatest scenes of war that can be conceived. If we look to the heights, Howe's corps ascending the hill in the face of entrenchments and in a very disadvantageous ground was much engaged. To the left the enemy pouring in fresh troops by thousands over the land and in the arm of the sea our ships and floating batteries cannonading them. Straight before us a large and noble town in one great blaze. The church steeples being of timber were great pyramids of fire above the rest. Behind us the church steeples and heights of our own camp, covered with spectators. The hills around the country covered with spectators. The enemy all in anxious suspense. The roar of cannon, mortars and musketry, the crash of churches, ships upon the stocks, and whole streets falling together in ruins to fill the air; the storm of the redoubt, with the objects above described, filled the eye, and the reflection that perhaps defeat was a final loss to the British Empire and to

America to fill the mind, made the whole a picture and a complication of horror and importance beyond anything that ever came to my lot to be witness to."

In the American lines the young farmers writhed impatiently at the slow British advance. Behind them their officers paced grimly up and down, talking to them in low, reassuring tones. Almost everyone between the rank of colonel and captain was a veteran who knew how to handle green troops. Behind the rail fence lines, Putnam rode up and down on his horse, roaring, among other things, the words which were to symbolize Bunker Hill for later generations. "Don't fire until you see the whites of their eyes, then fire low. Take aim at their waistbands. You're all marksmen, men, and there's not a one of you that can't kill a squirrel at a hundred yards. Reserve your fire and we will destroy every one of them. Aim at the handsome coats. Pick off the commanders." The other officers were repeating the same phrases. The "whites of their eyes" was not original with Putnam. It had been first used by Prince Charles of Prussia fighting the Austrians at the Battle of Jägerndorf, in 1745.

Down on the Mystic beach Stark was less voluble, but no less authoritative. He sprang over the stone wall and hammered a stake into the sand forty yards in front of them. "Not a man is to fire until the first regular crosses that stake," was his order. "Watch their gaiters. When you can see their gaiters clear, that's when to shoot." Here he shrewdly persuaded his marksmen to aim low, so that the recoil of the musket, which inevitably threw the gun up, would send the bullets into the groin or chest.

At the rail fence Putnam coped with the problem of desertion in his own highly individual fashion. As the British began their advance, one of his Connecticut men suddenly said he felt sick and needed water. He asked permission to withdraw. He was an older man who had served with Putnam against the French. But fifteen years of peace had sapped his fighting spirit. "I need you here," Putnam said, "to show these young fellows how to fight." The man refused the compliment and insisted he was too sick to carry on. He tried to edge past Putnam into open ground beyond him. Putnam pointed his sword at him, all friendship gone from his voice: "Get back into that line or I'll run you through on the spot." The man did not move. Putnam jabbed him in the shoulder with his sword. The man still did not move. With an oath Putnam sank the tip of the sword into his arm until blood flowed. "Do you believe me now?" he bellowed. The man stumbled back to the fence. "If anyone else is thinking of leaving," Putnam said, "he'll get more than the tip of this sword." It was a part of Putnam's personality his young hero worshipers had never seen before.

In the redoubt Prescott was having his troubles. As Pigot's men came within range and began firing, a few of the more impulsive militiamen could not refrain from pulling their triggers. Prescott swore he would put the next man to death who fired against orders. "If you believe in me enough to follow me here," he roared, "believe me now when I tell you that every order I give you has a reason and must be obeyed without question." While he spoke, Lieutenant Colonel Robinson sprang up on the parapet and ran along it, kicking up the leveled muskets, while British bullets flew around him.

The British light infantry moved steadily down the beach at a brisk five-mile-an-hour clip. Above their heads gleamed a forest of bayonets. They were under orders not to fire a shot, to sweep the Americans off the beach with these fearsome fourteen-inch blades alone. It was a perfectly reasonable order. For thirty years British bayonets had sent the best troops in Europe fleeing for their lives. Certainly it was logical to suppose the same tactics would work against troops who had never seen those bayonets come at them, level for the thrust.

On they came and now the American position was in clear view—an insignificant pile of stones barely knee-high. Hardly an impressive fortification to these tough professional soldiers. They could see the Americans crouched behind their little wall, a tall farmer standing behind them, dressed in brown, dirty-looking homespun. Not even their officers were in uniform. Now at a barked command the companies opened out as far as the beach would permit them—about fifteen men to a rank. Their bayonets went down into the charge position and with a roar the 350 picked troops, the best men in William Howe's army—surged forward, past the stake which John Stark had driven into the sand.

The American barricade seemed to explode—the simultaneous crash of muskets was louder than the roar of a cannon. The two front ranks of the Welch Fusiliers were turned back as if a giant leaden fist had struck them—the metaphor is not far from the truth. Those fearful one-ounce balls smashed through the company, flinging two-thirds of them onto the sand. Incredibly the remnant tried to go forward only to meet another blast of fire, which left a bare half-dozen on their feet, bewildered and dazed.

Behind them came the men of that other tradition-proud regiment, the King's Own. As coolly and calmly as if they were on a parade exercise, they moved through and over the dead and wounded fusiliers and plunged forward, to take ferocious revenge for the unexpectedly accurate American fire. Now was the moment when regular troops proved their superiority over amateurs. Behind the haze of musket smoke the farmers would be frantically trying to reload, in those ten simplified, but still torturous motions, when those fearsome bayonets came at their throats. But the King's Own advanced barely fifteen yards beyond the fusiliers when they, too, were struck by a blast of lead almost as destructive. Cries of dying and wounded men echoed across the empty waters of the Mystic. The remnants of the company hesitated, bewildered. Behind them, the men of the Tenth Regiment surged forward. These were the tough snarling regulars who had decimated the minute company at Lexington, in spite of all Pitcairn could do to stop them. Surely they would get home with the bayonet. One volley was expected, two was possible, but three before a charge went home was unheard of in 1775. But the impossible happened there on the Mystic beach. The regulars of the Tenth met the same sheet of leaden death which had laid waste the Welch Fusiliers and the King's Own. Desperately they tried to keep moving forward but it was an impossibility. There was not enough left of the company to form a solid line.

How did the Americans do it? Part of the secret was the Hampshire men's frontier marksmanship. But another part of the answer lay in British army files in a book written by Robert Rogers describing the tactics he had worked out for his rangers. In the passage devoted to repelling a frontal attack, Rogers emphasized the importance of maintaining a "continuous fire." This was to be achieved by having "the front fire whilst the rear reserves theirs till the front has discharged." This formation was not unknown to the regiments of the British army. In fact, the reserve of Cumberland's army at the Battle of Culloden on April 16, 1746, had broken the charge of the Scottish Highland clans in this very way: the front rank kneeling, the second rank stooping, the third rank upright and each rank in turn firing successive volleys so that the front rank was reloading by the time the rear had fired. But the formation had never been adopted by the British army as a whole. They had found their Brown Bess musket so superior to European models, especially in rapidity of fire, that only in special situations had they been

forced to worry about such defensive niceties. Howe's men
forgot two things on the Mystic beach. Behind that stone wall
crouched men armed by and large with the same rapid-fir-
ing British muskets. Commanding them was John Stark,
Robert Rogers' most trusted captain. Stark had stationed
his men in three ranks and undoubtedly the "rear reserved
theirs." Hence the uncanny succession of deadly volleys.

Now all Stark's men were firing as fast as they could reload, ignoring the cloud of musket smoke before them. On
this narrow beach all they had to do was fire low and
straight ahead and the bullet was sure to find a target in
that tangled mass of men in front of them. Moreover, they
were firing their traditional "buck and ball"—four pieces
of buckshot to every bullet—making their every shot all the
more terribly effective.

The men of the Fifty-second Regiment came forward now,
reluctantly, appalled by the carnage in front of them. Their
officers had to shout and curse them into motion. No wonder.
Ghastly holes were torn into their lines before they even
reached the shattered remnants of the Fusiliers and King's
Own. It was too much. The column could not go another
step into that murderous fire. It was like asking men to
walk into a furnace. The front lines wavered and broke,
the rear ranks piled up against them. Frantically the officers
tried to straighten them again, smashing at them with their
swords, but it was hopeless and they knew it. Men were still
dropping all around them. They had to get out of range of
that terrible fire. The order to retreat was given and William Howe's light infantry wheeled and all but fled down
the beach leaving ninety-six men dead on the sand in front
of John Stark's stone barricade. "I never saw sheep lie as
thick in the fold," was Stark's grim description of the
scene.

Up on the bank Howe's grenadiers were still smashing
down those stubborn stone fences when a white-faced aide

came panting up to him and reported the terrible results of the assault on the beach. Though he retained the cool aplomb of a major general, Howe must have shuddered inwardly. He suddenly found himself with no other maneuver left but a frontal assault on entrenched troops who outnumbered him along the rail fence almost two to one. But there was no alternative except retreat, and that was unthinkable.

Grimly Howe gave the order. An aide raced to deliver it to Pigot. "Attack all along the line."

12

IN THE 100-yard gap between the rail fence and the American breastwork, a sweating, cursing Israel Putnam now became a one-man artillery regiment. Captain John Ford's company had dutifully towed Callender's two cannon into line, but they knew nothing about firing them. Putnam had to go it alone. When he tried to ram the charge home he discovered Callender had, obliquely, told him the truth about his lack of cartridges. None of them fit. With a snarl of rage, Putnam slit one open and dumped the powder down the barrel with a ladle. Then he rammed home the wad and ball and sprinkled the touchhole with the highly explosive priming powder. Since the artillerymen had all disappeared, he had no linstock for his match. He simply struck it and shoved it into the touchhole, taking a substantial risk of blowing his arm off, or at least burning it terribly, if the priming powder flashed back. But his luck, as usual, was good. The cannon roared and the ball went whistling toward the British lines.

Putnam's first few shots, at the very beginning of the British advance, went wildly far from the mark, whistling over the heads of the regulars and landing in Boston Harbor.

The British ignored him totally and continued their slow, stately progress. "Gods curse you," Putnam roared at his unfaithful gun and ladled another charge into the now smoking barrel. But when he shoved the ball home, it stuck, halfway down. Without a sponge or a wormer, Putnam was unable to clean out the burned scraps of the old wad from the first two shots and they had clogged the barrel. With a bellow of rage, he flung all his considerable weight against the stubborn metal. With a dull crunch, the barrel split all the way down the side.

Now Putnam's language was as purple as his face. Frantically he ladled powder into the other gun and rushed to his saddlebags. From them he poured 200 or 300 musket balls down the muzzle of the cannon. "Damn the shot anyway," he rumbled to himself. "A taste of canister will do us a lot more good." He waited now until the British were about 200 yards away and the grenadiers' line was disrupted by the brick kilns. As they were re-forming on the other side, Putnam shoved his match into the touchhole. The cannon crashed and a hail of musket balls tore a gap in the grenadiers' ranks. "There's a lane through 'em." Putnam roared. The men near him gave a cheer.

But the gap was immediately filled and the two scarlet lines plodded forward again. Putnam realized command was more important than canister fire if his raw troops were going to make a stand. "Who knows how to charge these pieces?" he roared, looking around him. Men from Moses Little's regiment were closest, and Privates Halliday and Dutton, of Newburyport, volunteered. With them came a British deserter named Hill, who had had some artillery experience. "Fire until she melts, lads," Putnam shouted and sprang on his old white horse to take charge of the battle line.

Though the young New Englanders were shocked by the oaths with which Hill accompanied every command, they obeyed his orders, and within a hurried minute had the gun ready to fire. Putnam had taken his saddlebags with him, so they went back to solid shot. The first two tries were absurdly high but the young citizen-soldiers liked the noise and cheered anyway. In language which matched Putnam at his purplest, Hill told them to lower their aim. The next shot went smashing through British ranks, directly in front of them. "Yah, Yah," Hill roared, pounding his amateur gunners with profane glee. "You have made a furrow through them." Other men rushed to assist them now. One youngster eagerly ladled another charge down the muzzle. As he did so, a puff of flame came gushing out and struck him in the face. In the uncleaned barrel there must have been scraps of still burning wad, and they ignited the powder. Moaning in agony, the boy was carried off the field and everyone abruptly lost his ambition to be an artilleryman. The American gun was silent as the British came on steadily.

Now the grenadiers were throwing down a fence only a hundred yards from the American lines. Though this was the outside limit for effective musket fire, some of the self-confident New Hampshire sharpshooters could not resist opening up on them. They were stopped, after five or six scattering shots, by a bellow of rage from behind. Israel Putnam loomed over them, waving his sword. "Gods curse you," he roared. "I swear the next man who fires I'll take his head off."

Burdened by their full packs and drenched with sweat by the ninety-degree heat, the grenadiers lumbered forward behind Howe's striding figure. Now they were within seventy yards, just getting over another fence; Lieutenant James Dana of the Connecticut troops opened up, "to draw their fire." Other officers did the same thing. It worked very well. The grenadiers interrupted their advance to fire an answering volley. Behind them the Fifth and Fifty-second Regiments, caught by surprise, blundered into the grenadiers, and there were several moments of very unmilitary confusion. "The bayonet. The bayonet," Howe roared. Cursing, the General, aided by Lieutenant Colonel James Abercromby, re-formed the grenadiers and ordered them not to fire again under any circumstances. Howe was finding out that he was not commanding seasoned troops. Most of the enlisted men in these British regiments were in their first fight at Bunker Hill, and the few who had seen action were softened by years of peacetime duty.

Howe must have been aware that he was taking a calculated risk attacking in a long open line along the entire 200-yard front. Almost twenty years before, Wolfe, the master under whom he had learned his tactics, had written: "If an entrenchment is to be attacked, the troops should move as quickly as possible toward the place, not in a line but in small firing columns of three or four platoons in depth, with small parties between each column who are to fire at the top of the parapet when the columns approach to divert the enemy's fire. It is of little purpose to fire at men who are covered with an entrenchment, but by attacking in the above manner one may succeed."

Howe's use of the line was based on his now shattered plan to turn the flank of the rail fence defenders and hit the Americans in the rear with his light infantry. *Then* his grenadiers would have charged from the front—with bayonets leveled. As we have already seen, Howe never intended them to make a genuine assault in the long open line.

By the time Howe learned of the debacle on the Mystic's beach, was it too late to fall back and re-form his men into Wolfe's columns? For one thing, he probably told himself it would be bad psychology to give them a look at the ruined light infantry. For another, Howe probably attributed the failure of the light infantry to their own incompetence and lack of training more than to any remarkable ability on the

American side. So he made the impulsive, on-the-spot decision
to go forward in his extended double line, relying on the
bayonet. It was a daredevil's decision; it was not a good one.
On Morton's Point, a half mile away, the farmers crouched
behind Stark's low stone wall may have looked like a handful. But here, within musket shot of the rail fence, Howe
should have been able to see there were at least 1,500
determined men with muzzles leveled. Against them he was
sending little more than 900 grenadiers and infantry.

For the opening charge the odds were even worse. It was
led by the grenadiers alone—some 350 men, in ten companies. One of the myths of Bunker Hill—that a handful of
Americans stood off vastly more numerous British attackers
—was in ironic reversal here.

Still, the order was given and the grenadiers came on
through the hay, only to find another fence. Once more they
smashed their way through it. A moment after they re-
formed on the other side and lowered their bayonets for the
charge, Israel Putnam's voice rang out on the other side of
the rail fence: "FIRE!"

The grenadier officers and men who survived that first
blast said the earth seemed to buckle. A curtain of flame
raced down the fence, followed by a great gush of musket
smoke. It was like a volcano exploding. The stunned survivors in the British line were frozen with the shock; they
stood there staring stupidly at the massive gaps in their ranks
and their fellow soldiers on the ground, some twitching in
death agonies, others screaming helplessly, a few crawling
like animals for safety.

To Ralph Farnum, crouched with the New Hampshire
men behind the fence, the most frightening sound was not
the crash of the muskets, but the first scream of agony from
those British grenadiers. Eighty years later, when he was
105 years old and the last survivor of Bunker Hill, it would

be his most vivid memory. "It was louder than the firearms," he said and he confessed that he got sick before he could pull his trigger again.

For the next fifteen minutes, through that field of un-mown hay before the rail fence, William Howe, the master of light infantry maneuver, found himself engaged in one of the most ghastly frontal assaults in the history of warfare. Again and again the companies of grenadiers, and after them the men of the Fifth and Fifty-second, plunged forward to collapse in tangled heaps or stagger back, bleeding and terrified by a fire more destructive than anything their veteran officers had seen on Europe's most sanguinary battle-fields. Some companies of light infantry, re-formed by Colonel Clarke, were fed into the maelstrom and suffered a similar fate.

One British officer, recalling it later, said: "As we ap-proached, an incessant stream of fire poured from the rebel lines. Our light infantry were served up in companies against the grass fence without being able to penetrate. Indeed how could we penetrate? Most of our grenadiers and light infan-try the moment of presenting themselves, lost three-fourths and many nine-tenths of their men."

This is what the rail fence seemed like, to a man who was in front of it. To those behind it, the shooting was more spasmodic. After the first coordinated blast of musketry, the Americans loaded and fired individually, and the targets were not quite so evident. Musket firing was smoky busi-ness, and from the first volley there was a white haze drifting along the fence, through which the men fired at the shadowy figures of the charging regulars. But their aim did not have to be good. With over 1,500 men firing three shots a minute, those 350 grenadiers had to survive a theoretical total of 67,500 bullets to reach the rail fence with their bayonets during the fifteen minutes of the doomed assault. Actually, the attack probably lasted closer to ten minutes and since the Americans obeyed their militia training, and "took good sight," the average rate of fire was closer to two shots a minute. Yet this still comes to some 30,000 bullets poured at William Howe and his grenadiers, in ten awful minutes.

The results were written in blood. The King's Own Grenadiers lost all but four of their men; there were only eight of the Fifty-second's Grenadiers left standing; in the Tenth, forty men fell. The grenadiers of the Welch Fusiliers suffered as terribly here as their light infantry comrades on the beach. Forty-four out of forty-nine officers and men were flung to the earth by the murderous blasts of buck and ball pouring from the New Hampshire and Connecticut guns. On the right of the fusiliers the Thirty-fifth Light Infantry Company which had been one of the rearmost in the attack on the beach and emerged unscathed, charged into the billowing smoke before the fence and reeled back with twenty-five of its thirty privates dead or wounded. Not far away, their brother company of grenadiers was losing thirty-four officers and men.

The senior and junior officers and the veteran sergeants exposed themselves fearlessly in this maelstrom of bullets to encourage their inexperienced troops. It is hard for us to imagine a man standing upright in this fire, scorning the cover of fence or foxhole, but this was military tradition expected of every soldier in 1775. They paid a fearful price for their courage. Putnam's old friend, James Abercromby, fell with a bullet in the body. (As his men carried him to the rear, they could hear shouts from the American lines: "Colonel Abercromby, are the Americans cowards now?") Every officer and sergeant in the Thirty-fifth Light Infantry was killed or wounded. Every officer in the Tenth Grenadiers went down. Part of the reason was the explicit orders from Putnam and the other American veterans to pick off the officers in their "handsome uniforms." It was a command the sharpshooters in the American ranks obeyed with savage delight. Henry Dearborn tells of his men shouting excitedly to each other, "Look, there's an officer. Let's get a shot at him. Ho! You missed him. Let me try."

Howe's staff, clustered about him in the best military tradition, suffered terribly. Lieutenant Page, his engineer, was struck in the ankle by the first volley and carried back, his leg shattered. Lieutenant Jourdain, his naval aide, died with a bullet in his head. Captain Sherwin, his personal aide, toppled into the grass with a bullet in his chest.

No army in the history of the world has seen its forward units suffer eighty per cent casualties and remained a coherent fighting organization. These British troops were no exception. Hysterically, all thought of a charge forgotten, the remnants of the grenadiers and the less mauled Fifth and Fifty-second sent volley after volley crashing through the dense smoke that shrouded the American line. Their aim was deplorable. Henry Dearborn, fighting on the extreme right of the rail fence, said, "forty-nine out of fifty of their bullets went six feet over our heads." After the fight, his men noticed the higher branches of some trees, directly behind them, were shredded by the atrocious British marksmanship, while the trunks and lower branches were untouched. The Americans, true to their frontier training, kept their heads down. The field officers, standing upright behind their men, were much more exposed to this high-flying fire. Colonels Brewer and Nixon were hit and had to leave the field. Nixon's Lieutenant Colonel, William Buckminster, was smashed off his feet by a ball through the shoulder, which was to leave him a cripple for life. Captain Isaac Baldwin of Hillsborough, New Hampshire, was hit in the chest. He stayed with his men and loaded and fired his musket three more times before he collapsed. "You'll beat them boys," he gasped in farewell. "I'll be back as soon as the doctor tends this." He died that night.

Above the crash of the muskets along the New Hampshire

line rose the enormous roar of Major Andrew McClary's voice. From the moment they opened fire he never stopped a continuous bellow of encouragement. His six-foot-six frame towered over the kneeling defenders of the fence and presented a likely target to the high-firing British muskets, but he remained utterly contemptuous of the balls whistling around him. He was one of those great animal men, like Putnam, who have almost a faith in their own invulnerability.

Howe was the same kind of man and he was exhibiting the same kind of courage on the other side of the fence. His size and his uniform made him a perfect target, and no less than twice in this first assault he was left utterly alone as his regulars broke and fell back. With Americans under orders to pick off the officers, it was all but miraculous that he survived.

The second time Howe found himself alone he knew that the fight before the fence was won for the moment by the Americans. There were simply no more companies in any semblance of order to continue the attack. Behind him his once crisp battalions milled in total confusion, firing sporadically at the American lines, almost beyond the control of their officers. As he returned through the hay to restore order in his demoralized men, Howe must have found himself hoping with a desperation he never expected to feel that Pigot's assault had better luck. He was quickly informed that the news from Pigot was almost as bad as his own.

Behind Pigot's double line of marines and infantry, Charlestown now sent great tongues of flame leaping up into the blue sky. The steeple of the church was wreathed in fire. But the flames had not yet reached the outskirts of town and there some snipers still lingered, to "gall him exceedingly," as he began his first real assault against Prescott's fort. He had already come close enough to begin a fire fight with the defenders, while waiting for news that Howe had

swept through the fence. Now, as he ascended the brutally
steep hill, he found another obstacle: the Americans who had
been driven out of Charlestown by flames and Pitcairn's
attacks had taken up positions in buildings and along walls
to the rear of the redoubt. Again the exasperated brigadier
was forced to refuse his flank and carry on a small war with
these harassers, while pressing home the attack on the fort.
Pitcairn and his marines were given the assignment once
more, supported by the Forty-seventh Regiment.

Some of the most damaging fire was coming from a loopholed barn, about 100 yards to the rear of the redoubt.
Closer in there was Warner's incomplete company, still
holding their posts and supported now by an irregular
crowd of single volunteers who had become separated from
the companies or wandered on the field individually when
their friends refused to cross the Neck. It was a short, vicious
fight, and the Royal Marines won again. Warner's little
company made a heroic, largely unrecorded stand behind
their stone fence and paid a fearful price for it. Seventeen
out of twenty-two were killed or wounded. The barn was
also flushed by bayonets in a brief ferocious struggle. Benjamin Walker and his volunteers were among those routed
again. This time the tireless guerrilla captain decided that
the position was indefensible, and with nothing left of his
company but one man, Jacob Frost, he drifted around the
lines and took a post along the rail fence, where the Americans were doing much better. The travels of this peripa-
tetic captain are a comment in themselves on the chaotic
state of American command during the day.

In the redoubt, Prescott could do nothing for these routed
supporters of his right flank. But he must have thanked God
for their help. By diverting almost one-fourth of Pigot's
troops, and protecting the rear of the redoubt, they vastly
simplified the defense of his little fort against the enveloping frontal attack. He was able to mass his fire power on two

sides instead of three, and he needed every gun he could muster. Here the rail fence situation was reversed. The British were attacking with over 1,000 men; in the fort, Prescott had barely 300. Another 300 were manning the breastwork outside.

Pigot sent the Thirty-eighth and Forty-third Regiments under Major Small against the eastern side of the fort and the breastwork; on the south or Charlestown side, it was the marines and the Forty-seventh. This meant the attack was separated by the turn of the hill, and the two regiments on the Charlestown side were heavily preoccupied by the irregulars on their flanks. The two wings failed to hit the fort simultaneously, and Prescott shrewdly manipulated the youngsters inside his walls to take advantage of this miscoordination. The Thirty-eighth and Forty-third closed first, firing volleys by platoon as they came. Pigot made no attempt to stop them, although their bullets were more futile here than the grenadiers' fire before the rail fence. The Americans simply crouched on their firing platforms, their heads down, and the British lead crunched harmlessly against their solid earth walls.

Now the red ranks were close enough for Prescott to see the sweat gleaming on their faces. The colonel had reinforced the wall with men from the south parapet, so his ranks were more than full. "Fire!" he snarled, and the redoubt and breastwork came alive with belching muskets. It was the beach and the rail fence all over again—broken men, screaming and groveling on the ground and the remnants of the first rank recoiling into the second and throwing the whole attack into a cursing tangle. "Now—to the other side." Prescott rushed his reserve to the south wall, and a moment later the oncoming companies of the marines and Forty-seventh received a similar blast.

Pigot's men showed the soldierly courage their comrades were displaying, at the same time, before the rail

fence. The companies toiled up the steep slope into the
curtain of smoke around the redoubt; then a man would
drop, then another, and another would stumble backward,
clutching his arm or his leg in agony. Here too, in spite of
the haze, the American fire was accurate and intense beyond
all reasonable expectations. In the ten to fifteen minutes
they fought in this first assault, Prescott's 600 men fired at
least 12,000 bullets. Yet Pigot's casualties were only half of
what Howe's men were suffering. Shooting down a hill
makes for more difficult aiming, and there was the inevitable haze from their own muskets. Yet they hit home often
enough to take the heart out of the attacking infantry, who
also had their packs, the heat, the brutal slope and stone
fences to contend with on their side. The regulars soon lost
all appetite for charging and simply blazed away with their
muskets at about sixty yards, hitting no one. Prescott's men
excitedly returned them shot for shot, until Joseph Warren
and the colonel both abruptly ordered them to hold their
fire. It was difficult to hit anyone with a musket at sixty
yards, and the haze made it next to impossible. They were
wasting precious powder and ammunition.

To Pigot and his men outside the redoubt the sudden silence was a hopeful sign. They thought the Americans were
retreating and with a cheer they surged through the smoke
again. This time Prescott waited until they were barely
twenty yards away. "Fire!" he roared, and the redoubt
bristled with blazing muskets at point-blank range. The
blast tore terrible gaps in the British front rank and the rest
recoiled in outright terror. Only magnificent discipline
held them in formation. Ruefully Pigot gave the order to
retreat. They fell back down the hill for about 200 yards,
firing defensive volleys as they went.

This was the story William Howe heard as he struggled
to bring order into his milling men before the rail fence.
Shocked though they were by the beating they had just taken,

the habit of discipline was stronger. They formed up, even the frightening remnants of the grenadiers and light infantry companies, each numbering only six or seven men. The five men of the Thirty-fifth Light Infantry, without an officer or a sergeant, were proudly led by their eldest private. Grimly Howe promised them that if they withheld their fire and got home for one bayonet stroke, the Americans would run like rabbits. On Pigot's side of the field, however, there is no record of any particular emphasis on the bayonet in the first two assaults.

Very little time elapsed between the first and second assaults; not more than five minutes. To many of the men in the redoubt it was all one continuous fight. The British simply fell back, re-formed and came on again, with a squeal of fifes and a rattle of drums. Once more they began their rolling volleys by platoon. Their aim was still high and wild, but one shot did serious damage. Major Willard Moore, the commanding officer along the breastwork, was hit in the thigh. The ball tore away the muscle and he could not stand. As two of his officers carried him to the rear, another wild British bullet, again far over the heads of the men at the breastwork, struck the unlucky major in the lung. His men wanted to carry him off the field; but he knew he was dying. He asked to be placed in the shade of a tree behind the redoubt and gallantly ordered them back into the lines.

In the redoubt, Sergeant Benjamin Prescott, the colonel's nephew, was hit in the shoulder as he peered over the parapet to get a look at the advancing red line. The tough young farmer showed he was Prescott stock by concealing it from his uncle as the colonel moved by him down the firing wall, repeating to man after man: "You drove them back once. You can do it again. Hold your fire until you get the order and don't shoot until you have a target." This time not a man disobeyed. In their pouches they were all finding an

alarming shortage of musket balls. To piece out their supply
they snatched up bits of nails and round pebbles and anything else that would go down their gun barrels.

On came the scarlet line, enveloping the breastwork and
the redoubt in its extended arms, like a giant creature. At
least, this was the view from Boston. (Howe's men, moving
against the rail fence, were invisible behind the hump of
Breed's Hill.) Across the city's hills and rooftops a pano-
rama of emotion flickered. Up on Copp's Hill young Peter
Edes, in full view of generals and Tories, jumped up and
down and shouted: "Now they'll get it again. Watch now.
Watch. Give it to them boys. Give it to them." Beside him
Burgoyne admired the soldierly perfection of the British
formations and marveled at a battle fought like a drama in
an amphitheater. From Beacon Hill, saintly Andrew Eliot
watched and prayed for the brave men dying on both sides.
Vengeful Ann Hulton beseeched the Almighty for the total
annihilation of the rebel scum. In the North Church tower,
from which the fateful signal to Paul Revere had been
flashed sixty days before, Thomas Gage watched through a
field glass. He had planned to direct the battle from Province
House. But not even his natural talent for patience could
bear the suspense; too much depended on those scarlet figures
moving up the green hill so slowly now.

To the men breasting the steep hill in the beating afternoon sun, things were not quite so picturesque. The Americans crouched in their fort, invisible and silent. Along the
breastwork there was the long line of leveled muskets, with
the round provincial hats peeking above them. In the tall
grass there were the still bodies of friends with whom they
had eaten and drunk for years. With magnificent discipline
they stepped over these silent figures; several stirred and
cried out for help, water; not a head turned. Only when
they reloaded after a volley did the British stop their geo-
metrical advance. On the south side not even the loss of a

man here and a man there from the few snipers still in blazing Charlestown disturbed them.

Before the rail fence Howe's thinned battalions moved forward but with not quite the same determination. The Fifth and Fifty-second Regiments were bearing the brunt of the attack now, with little more than token support from the grenadiers and light infantry. Howe could not have mustered more than 600 men, and he was moving again against the solid line of 1,500 muskets; scarcely a dozen Americans had been wounded, and Putnam was still there, on his white horse now, forbidding a man to leave the line as long as he could fire a gun. When one of his Connecticut soldiers tried to help a wounded man to the rear, Putnam pointed his sword at him and roared, "Gods curse him, he can walk. Get back to your post." A few seconds later he found one of Doolittle's soldiers cowering behind a haystack, several dozen feet to the rear of the firing line. With a bellow of rage, Putnam sprang off his horse, no doubt delighted at the chance to get even with the "do-nothing-at-all" regiment. *Whack!*—the flat of his sword went across the slacker's shoulders like a whip. *Whump*—another swing caught him in the rump as he scampered back into the lines, howling for mercy.

Being outnumbered was nothing new to British infantry. They came on, until the dead of the first attack could be seen in the unmown hay. This time, Howe varied his strategy just a little. The 100-yard gap between the rail fence and the breastwork became his target, rather than the bristling center of the rail fence line. There was a swamp directly in front of it, but behind it there were only the three small flèches, constructed under Gridley's direction at the last moment. Again Howe himself led the advance, striding fearlessly at the leveled muskets. What was left of his staff courageously clustered about him, ready to receive his orders and protect him, if possible, from injury. Behind him Captain Harris and his dashing lieutenant, Lord Rawdon, led their decimated grenadier company. Not far away, Captain Evelyn of the Fifty-second, his company still fairly intact, pondered the mystery of how these cowardly Americans stopped the grenadiers. His soldiers were undoubtedly thinking the same thoughts.

For a moment, before the rail fence and the redoubt, the only sound was the roll of British drums and the shrill call of their fifes as they came forward. Thinking of their dwindling ammunition, the American officers withheld the order to fire until the scarlet line was less than thirty yards away. Then, from Breed's Hill, down the slope to the rail fence, the Yankee voices twanged: FIRE!

Again the blast of lead tore into the first British rank. But now they expected punishment. They closed the gaps and lumbered forward, with incredible courage. Two of the five privates from the Thirty-fifth fell, and the last three still advanced. Then the grenadiers, as they swung to the left around the head of the swamp in an attempt to flank the rail fence, received their coup de grâce. The men in the flèches, firing from their raised bank, poured in a terrible fusillade on them which utterly annihilated any hope of their winning the fence with the bayonet; there were not enough of them left in any kind of order to make an attack. Grimly, the Fifth and the Fifty-second shoved past them at the now smoke-shrouded American line. Again through the murk the muskets flared and these regiments paid a price for their courage almost as fearful as the grenadiers. Most of the 144 enlisted men lost by the Fifth and the 100 lost by the Fifty-second fell now as they struggled through the hay toward the fatal fence. Captain Evelyn's company was torn to shreds before his unbelieving eyes.

Up at the redoubt, Pigot was doing no better. More snipers were tormenting his flanks. His six companies of light infantry and grenadiers led the way against the

Charlestown side of the redoubt and his other regiments were positioned as before. The picked troops met the same blood-curdling frustration their comrades met under Howe; a blast of massed fire which sent them reeling back down the hill. The rest of the regiments staggered under similar shocks, but they kept coming forward.

On the eastern side of the hill, Putnam's old friend John Small, Pigot's brigade major, led on the Forty-third and Thirty-eighth. A bullet tore into his arm. He shifted his sword to the other hand and roared his hesitating troops into motion again. American guns blazed through the smoke and men fell, clutching at the agonizing wounds caused by the Americans' homemade musket balls. On the other side of the hill, Pitcairn ignored a flesh wound and lashed his marines into line with a torrent of magnificent oaths. But not even they were inclined to take the kind of deadly punishment Prescott's men were giving them. All around Breed's Hill the British attack ground to an anguished halt. Only a few veterans followed their officers into the swirling smoke. Even these bravest found that courage alone was not enough. Raw troops should, by all the laws of military logic, panic when they see the enemy within ten yards. But Prescott's men clung to their parapets with a ferocity which defied all the rules of eighteenth-century warfare. The sergeants and captains fell less than five yards from the walls and a few were in the ditch when bullets fired at point-blank range ripped into them and literally tore them apart. It was too much for the rank and file. Those who were still on their feet fled outside the deadly perimeter of musket smoke and joined their comrades in firing futile volleys at a relatively safe eighty yards.

Down at the rail fence, William Howe for the third time found himself standing utterly alone. Around him grenadiers lay sprawled in the contorted postures of painful death, their elaborate bearskins gleaming blackly in the tall

hay. Beside him, the last of his staff officers, the just arrived
Captain Addison, lay dying with a bullet beneath the
heart. The general's beautiful white breeches were covered
with ugly blotches of blood. But it was the blood of his officers and men. He was still miraculously untouched.

Desperately he pointed his sword toward the American
lines. "Once more men, once more. Show them what English
soldiers can do." One last time two companies—or more
correctly, two collections of companies thrown together from
remnants—formed into line beside him. The American muskets blazed. Men dropped and the line wavered, stopped and
a shudder ran through it as if it were a living organism. The
survivors turned and fled.

A great shout of victory went up from the American lines.
Men began leaping over the fence to pursue the shattered
British, but Stark and McClary sternly stopped them.

Standing there alone, with the musket balls still whizzing
around him, William Howe experienced for the first time
the possibility of personal defeat, and something deeper
than defeat. Throughout his military life he had been a
daredevil who took the long chance and had always succeeded. He had seen men die under his command but he
had never seen them slaughtered. He had seen it now.
"There was a moment," he said, "I never felt before." Howe
was not a talkative man. But there are times when untalk-
ative men can say more in a terse sentence than a writer
like Burgoyne can say in a dozen windy paragraphs. This
was one of those times.

"Once more men—" But his voice failed him. Of his 750
grenadiers and light infantry 450 lay dead and wounded on
the Mystic beach and in the grass before the rail fence. Not
even William Howe, the daredevil of Quebec, could call
men forward again after such losses.

Once again he turned his back on the American lines and
followed his retreating troops.

The moment the British broke before the rail fence, Israel Putnam spurred his horse around the swamp and up the rear slope of Breed's Hill, where there were still sounds of firing. He came charging up to the breastwork, not far from where it joined the redoubt, and saw that here, too, the fight was over for the time being. The battered British regiments had, for all effects, fallen back. Only scattered musket shots were being exchanged on both sides.

At this moment, a breath of wind parted the haze before the American lines, and Putnam saw, not twenty yards away, a lone British officer shouting futile orders at his retreating troops. "There's an officer," one of the Massachusetts men behind the breastwork shouted. "Let's get him," another howled. Putnam peered, in the dissolving haze, and suddenly unleashed a bellow of horror. It was his friend John Small. In the same moment, the major seemed to recognize his old comrade and saw the leveled muskets. To run or duck was beneath the dignity of a British officer. "I prepared myself for death," was how Small described it later. But as trigger fingers tightened, Putnam sprang forward and knocked up the American guns with his sword. "For God's sake spare that man," he shouted. "I love him as a brother." Small bowed his thanks to his friend and followed his men down the hill.

Before the rail fence, where Howe was wearily plodding through the tall grass toward his shattered regiments. His back was a challenge to the frontier marksmen, and they blazed away at him as he went. But his charmed life persisted. Not one came close to him.

His valet, Evans, was not so lucky. In the finest traditions of the British manservant, he greeted his sweaty, blood-smeared general with a napkin-wrapped bottle of cool wine in one hand and a goblet in the other. Bullets still whizzed around them as they met, but Evans was as magnificently contemptuous of them as his master.

"Some wine, General?"

"Thank you, Evans," said Howe.

Evans began to pour a cool sparkling glass. But it never reached the general's lips. The hot, thirsty defenders of the rail fence cut loose with a furious volley. A ball shattered the bottle and another caught Evans in the arm and spun him around like a top.

Howe sent him staggering back to the boats and rejoined his beaten battalions. If there had been demoralization before, now there was chaos. Many of the men flung down their muskets and swore they would not go forward again, if their officers killed them on the spot. Ignoring them, Howe assembled Pigot, Small and his other senior officers for a council of war. Several immediately told him that it would be "criminal" to send the men against such fire again. "Butchery," another officer said.

There was a moment I never felt before. Howe stared in baffled perplexity at the American lines. Was it possible that his lucky star, which had risen so smoothly and so superbly on his military exploits, was to be suddenly extinguished by a collection of farmers in shirtsleeves? He could hear the laughter in the London coffeehouses, the acid denunciations in Parliament—a major general of the British army with 2,300 picked troops defeated by militiamen, by those despised Americans who had never before been able to defend themselves against either the French or the Indians.

"We will go forward once more, gentlemen," Howe said.

13

DAZED from the crash of muskets so suddenly stilled, the citizen soldiers peered over the top of their little fort, their guns still at ready. The light breeze quickly cleared the haze of dust and powder smoke, and there, in the brilliant sunlight, they beheld an almost incredible sight. Red-coated bodies lay everywhere now, some near the ditch, many in the tall grass beyond it; a few of the bravest sprawled awkwardly over the obstructions in the ditch itself, a bayonet thrust away from the redoubt. Beyond the dead, midway down the steep slope, the red line was retreating again, not in good order this time, but in shattered clumps and fleeing strays, looking more like a band of hapless refugees than an army. Everywhere there were wounded, some being carried but most limping, stumbling, clinging to arms and shoulders of those near them. Others had turned their backs and were frankly running. A hoarse triumphant cheer rose from the parched American throats. For a magnificent moment they forgot their thirst, their weariness, their suspicions of treachery and betrayal, in the first flash of American military pride.

Across Boston Harbor, beside the booming battery on

Copp's Hill, Major Generals John Burgoyne and Henry
Clinton watched with even greater disbelief the collapse of
the British attack. The elegant Burgoyne confined himself
to exclamations of dismay. To his calculating eye, the day,
which had begun so gloriously, was rapidly becoming a
major military disaster. Privately he had no doubt thanked
his gambler's luck—and General Gage—for limiting him to
the role of a spectator. Let William Howe bear full responsibility for this blot on Britain's martial prowess.

Not that Burgoyne could have done anything, even if he
were inclined. Clinton was second in command, and Gage
had given him authority to send Howe any reinforcements
he might need. The excitable Clinton now proceeded to not
only send the reinforcements, but lead them as well. The
sight of British regiments in flight had filled his professional soldier's heart with rage and horror. Flinging down
his telescope, he rushed from Copp's Hill to the North
Battery and ordered the reserves there, 500 Royal Marines of
the Second Battalion, and the Sixty-third Infantry Regiment,
to embark immediately. He sprang into one of their boats
and urged them across the narrow river with all possible
speed.

The marines and infantry headed for the blunt tip of the
peninsula, Morton's Point. Clinton ordered his oarsmen to
land him nearer burning Charlestown. A large group of
wounded, perhaps 200, hit in the assault on the redoubt, had
come straight down the hill and collapsed there, waiting for
boats to take them back to Boston. It was by no means a safe
haven. Though flames and smoke seemed to have engulfed
the entire town of Charlestown, some of the Yankee snipers
still ignored the conflagration. As Clinton's boat touched the
shore, the man beside him toppled over with a choked cry,
blood spurting from a wound in his neck. Before the rest
could scramble to relative safety on the beach, another man
went down with a ball in the chest.

Ignoring the snipers, Clinton strode onto the beach and surveyed the wounded. Most of them Royal Marines, they lay, sat and squatted in attitudes of abject defeat. Many of them had lost their hats. Their once immaculate red uniforms were dirt smudged and sweat stained. They were obviously men who had tasted the Yankee's fighting spirit and wanted no more to do with it. But Clinton reminded them that they were also British soldiers. Vigorously he called on every man who had an ounce of strength or courage left to join him in another assault. "To their honor," Clinton wrote later, "there were many." In the finest tradition of the British army, the men rose to his challenge. Singly, then in twos and threes, they struggled to the shore where Clinton stood and he formed them into a column, "with as much show as possible to impress the enemy."

Out on the battlefield William Howe was calling on every scrap of knowledge he had as a soldier to rescue his victory. The artillery was hauled out of the muck, where it had rested, all but useless, for the first two attacks, and carefully placed, under his personal direction, well forward, along the shore of the Mystic. It was uncomfortably close to the American lines as far as the artillerymen were concerned, but they were ordered to stand their ground on pain of instant death. From where they were to fire, Howe calculated, they would be able to enfilade—fire along the flank—of the breastwork. Not all the way up to the redoubt, but far enough to demoralize the troops manning this troublesome barricade. By now, they had brought a fresh supply of six-pound balls from Boston and were finally ready to give him genuine support. They could also rake the rail fence with grape, if necessity demanded it.

Quickly but clearly, Howe outlined his plan for the attack. The light infantry, the grenadiers and the Fifth and Fifty-second would proceed against the rail fence, as they had for the first two assaults. But just before they reached the point where they committed themselves to attack, they would wheel and all the strength they could muster would go against the breastwork and the front of the redoubt. Pigot would simultaneously attack the redoubt on the Charlestown side. Before the rail fence there would be nothing but a screen of light infantry, to lay down a diversionary fire.

Next, Howe turned to his men and told them to drop their packs. When many also flung aside their greatcoats, he did not object. He knew that his position was critical. If the rebels beat them back once more, neither appeals to honor nor threats of death could drive these men up this hill a fourth time.

Out in the harbor he could see the reinforcements rowing slowly toward Morton's Point. It would take another twenty minutes for them to disembark and reach his advanced position. Could he wait for them? William Howe decided he could not. On Bunker Hill there was a growing mass of Americans obviously hesitant to commit themselves to battle. If he remained inert for another twenty minutes, they might well decide to join their comrades in the lines, and then disaster would be guaranteed. The same reasoning forced him to give up on Colonel James and the two floating batteries, which could have swept away the Americans before the rail fence. Howe could see them, torturously making their way around Morton's Point. They had another half mile to go against the tide in the Mystic. It would take them at least thirty minutes. Somehow he would have to win with the men and guns he had around him and nothing else.

Up on Breed's Hill, Colonel William Prescott studied his citizen soldiers. Faces streaked with gun powder and lips caked with the fine dust that rose incessantly from the dirt floor of their fort, they were unmistakably weary. The sleepless night and twelve hours of furious entrenching and now almost a full hour of fighting was more than the toughest veteran could be expected to endure. The weather was doing them no favors. The sun still blazed pitilessly in the blue June sky, and the walls of the redoubt seemed to concentrate the oppressive heat, until the air inside became tropically thick and moist. They had drunk the last of their rum hours ago and for food still had nothing but leftover salt pork, hardly the right nourishment for men with burning thirsts. From Cambridge had come not a dram of the promised supplies.

Still Prescott was certain his lean young farmers could summon up reserves of strength and endurance. Of much more concern was the low state of their ammunition supply. A check revealed that few men had more than three rounds of powder left. Equally depressing was the depletion of fighting men. There now remained barely 150 in the redoubt. Throughout the first two attacks every time a man was wounded, three, four and five friends nearby him seized the opportunity to assist him to safety on Bunker Hill, or points west. The suspicion and distrust of their leadership at Cambridge which the citizen soldiers had so vociferously expressed before the fighting started had as much to do with this desertion as simple cowardice. Now, as they fought on without a sign of help forthcoming from Cambridge, even the brave men who stood by the unwavering Prescott began to have doubts. All around them the British cannon continued to rain steel on the peninsula. Below them on Morton's Point they could see fresh troops landing.

As the tall, balding colonel passed down the line, complaints and querulous questions fell on him from all sides. Would there be another attack? If the generals in Cambridge couldn't spare water, why didn't they send beer? If General Ward would not send reinforcements, couldn't he at least send replacements for the deserters? How long would the British keep fighting? Where could they get more powder?

Prescott said nothing. Quietly he ordered Lieutenant

Colonel Robinson to slice open three useless artillery cartridges left behind by Captain Gridley, and distribute the powder to those who needed it most. Then he sprang to the wall of the redoubt. "I tell you men," he roared above the continuing British bombardment, "if we check them once more they will never come back. The best soldiers in the world cannot take the losses we have given them." Down the line grimy faces came aglow and the defenders of Breed's Hill answered with a brief cheer.

Prescott with his ferocity was not the only man in the redoubt who played a vital role in keeping up American courage. Warren was there too, laughing and joking the men out of their uneasiness with his cocky gaiety. "Lick them once more, boys, and they'll never come back. We can drink tea in peace for the rest of our lives."

American spirits needed such lifting. To Peter Brown and Amos Farnsworth and Peter Salem the scene before them now was anything but a herald of victory. Below on the right the town of Charlestown burned fiercely. The steeple of the church toppled with a great crash and a gush of flame; the roofs and walls of every house were enveloped with darting orange tongues, and a huge pall of smoke drifted slowly out across the harbor. Down at the base of the hill the Americans could see the British officers, their gorgets glittering in the sun as they bowed their heads in a grim conference. On the water the sloops and ships of the line still poured a thunderous and relentless cannonade on hapless Charlestown, the Neck and every other part of the peninsula where an American showed his head. The roar of the guns no longer bothered the men on Breed's Hill; the sound had become routine, like heat and thirst and weariness. But nevertheless their thunder must have remained a symbol reminding them with every blast that they were challenging with their little fort and puny muskets the might of an empire.

Thus far Prescott's casualties, in comparison to the British, were negligible. He had less than two dozen wounded and only two or three killed. Benjamin Prescott's shoulder wound, which he received during the second assault, had by now soaked his sleeve with blood. During the lull his uncle noticed it and ordered him to the rear. The youngster protested violently. As long as he could lift a gun, he wanted to keep fighting. His uncle compromised: he was permitted to remain in the redoubt, but not on the firing line. "You have done enough for one day," the colonel said. The stoic sergeant reluctantly obeyed.

Behind the redoubt Major Willard Moore was suffering the "death thirst." One of his sergeants, who had helped carry him from the breastwork to the shelter of the redoubt, hailed the regiment's drummer boy, Robert Steele. "You are young and spry," he said. "Run in a moment to some of the stores and bring some rum. Major Moore is badly wounded."

This was no small order, with British batteries covering Charlestown peninsula with a thunderous rain of shot and shell. But Robert, and Benjamin Ballard, a Boston boy of his own age, obeyed without an instant's hesitation. Outside they thought for a moment of descending to blazing Charlestown, the most likely place to find rum. But the town looked a little too hot for comfort. Fortunately Benjamin knew the area well and suggested they make a dash to the Neck, where there was a public house which would undoubtedly be glad to donate a pint to the cause.

As the two boys raced down the shell-torn rear slope of Breed's Hill and skirted Bunker Hill just behind them, they were bewildered to see what looked to their inexperienced eyes like thousands of fresh American troops on Bunker, not one of whom was making the slightest attempt to reinforce the weary handful of fighters on Breed's. The boys were not dreaming. They had the dubious privilege of

seeing, close up, the climax of the monumental confusion
behind the American lines.

In the lull after the second assault, Israel Putnam's mind
had immediately turned to his second line of defense on
Bunker Hill. He had mounted his weary old white horse
and spurred him once more up the half mile of sloping
ground between the two hills. There were men on Bunker
—just what the powder-shy troops in the line could use.
But when he reached the top, the fiery Connecticut campaigner had a rude shock.

These men on Bunker Hill were not acting like soldiers.
At least 500 of them were in the vicinity, but the ships of
the line and the battery on Copp's Hill had done more for
the royal cause than the eye of the civilian observer could
perceive from a Boston rooftop. The continuous stream of
shot and shell the British gunners poured across the hilltop
had thrown these green troops into chaos. They crouched
behind rocks and trees or lay prostrate on the ground, all
semblance of company and regimental order gone. This was
not too surprising, but what really outraged Putnam was
the conduct of the officers.

Samuel Gerrish was the senior officer in sight. The corpulent, talkative colonel had marched his men through the
fire on the Neck, but the more intense bombardment on
Bunker had shattered his nerves. He lay on the ground,
moaning that he was too exhausted to advance. Putnam
called on his captains to lead the men forward without their
colonel. They refused. The battle was as good as lost, they
whined. The artillery had retreated or given up, had it
not? They were not going down there to be slaughtered. Putnam went almost berserk with rage. Cursing, roaring, all
but foaming at the mouth, he rode up and down Bunker
Hill, flailing at the laggards with his sword. One unlucky
captain failed to duck, and Putnam broke his sword over his
recalcitrant head. But no amount of violent language could

pull these terrified men together. Probably it only demoralized them a little more. If any of them had some twinges of conscience, they told themselves that Putnam was a Connecticut man and had no authority to give them orders anyway.

Only two men responded to Putnam. One was Christian Febiger, a Dane, with considerable military experience in Europe. Gerrish, when his original group of captains had revolted against him, had had to recruit anyone and everyone he could find to retain his colonelcy; Febiger had been serving as Gerrish's adjutant. He now rallied a group of men near him with the aid of another professional soldier, Thomas Doyle. Only a few months ago Doyle had been a member of General Gage's army; his Irish antipathy to England, plus the invitations of the provincials, had persuaded him to desert. Coolly ignoring the cannon, he and Febiger collected a company of men and marched them down the hill. They took up a post in the gap between the rail fence and the breastwork, where everyone, including Putnam, thought the main British effort would come, as it had in the first two assaults.

On the other side of Charlestown Neck the situation was no better. Colonel Scammans had marched his men to Lechmere Point to repel the British assault Artemas Ward feared there. But he was hardly needed. There were already two regiments there—Jonathan Ward's and Sargent's. A messenger finally caught up with him and told him to go to the hill. With almost inexcusable stupidity, he marched his men to Cobble Hill, a feeble elevation on the landward side of Charlestown Neck, and then sent word to Putnam, on Bunker Hill, asking if he were needed. One reason why he may have thought Cobble Hill was an important post was the company he found already ensconced on it.

Major Scarborough Gridley, the colonel's older son, was demonstrating that nepotism in the armed forces is a ruin-

ous vice. He had been ordered to advance to the battlefield, but when he saw the shot bounding across Charlestown Neck, he decided he could do as much good by marching his guns to Cobble Hill on the safe side of the Neck and
engaging in an artillery duel with the bombarding *Glasgow*
and *Symmetry*. His captain, Samuel Trevett, was so disgusted by this cowardice that he defied Gridley's orders and
led his men and two guns across the Neck to the fight. A few
minutes later, Colonel James Frye came along, leading one
of the companies from his regiment which had been withheld from Prescott's force last night. "Major Gridley," he
said. "What are you doing here? They need those guns on
Charlestown." Gridley insolently replied that he thought they
were more useful right here. Frye had no authority to con-
tradict him; he shrugged and departed for the battlefield,
and Gridley began unlimbering his guns for his idiotic target practice. He must have known he was being ridiculous—
the two ships were at least a mile away and even at close
range Gridley's four-pound guns could have scarcely dented
their planking.

A moment after he opened fire, along came Colonel
Mansfield and his regiment, bound for Bunker Hill. Apparently not satisfied to make a fool of himself alone, young
Gridley hailed the colonel and ordered him to take a position on the hill with him, to "protect" his guns. Since the
young man was considered a great authority in the army,
thanks to his father's reputation, Mansfield promptly obeyed
him. Scammans arrived a few minutes later, so the two colonels and their 700 men with full ammunition pouches sat
out the battle watching Gridley fire his pop guns at the two
ships.

On Prospect Hill, Colonel Thomas Gardner paced up
and down in a fury of frustration as the sounds of firing
rolled across the fields from Charlestown. He had been one
of the most ardent advocates of this adventure and he wanted

to share as equally in the danger. But no orders came from Artemas Ward. Frantically Gardner sent a messenger racing to headquarters begging for permission to advance. He wanted to expiate, once and for all, the memory of that humiliating retreat before Lord Percy's cannon.

One company in Gardner's regiment was even more impatient than the colonel. They were all from Charlestown. Most of the men had not been home since April 19, when they had marched with their minute company to join the fight along the Lexington road. When Lord Percy retreated to Charlestown, their wives and children had fled a few minutes before he arrived, because they were afraid his troops might take out their frustration on them. Twenty-year-old Timothy Thompson, who was the company sergeant, was typical of the rest. He owned a carpenter shop and a house on Charlestown's Back Lane, and his young wife Mary had left a pot of beans on the stove and loaves of bread in the oven when she fled with her father and friends. They met Percy crossing the Neck, and a young boy in their party was killed by a potshot from an angry regular. Now these Charlestown soldiers could see from their hilltop the flames consuming their homes and shops and they became incoherent with rage and frustration. Twice their captain, Josiah Harris, went to Colonel Gardner and begged him to let them march to the fight alone. But the soldierly colonel refused. They must wait for orders. Finally, the word came, on the lips of an all but breathless messenger. "Advance!" With a cheer the men surged forward on the double.

After them came Colonel Jonathan Ward's regiment, those same rugged men from Worcester who had done so much to spread the revolution across Massachusetts. They too had been sending messengers asking General Ward's permission to advance from Lechmere Point. They were several hundred yards behind Gardner and they paused to let his men get across the Neck. As they stood in the road a horseman rode up and shouted: "Who gave you orders to advance?"

"General Ward," was the reply.

"The Committee of Safety countermands it," the messenger shouted and galloped away. No one, in the excitement, was later able to identify him, though several of the men said he was Dr. Benjamin Church. Few of these Worcester men were likely to know the plump traitor; it is very possible that it was he sowing confusion up and down the American lines, as he had tried to do before.

Colonel Ward was perplexed. The Committee of Safety had absolute authority. Did he dare to refuse the order? Captain Seth Washburn, one of his more pugnacious officers, decided for him. "I don't care who gave that order," he swore, "I say it's a Tory order, and we should ignore it." Without waiting for Colonel Ward, he led his company across the fire-swept Neck on the dead run. Two other companies followed him and Ward, mortified to stay behind, left the rest of his regiment in the road and raced after them.

Over in Roxbury, opposite Boston Neck, were 7,000 of the best troops in the American army. Throughout the afternoon, Artemas Ward remained fearful that the British might launch an assault at this gateway to Cambridge, and Lord Percy, in charge at Boston Neck lines, did his best to maintain the illusion. Every cannon he had thundered away at the American positions. General Thomas was so alarmed he felled trees across the streets of the town, and one regiment took up a post of ambush in the Roxbury cemetery, with two cannons "placed to give it to them unaware, should the regulars come." But the regulars did not come; they had no men to send. The only casualty was the daughter of John Trumbull, the Connecticut governor. She arrived in Roxbury that day to join her husband, Colonel Jedediah Huntington, and was so terrified by the bombardment that she went insane and died several days later.

Ward himself was so concerned over a possible attack from this direction that he left his headquarters early in the afternoon and examined the Roxbury defenses personally. Thomas, who had done little in the way of building fortifications, undoubtedly told him once more that he could not spare a man.

Colonel Gerrish and his men on Bunker Hill were not the only malingerers. Captain John Chester, the soldierly head of the Wethersfield, Connecticut company, tells of waiting impatiently with the other Connecticut men at the Red House Fort and finally being ordered to the field, after the fighting started. (Before they marched they covered their blue uniforms with their homespun farm clothes; they were the only company in the army with uniforms and they felt they might make conspicuous targets.) As they came down Cambridge Road to the Neck, Chester tells of seeing whole companies without so much as a corporal commanding them. "One in particular fell in the rear of my company and marched with us," he related. "The captain had mustered and ordered them to march and told them he would overtake them directly but they never saw him until the next day."

As Chester's men came up Bunker Hill the conduct and deployment of the American troops there made his blood boil. More than once he saw as many as twenty men carrying away a man wounded by the British bombardment when "not more than three could take hold of him to advantage." The rest of the troops were on their bellies behind rocks, haycocks and apple trees, completely disorganized and uncommandable. One large body of troops, led by an officer, passed Chester, going the wrong way. The young Connecticut captain thought this was strange and asked them what they were doing.

"Retreating," said the officer in charge.

"By whose order?" Chester asked angrily.

The officer admitted he had no orders and began to march his men on down the road toward Cambridge. With a roar of rage, Chester ordered his men to cock their muskets. "Either you get up that hill," he said, "or I will order my men to fire on you." Grumbling, the slackers obeyed; Chester never saw them again, but it is a safe bet that they easily lost themselves in the tangle of regiments on Bunker and did no fighting.

Another story, a curious mixture of cowardice and courage, comes from Oliver Morseman, a private in Colonel Asa Whitcomb's regiment. When Gardner's regiment advanced, 100 of the Whitcomb men under the leadership of their major decided to follow them, although they had no orders to do so. But when they reached Charlestown Neck and saw the cannon balls whistling across it, the major lost his nerve. "We have come without orders," he said. "Every man return to camp." Out of the ranks stepped Captain Benjamin Hastings, nearly seventy years old. "Boys," he said, "you that are not afraid follow me, for I will go onto that hill or die in the attempt." Morseman and thirty-three others followed the veteran and joined the men behind the rail fence.

Meanwhile Robert Steele and Benjamin Ballard, on their quest for water for the dying Major Moore, arrived gasping for breath among the cluster of houses near Charlestown Neck. Cannon balls from the *Glasgow* and *Symmetry* whirred over their heads, and ringshot fell hissing all around them. But they were oblivious to the fact that they were now in a prime target area. They found the public house readily enough and were curiously surprised that there was not a customer in sight. "I stamped and called out to rally some persons," Robert reported. A voice answered from the cellar. The boys told him they were in search of rum and the voice in the cellar told them they could take anything they pleased. Shouting above the roaring guns, Robert, with a wonderful combination of courage and innocence, said: "Why do you stay down in the cellar?"

"To keep out of the way of the shot," the voice replied hollowly.

Robert seized a brown, two-quart earthen pitcher and had filled it almost to the top from one cask, when he found it was wine. He threw it out and tried the next cask, which by good fortune was the much needed rum. Benjamin Ballard, meanwhile, found a pail and filled it with water. Lugging their liquid loads, the two boys trotted out into the bombardment which had made cowards of captains and colonels and began the perilous hike back to Breed's Hill.

Down on the water's edge, General Clinton had almost completed the quarter-mile march to the field of battle with his shambling, bloodstained column of wounded volunteers when Howe's revived field artillery began blasting away at the American lines. Howe did not know Clinton was coming. From where he stood, on the other side of Breed's Hill, his colleague was invisible. He pointed with his sword at the rail fence, and his double line surged forward once more. Most of the regulars were fighting in their shirtsleeves now, like their American cousins behind the barricades.

That these men, whose losses were already among the heaviest of any British army in history, should go forward once more, against an enemy whom they believed outnumbered them three to one, is a magnificent tribute to their soldier's creed. When a French marshal, a few years later, remarked, "the British infantry is the greatest in the world. Thank God there is so little of it," he was thinking of the kind of courage William Howe and his soldiers displayed at Bunker Hill. Fortescue, the official historian of the British army, says bluntly that their return to a third attack, after the fearful losses they had taken, makes Bunker Hill "one of the greatest feats of arms ever credited" to the British soldier.

On they came, Pigot and his men again breasting the murderous slope of Breed's Hill, while the flames of Charlestown roared almost at their backs. There were few snipers left now. The fire had reached the outermost buildings. The marines had cleared away the opposition along the stone walls behind the redoubt. The few men that might have hung on there had been persuaded by the first two assaults that they were more needed at the rail fence.

Everything in Howe's advance certainly seemed to suggest this was a sound assumption. His battered grenadiers and light infantry were marching once more into the same muskets that had twice smashed them back so savagely. Suddenly the artillery, which had been firing more or less indiscriminately at the breastwork and the fence, advanced to within 900 feet of the rail fence lines, wheeled and opened up entirely on the breastwork. From this new position they were as Howe predicted able to enfilade the lower half of the breastwork. As grape and solid shot poured down their line, the Doolittle regiment, from which most of the men at the breastwork came, panicked. Their commanding officer, Willard Moore, was dying behind the redoubt. There was no one to steady them. They could have held part of the breastwork—to enfilade the entire line the British artillery would have had to fire from behind the rail fence. But they did not stop to consider such tactical niceties. Some simply took to their heels. Most of them scrambled wildly up the hill to the comparative safety of the redoubt.

For a few moments, the Americans had artillery to answer this deadly fire. Captain Samuel Trevett arrived with his two guns and unlimbered in the gap between the breastwork and the rail fence. Colonel Gridley himself took charge of the little battery. But not even he could do anything with another group of untried inexperienced gunners. The veteran British artillerymen answered the first American rounds with a furious barrage of shot which smashed one of Trevett's guns and sent his men fleeing for shelter. He,

Gridley and seven loyal men were left with a single gun. Then a bullet from a British musket caught Gridley in the thigh and Trevett had to detach two of his men to carry him to the rear. The young captain struggled to man his gun, but his men, completely unnerved by the continuing British fire, were all thumbs. There is no record of them getting off another round before they were forced to run for their lives by William Howe's surprise.

Moments after the artillery began hammering the breastwork, orders were shouted along the British lines, and the advancing ranks swung sharply to the left. All but the light infantry shifted their attack from the rail fence to the breastwork and the redoubt. Before the rail fence the light troops laid down a screen of diversionary fire, which immobilized Stark and his men. It was a neatly planned maneuver. But Howe once more discovered he was dealing with poorly trained troops, not as dependable as the veterans he had led under Wolfe. As the ranks swung to the left, they opened and fired a rolling volley. To the general's horror, the men in the rear ranks, firing up the hill at an angle toward the retreating defenders of the breastwork, sent most of their bullets into the backs of the regiments ahead of them.

"Cease fire! Cease fire!" Howe shouted, frantically smashing at men near him with his sword. "Your one hope is your bayonets, men. Your bayonets."

All along the line officers restored order at the point of their swords. Not even the penultimate frustration of shooting each other could stop the British now. They surged forward again, some of their sergeants shouting, "Conquer or die!" The honor of the army, the fate of the empire, trembled in the balance.

Up in the Breed's Hill redoubt, Prescott saw, at a glance, what Howe was doing. With barely 400 men, including the refugees from the breastwork, the Massachusetts colonel was left to repel a three-sided assault from almost 1,500 regulars. For a moment Prescott must have looked with desperate hope toward the rail fence. There were over 1,500 men there. Could they attack Howe from the rear and throw him into total confusion? The New Hampshire and Connecticut men did not move from behind their barricade. They were busy answering the light infantry shot for shot, and they did their best to knock out Howe's artillery. All of the gunnery officers and nine of their men were wounded before the day was over.

The last thing green troops learn is when to attack. Moreover, the field artillery was alert to the possibility and Stark would have had to lead his men through a hail of deadly grape. The New Hampshire veteran undoubtedly had a healthy respect for those light infantry skirmishers, even if there were barely 150 of them. He knew, too, that regular troops, trained to obey orders promptly, can wheel and meet a new adversary with no trouble whatsoever, and Howe would certainly have been delighted to see his rail fence tormentors venturing into the open field where his regulars could get at them with their bayonets. So Stark was forced to let Prescott fight on alone.

In the same crowded minutes, Gardner and his men arrived on top of chaotic Bunker Hill to find Israel Putnam still storming and cursing at the fragments of companies and regiments cowering in terror of the British bombardment. Putnam had given up all hope of getting them into the lines and had returned to his obsession of the morning: to complete the flimsy fortifications he had begun on Bunker's crest. He could not command even this much cooperation from the panic-stricken Massachusetts men. God Himself probably could not have gotten them to stand erect and swing picks and shovels with those fearsome British cannon balls hissing around them. Almost distracted with rage, Putnam took one look at Gardner's well-officered, disciplined companies and ordered him to work on the unfinished entrenchments. It seems incredible that Putnam could have given such an order while Prescott, a quarter of a mile away, would have traded his farm for the fresh ammunition and powder in Gardner's pouches.

Here Putnam was hamstrung by the total absence of staff officers in the American army. He had no idea what was happening in the redoubt. He was also the victim of his own inexperience. Never had he and Prescott discussed, much less attempted to work out a coherent plan for a withdrawal to Bunker Hill. Prescott's mind was inflexibly set in the opposite direction—to hold his fort on Breed's Hill to the last man. Moreover, Putnam was soon to discover that it was not easy to withdraw several thousand men to secondary positions under fire. These were tactics far better suited to a small, well-knit body of rangers. But the order was given and the obedient Gardner told his men to stack their muskets and go to work with the entrenching tools.

In the redoubt, Robert Steele and Benjamin Ballard had just arrived, bearing their borrowed rum and water. "It went very quick," Robert recalled later. And added: "We found our people in confusion and talking about retreating." Prescott grimly confined the retreating to talk. Quickly he filled the gaps in his firing line with the men from the breastwork and sternly ordered every man to hold his fire until he gave the command. This time no one disobeyed. Veterans now, they crouched on their firing platform, heads down, while artillery fire and musketry from the advancing red ranks rattled harmlessly against the solid log walls.

The British fire was not completely harmless, however. Young Sergeant Prescott, who probably never had the slightest intention of obeying his uncle's order to remain in the rear of the redoubt once the fighting started, seized a musket and rushed to take his place beside his men on the firing line. As he charged past the square mouth of the sally port, a one in a thousand shot from the field artillery cannon struck him in the body, mangling him terribly. He died instantly.

Outside on the slope the oncoming British ranks were suffused with a strange, almost wild enthusiasm. In our era of automatic weapons the frontal assault seems as hopelessly out of date as a knight in armor, but there was a certain logic in the maneuver which almost had to be experienced to be understood. The glitter of arrayed bayonets, the relentless beat of drummers, swept a man out of himself into emotion that was half pride and half courage. He lost consciousness of himself as a target and became part of an invincible wave. Or so his general hoped.

On came the scarlet ranks, to a quickening drumbeat now, past the bodies of their dead without so much as a glance. Occasionally a man slipped on grass that was wet with blood. Otherwise there was not the ripple of a break in the geometric line. Then, with their bayonets in the classic position, they hurled themselves forward at the uncannily silent rebel fort.

Inside the redoubt Prescott was like a coiled spring. "Remember," he snarled, "every shot must count. Don't fire unless you have a target."

The click of cocking hammers filled the sultry air.

"Now."

As one man the Americans rose up on three sides of the redoubt, their guns leveled. There was the scarlet line less than thirty yards away.

"Fire!" Prescott snapped.

Every finger pressed a trigger simultaneously. The redoubt belched flame and smoke and everywhere there were huge gaps torn in the British front rank.

For the stunned regulars, it seemed like the first two assaults all over again. All along the line regiments wavered as wounded men fell crying for help and others stumbled over them and the bodies of new dead. Then, whipped by the drumbeat and the roars of their officers, they closed the gaps and came on again.

Once more the redoubt belched flame and men toppled like wooden soldiers in a windstorm. Veteran Major Spendlove slumped to the ground with a bullet in his chest as he shouted the Forty-third into the musket smoke. Major Arthur Williams of the Fifty-second toppled as he sprang across the ditch. But Captain Harris and Lieutenant Rawdon led a patched-together company of grenadiers past these senior officers into the ditch and up on the berm—the narrow ledge of earth between the wall of the redoubt and the ditch. Ordinarily this was tantamount to victory. "There are few instances of regular troops defending a redoubt until the enemy were in the very ditch of it," Rawdon wrote later. A musket ball sizzling through his catskin cap quickly convinced the young Earl and his captain that Prescott's men were uninterested in fighting by the professional soldier's rulebook. They continued to man their firing walls and pour shot after shot into the grenadiers and infantry who were in the ditch or hesitating beyond it.

Harris answered courage with courage. Shouting for his men to follow him, he started to scale the ferociously defended barrier. Twice he got his leg over it and was smashed back by the defenders using their muskets as clubs. The third time a gun went off less than a foot from his head and a ball cut a vicious furrow through his scalp. He toppled back into Rawdon's arms unconscious. Rawdon thought he was dead and began to drag him off to the right, so he would not be trampled. The movement restored Harris to consciousness, and he groaned: "For God's sake let me die in peace." Rawdon ordered four grenadiers to take the captain back to the boats.

At the same time he saw Major Williams writhing in agony in the ditch and ordered young Ensign Hunter to get a surgeon for him. By now Hunter and a few other officers and men were also crouched under the wall of the redoubt. The other officers seconded Rawdon and told the ensign to get a surgeon for the dying major. The white-faced teen-ager simply shook his head. "Though a very young soldier," Hunter says, "I had sense enough to know that I was much safer close under the works than I could be at a few yards from it, as the enemy could not depress their arms suffi-ciently to do any execution to those that were close under, and to have gone to the rear to look for a surgeon would have been almost certain death; indeed, the Major was not a very great favorite with me as he had obliged me to sell a pony that I had bought for seven and sixpence."

Harris' grenadiers, returning in the crisis the kindness and consideration he had shown them, obeyed Rawdon with-out question and carried their captain into the line of fire, toward the boats. Before they had gone ten yards, three of them were wounded, one of them seriously, but they did not stop until they had Harris safely out of range.

In front of the redoubt, Rawdon, Hunter and the other officers were still trapped beneath the walls while most of their troops milled in confusion on the edge of the ditch, forgetting their orders to rely on the bayonet and firing at the Americans on the wall. Pigot, on the left, was having the same trouble. The marines and the Forty-seventh had closed to within ten yards when the wall came alive with Americans and another volley threw the British ranks into a tangle of dead and wounded. Roaring and cursing, Pitcairn held his men with magnificent leadership, refusing to let them re-treat, begging them not to fire. "The bayonet. The bayo-net. Form up. Form up." He shouted. Without him, the marines would almost certainly have run. At this moment, Peter Salem thrust his immensely long gun over the para-pet; through the shifting smoke he could see, and probably hear, Pitcairn shouting to his men. Grimly, the young Negro took aim and pulled the trigger. Pitcairn clutched his chest and slumped to the ground. With a cry his son ran to his side. His father told him to return to his men but the young lieutenant refused, and with the help of two enlisted marines he carried Pitcairn to the boats.

Adjutant John Waller of the marines took over. "I had all I could do to form two companies on our right," he says, "which at last I effected, losing many of them while it was performing. Major Pitcairn was killed close by me with a captain and a subaltern; also a sergeant and many of the privates; and had we stopped there much longer the enemy would have picked us all off. I saw this, and begged Colonel Nesbitt of the Forty-seventh to form on our right in order that we might advance with our bayonets to the parapet. I ran from right to left and stopped our men from firing; while this was doing, and when we had got in tolerable order, we rushed on, leaped the ditch under a most sore and heavy fire."

On the right, Howe's officers struggled to get more men across the ditch, to support Rawdon and his little group beneath the walls. Howe himself was of no use. As the attack shifted from the rail fence to the redoubt, he was left in the rear, and as he came across the field after the charging troops, a spent ball, probably fired by one of the men at the fence, struck him in the foot. Major Small rushed to his assistance and supporting himself on Small's shoulder, the general limped after his men. Small himself had a ball in the arm, but he insisted on serving as the general's crutch.

As Howe's men charged into the smoke of the ditch, they saw one of the most amazing demonstrations of reckless courage in their experience. Above the breastwork loomed a tall, broad-shouldered young American, firing one musket after another in startling succession. Unlike the other defenders of the fort, who ducked to reload, he scorned the gesture; obviously other men were loading his muskets for him. The regulars soon saw why "the sharpshooter," as they quickly dubbed him, received such service. He was a dead shot and he aimed at nothing but officers. In the seven or eight minutes of confused fighting in front of the redoubt, one British soldier estimated he picked off no less than twenty. Finally a sergeant of the grenadiers charged through the smoke and fired at point-blank range. The sharpshooter was seen no more.

On all sides of the fort, Americans kept up a destructive fire as the British poured into the ditch and kicked and cursed their way through the obstructive jumble of fence rails and bushes and sticks the Americans had thrown into it. But there were no longer any volleys which could check with a massive stroke the whole advance. More and more men were running out of powder and musket balls; even the nails and bits of rock they stuffed into their musket muzzles were gone. They knew, now, it was impossible to stop the scarlet wave that was engulfing them. "Suddenly," reports Waller, the marine adjutant, "their fire went out like a spent candle."

Inside the redoubt there was desperation, but not a breath of retreat. In the crucible of this grim moment, these young farmers were transformed from a crowd of grumbling individualists into one magnificent body, animated by William Prescott's indomitable courage. They were Prescott's men and Prescott had sworn he would die rather than be captured. With amazing calm the colonel retained command. Someone found another artillery cartridge and this was ripped open and the powder distributed with frantic haste. Those with bayonets were ordered to man the breastwork when their powder ran out; they were less than fifty. A force of men without bayonets, led by Joseph Warren, Prescott stationed in the rear of the redoubt to fire on anyone coming over the top.

Onto the breastwork, on three sides, came the bristling

bayonets. Now, certainly, was the moment of surrender. No regular soldier fought on after his position had been carried by storm. But Prescott's men were still Prescott's men. The few with bayonets and others using muskets as clubs met the wave of steel head on. From the rear of the fort a last volley from Warren's detachment swept the right flank breastwork clean. But on the left, Pigot's men, the marines and the doughty little brigadier in the lead, were pouring over the wall unchecked. Pigot was too small to get a leg over the parapet, but he scampered up a tree just outside and swung himself over. Then the red tide was flowing over right, left and center, and the floor of the fort became a maelstrom of struggling, flailing bodies.

In an agony of frustration, Prescott shouted incomprehensible orders to his desperate men. "Twitch their guns away," he roared. "Use your guns for clubs. Let them have those rocks in the face." For a moment they were successful. They actually tore some guns out of British hands and began clubbing their owners with them. Others flung rocks and punched and kicked. The stunned British fell back a few steps. "Surrender, you rebels," shouted a captain. "We are no rebels," Prescott roared. But more regulars poured over the walls, and bare hands and rocks quickly proved no match for men trained to use the bayonet. Americans were twisted in agony on those fourteen-inch blades before Prescott's anguished eyes, and he himself was soon parrying thrust after thrust with his sword. "Give way men, give way," he shouted. "Save yourselves. Run quick, but don't run too thick. That way they won't have such good shooting."

Prescott himself refused to run. Again and again cursing British infantrymen lunged at him with their bayonets and he turned them away with his sword. His loose coat probably saved his life. In the four or five frantic minutes of melee in the fort, bayonets turned it into a shredded tatters, and even his waistcoat had long gashes in it. But his grim determination not to be taken alive carried him out of the fort into the open ground beyond. Even here, he refused to do more than "step long, his sword up."

Clouds of choking dust arose from the dry floor of the fort, making it almost impossible for the wrestling, cursing mob of men inside to tell friend from foe. The dust was so thick it obscured the exit and more than one American died because he blundered into a corner filled with British bayonets. Waller, the marine adjutant, described the bayonet work of the marines as "shocking"—on the lips of such a veteran the word covers a multitude of bloody deaths. But no matter where or how they died, the Americans died fighting. No quarter was asked and none was offered.

Many Americans leaped over the walls and fought their way through the milling regulars outside before they knew what was happening. Peter Brown was one of these. "I ran a half mile," Peter later wrote his mother, "while balls flew like hail stones and cannon roared like thunder." Captain Ebenezer Bancroft, one of those forlorn fifty with bayonets who were ordered to man the walls, had one shot left in his gun as the first British officer, Lieutenant Richardson of the Royal Irish, sprang up on the parapet. "The day is ours," roared Richardson. Bancroft rammed his bayonet into him and pulled the trigger. Richardson toppled backward off the wall, his shoulder shattered.

Beside Bancroft a man snatched up the dead Benjamin Prescott's musket and killed a captain of the Fifty-second as he came over the wall. But individual heroism from these few, such as Bancroft or Peter Salem, who was beside him with his bayonet, could not stop the next wave. In a moment, they were engulfed in the wild, dust-shrouded melee. Bancroft had his beloved French gun torn out of his hands. He in turn tore a musket out of the hands of a grenadier and killed him with his own bayonet. He lost this gun too and plunged over the wall. He landed beside a British soldier and started to run. In the first step, he realized that the regular would almost certainly shoot him in the back. Bancroft spun and smashed him in the face. The captain never forgot the astonished look the regular gave him as he toppled to the ground.

Blood streaming down his face, Colonel Bridge stumbled out of the rear of the redoubt after Prescott. A British officer had hacked him viciously on the head and neck with his sword. Black Cuffee Whittemore followed Bancroft over the wall. Outside he found a dead British officer. Though there were redcoats all around him, Cuffee with a true American passion for souvenirs, stopped to seize the officer's handsome sword, before running for his life.

Most of Prescott's men fought their way out the rear of the redoubt. They did not know it, but their lives were saved by Joseph Warren and a few of the men Prescott had stationed in the rear. Forming a solid block before the exit to the redoubt, they fought the British bayonets with clubs, rocks, sticks and fists and prevented the regulars from sealing off the line of retreat. They were a strange picture in the suffocating haze, the aristocratic Warren in his beautiful blue silk-fringed waistcoat and ruffled shirt, surrounded by the gaunt farmers in their homespun shirts and breeches. Prescott had sustained them all day with his steel calm, now Warren raised them to a pitch of pure ferocity. Never had the gasping, dust-choked British regulars seen such courage. It took them the better part of a minute to realize that they were alone in the fort, and Warren's rear guard was backing slowly through the exit, still fighting every step.

Outside the redoubt, the Americans found themselves surrounded by redcoats on three sides. Those who had not scaled the walls had poured around both sides, and those who had gone over the top were pouring out the rear exit behind them. But the British did not dare fire, because they were likely to hit each other. Slowly, Warren and his men backed down the slope. The doctor had a bayonet wound in the arm. He ignored it and with tears of rage on his face, he tried to rally some men to make a stand. Jonathan Clark, of Abington, who had been one of Warren's patients, begged him to retreat.

Warren was beyond reasoning; he shouted that he would never set the example to the "bloodybacks." Moses Parker and a handful of others stood with him. It was madness, of course. They had neither bayonets nor ammunition, and the entire British army was pouring down the hill toward them. Yet Warren's reckless courage saved some lives. The astonished British, seeing him summoning men to make a stand, hesitated for a few moments, long enough for most of the Americans to get away. Then an order was barked, ranks were formed and the regulars fired a massive volley. Warren was struck behind the ear as he turned to call one last time to his countrymen. He flung his hand to the wound and fell without a sound.

14

ALMOST certainly, there would have been some attempt to carry off Warren's body, if many of the Americans had seen him fall. But the first blast of British musketry which killed him wreaked equal havoc on those few who had lingered with him. Lieutenant Colonel Moses Parker fell with a shattered kneecap. James Dodge of Edinburgh, one of the last to leave the redoubt, fell with a ball in the body. Sixteen-year-old Corning Fairbanks died here, proving that courage was by no means limited to the veterans. Captain Henry Farwell was struck in the spine but somehow managed to stagger away. Amos Farnsworth took a ball in the arm but also stayed on his feet. Rugged Caesar Bason had one shot left and he flung up his musket, muttering to himself: "Steady Caesar, give 'em one shot more." A ball struck him in the thigh before he could pull the trigger. He staggered after Farwell and Farnsworth and a few hundred feet farther on he collapsed behind a fence. Captain Ebenezer Bancroft had his forefinger shot off. Lieutenant Spaulding of Prescott's regiment was struck in the head and died a few feet from Warren.

Now, minutes too late, Putnam saw the disaster overwhelming the redoubt. He had begun to descend Bunker's slope to regain his position of command at the rail fence when he realized that Howe was throwing all his weight at Prescott. "Gods curse them," he roared and spurred his horse furiously back up the slope to Gardner's men still digging in spite of the relentless British barrage. "Colonel. Your men. To the fort," Putnam shouted.

As Gardner led his men on the double down Bunker's slope, he saw the collapse of resistance in the redoubt, the sea of redcoats pouring over the parapets and around the sides.

Then the British formed and fired their first volley at the fleeing Americans. At close range their aim was moderately good. Men pitched forward under the impact of those murderous musket balls and others stumbled and were caught by those near them and were half carried, half dragged along. But some of the British fired as wildly as they had in the field before the grass fence and the bullets went over the heads of their running targets and fell among Gardner's regiment. One of the first shots struck the colonel in the groin. He collapsed in agonizing pain but managed to order his men forward. His grief-stricken son begged permission to carry him off but with spartan fortitude Gardner ordered him to the fight.

At the foot of Bunker Hill Gardner's men dropped behind trees and walls and stone fences and any other cover they could find and began firing ragged volleys at the oncoming British, checking them long enough to give most of the retreating defenders of Breed's Hill a chance to escape alive. Major Michael Jackson who was now commanding Gardner's troops was close enough to recognize a British captain with whom he had served against the French. "What, you damned rebel! Are you here?" the redcoated figure shouted and aimed his fusil at him. He and Jackson fired simultaneously. The ball caught Jackson in the side, but his belt deflected it enough to save his life. Jackson's shot also went home. The captain fell with a bullet in his chest.

Farther down the line John Chester's company went into action as the right wing of the British attack, seeing the resistance at the redoubt crumble, moved forward to encircle the retreating militiamen. For five or six minutes the fighting was as bloody as anything on the field that day. "We lost our regularity," Chester said later, "as every company had done before us, with every man loading and firing as fast as he could."

His lieutenant, Samuel Webb, who fought beside Chester, was more vivid: "My God, how the balls flew! When I was descending into the valley from off Bunker Hill at the head of our company, I had no more thought of ever arriving at the Hill again, than I had of ascending to heaven as Elijah did soul and body together, but after we got engaged, to see the dead and wounded around me, I had no other feeling but that of revenge. Four men were shot dead within five feet of me."

The fighting frequently shifted from point-blank musket duels to hand to hand. A regular came at Gershon Smith and Edward Brown, in Webb's company. He killed Smith with a bullet in the head and charged Brown with his bayonet. Brown fired his own gun, missed and seized the dead Smith's gun and missed with this one also—the regulars were not the only ones who missed at point-blank range. But Brown had the advantage of being fresh to the fight, while the Englishman had just spent an exhausting hour on Breed's Hill. As the regular sprang over the wall, Brown sidestepped the thrusting bayonet, tore the gun out of the man's hand and killed him with his own weapon.

The confusion produced comedy as well as tragedy. Captain Stickney of Newburyport was taking aim at the oncoming regulars when his colonel, Moses Little, ordered him to retreat. "The enemy's in the fort," he shouted.

Stickney said he was loaded and wanted to have "one more slap at them." As he took aim a grenadier came charging in from the side and bayoneted him in the thigh. "Accept quarter and you are my prisoner," roared the grenadier. "Not me," shouted the enraged Stickney. He started to run, and the grenadier grabbed the skirt of his coat. Stickney kept on running and left the regular standing there with the tail end of his coat in his hand.

The Americans had been firing their guns so fast they made no attempt to clean them before they rammed home the next charge. Normally a musket had to be cleaned after a half dozen firings or the burned powder would jam the barrel. Captain Abel Wilder of Doolittle's regiment, who like Stickney had fallen back from the breastwork to some fences on the rear of Breed's Hill, suddenly found his "long thin gun" completely stopped. Not far away, Captain Nathaniel Warner, still in the fight in spite of the battering his company had taken from the marines behind the redoubt, was taking aim through the smoke when his gun exploded in his face, showering him with metal. Although these are the only two certified reports, it is a safe bet that many other Americans were having trouble with their antiquated guns by now. Here is where the companies and pieces of companies which arrived late, such as Chester's men, the Gerrish detachment led by Doyle and Febiger and Jonathan Ward's men, used their full ammunition pouches and fresh guns with telling effect.

Seth Washburn and his men, from Ward's regiment, played a vital role in the rear guard along the rail fence. When the redoubt gave way, the stunned New Hampshire and Connecticut men suddenly realized they were now in danger of being cut off. A column of British infantry could seize that crucial crossroad immediately behind them and they would have to flounder through the fields along the Mystic shore to escape, while the British raked them from above. Still

Stark and Knowlton stood their ground until it was obvious that there was not an American alive on Breed's Hill; then they ordered their men to fall back, slowly. Their ammunition was almost exhausted, and Washburn and his men, with full pouches, moved in between them and the British to become a fighting rear guard. Beside them was the Charlestown company from Gardner's regiment. They had arrived too late to save their homes, but they were ferociously eager to take what revenge was available. Above Breed's Hill an enormous column of black smoke towered into the clear blue sky to remind them why they were fighting. Beside them fought the indefatigable Captain Walker and his man Frost, determined to get in one last lick of their own.

As they left the shelter of the rail fence, the British light infantry charged them with a shout, apparently regaining for a moment their old hope of cutting off the American rear. But a blast of fire from the rear guard changed their minds. Then the British artillery, delighted to find a new target, opened up, raking them and the retreating column of New Hampshire and Connecticut men with a shower of grape. Almost all the Connecticut and New Hampshire casualties were suffered in this retreat. Young Ashael Nims, of Stark's regiment, who had volunteered for the honor of Keene, fell here, with a grapeshot in his back, leaving his fiancée a premature widow.

Fighting from wall to wall, the rear guard fell back and the light infantry pursued them at a more cautious distance, keeping up a steady and by no means harmless fire. Here, at the last moment, Captain Walker's luck ran out. A ball shattered his leg and another smashed Frost's hip. They were left on the field; again, those who were last to retreat paid a harsh penalty for their courage.

Elsewhere Americans did a good job of carrying off their wounded. Two brothers, William and Jonas French, found

Prescott's captain, Henry Farwell, slumped against a fence. "I cannot live," he said. "Take care of yourselves." They ignored him, hoisted him up between them and carried him off. Captain John Davis of Frye's regiment, one of the defenders of the redoubt, was overtaken by a regular who confronted him with his bayonet and shouted, "You are my prisoner."

"I guess not," roared Davis and ran him through with his sword. A few feet farther down the hill he found a wounded private and hoisted him on his back. He carried him another 200 yards and began to stagger from exhaustion. Just ahead of them there was a board fence, which to Davis looked as insurmountable as a castle wall. "I don't see how we can get over that fence," he gasped. Just then, General Burgoyne on Copp's Hill solved the problem by sending a cannon ball smashing through it.

Captain Aaron Smith of Shrewsbury ducked behind a stone fence and began firing at the pursuing British. Beside him, when he looked down, he saw Caesar Bason, his leg drenched in blood. He was too weak to stand, but there was fight in Caesar yet. Together he and Smith set up a load and fire system; while Smith used Caesar's gun, the Negro reloaded Smith's weapon. Then Smith's gun was smashed by a bullet and the captain hoisted Caesar on his back and began retreating. But Caesar apparently was a big man and Smith was not. The pursuing British began gaining steadily on them and Smith began to run out of strength. "Put me down, Captain," Caesar said calmly. "I'm going to die anyway. You save yourself." The captain let him slide to the ground, but he could not desert him. Desperately he shouted to men rushing by, but in the thunder of cannon and muskets, it was impossible to attract anyone's attention. Only yards away he saw a squad of British soldiers coming on the double. "Go, Captain. Go," Bason said. "Next time you fight, give 'em one for Caesar." Cursing his own weakness, the captain joined the general retreat.

Not far away, Febiger and Doyle's men from Gerrish's regiment fell back in fairly good order, firing furiously. But on the slope of Bunker Hill, the Irish deserter toppled over with a British bullet in his chest—the only casualty the regiment suffered.

Seth Washburn's sergeant, John Brown, was shot through the thigh and the foot and was unable to walk. Captain Washburn lugged him on his back, with both their fourteen-pound muskets, until he was exhausted. Luckily he found the sergeant's brother, Perly Brown, and he and another man carried him to safety.

Private Isaac Livermore of this company had gone into action with a canteen of rum on his hip. As they retreated along the slope of Bunker, a British ball severed the canteen thong and it went rolling down the hill toward the pursuing British. Instead of congratulating himself for a narrow escape, the hotheaded private roared: "I'll be damned if I'll let the regulars have my rum" and went scrambling after it. He snatched it up barely a musket length from the amazed British and escaped in a shower of bullets. Others had equally close calls. Daniel Hubbard was very proud of his queue, which he wore braided and fastened in two strands. A bullet clipped one off. Washburn himself had a bullet through his cartridge box, another through his hat and four through his coat.

The refugees from the redoubt fled along the south road, which skirted the bottom slopes of Bunker Hill. The men from the rail fence, and the flèches, retreated in much better order up the road which ran across Bunker's crest. This was not, by any means, a place of refuge. Every available British gun was raining shot across the long semirectangular height. From the lower slopes of Breed's Hill the British infantry were adding their own wild volleys. The British were keenly aware that they themselves had supplied the Americans with the beginning of a fortification on the western end of the hill—the flèche which Percy's men had built the night after Lexington. They were determined to prevent the Americans from forming a second line of defense there.

They had little to fear. Barely three men in the entire American army had any thoughts about making a fight on Bunker Hill. One of them was Israel Putnam; it had been his idea from the beginning to fight the hill as hard as they had fought Breed's. But the British artillery had broken up all his desperate attempts to complete the fortifications. (The British flèche had never entered into his plans; it was, as far as Putnam was concerned, at the wrong end of the hill.) Now, wild with frustration, he rode up and down the crest pleading frantically with the retreating troops. Beside him old Seth Pomeroy, his musket shattered by a bullet, did his best to help him. But it was a hopeless task. The New Hampshire and Connecticut men, who had the discipline to make a fight, had no more ammunition. What remnants there were of the scrambled Massachusetts regiments lacked the discipline. The detachments of the fighting rear guard which retreated over Bunker probably numbered less than 400—not enough to handle almost 2,000 regulars, 800 of them fresh troops. The Second Marines and the Sixty-third Regiment now had landed and moved up to join Howe on Breed's Hill.

Even if the numbers had been equal, it was foolish to expect raw troops to stand in the open against regulars under such ferocious fire. A man was cut in two by a cannon ball. The concussion from another shot ripped off Colonel Jonathan Ward's cartridge box and threw him up in the air. Others fell in the continuous shower of musket balls. "The brow of Bunker Hill," said Major John Brooks, "was the place of great slaughter."

Ignoring the flying lead as usual, Putnam reined his horse in front of his unfinished entrenchments and swore he would not retreat a step. "For God's sake, stand and give them one shot more," he thundered at the men streaming by him. "Stand. We can stop them yet." Only one man, a Connecticut sergeant, paid the slightest attention to him. Determined to protect his general, he stood by him until the British were within ten paces, firing as they came. He fell with a ball through the heart. Putnam, with the miraculous luck which had protected him all day, was not touched. The sergeant's death shocked him into realizing the folly of throwing himself away for mere heroics. Besides, there was still hope of organizing a counterattack on the other side of the Neck. To the frustration of the British company, who were now but a bayonet-length away, he spurred his horse down the hill to join the general retreat.

Elsewhere on Bunker, Captain Samuel Trevett of the artillery, who had lost his two guns at the rail fence, saw Captain Samuel Gridley's two abandoned field pieces. One was too damaged to move, but with seven artillerymen of his company who remained with him, plus about thirty infantrymen, they began to drag it off. A British company came at them on a dead run, determined to stop them and to capture the prize. They fired a volley at point-blank range and Trevett's men threw up their hands, certain that they were dead, but the British hit only one man and while they reloaded, Trevett and the others dragged the gun down the north slope of Bunker to safety. It was the only one of their six cannon the Americans were able to save.

Colonel Gridley was carried to his sulky, which he had left on the western slope of Bunker Hill near the American hospital. Halfway down the hill, he was forced to abandon his transportation because the road was so badly torn up by the artillery fire. A moment later an explosive charge killed the horse and riddled the sulky with metal.

At the base of Bunker Hill Putnam and Prescott met face to face for the first time since the battle started. "Why did you not support me, General, with reinforcements as we agreed?" Prescott asked bitterly.

"I could not drive the dogs up," Putnam roared.

"You might have led them up," Prescott said and stalked onward.

The British pursuit was almost as chaotic as the American retreat. Were it not for the arrival of Clinton at the head of his heroic column of wounded volunteers, it probably would have lacked what little order and energy it did have. Howe welcomed Clinton effusively when he appeared beside him on Breed's Hill. The man who had helped conquer Quebec looked and acted more like a loser than a victor. All he could talk about was how close they had come to catastrophe. "My left was totally gone, totally," he said. His face was white with exhaustion and his exquisite uniform was a rumpled, sweat-stained, blood-spattered mess. He seemed incapable of commanding the troops around him. Clinton was so shocked by the situation that when he made notes on it for his memoirs he put the words in cipher: "All in confusion officers told me that they could not command their men and I never saw so great a want of order."

Pigot was vigorously pursuing the Americans from the redoubt along the south road, where his chief opposition was Gardner's regiment. But he was unable to do anything about Bunker Hill, where Putnam was then obviously trying to organize a stand. It was Clinton who with Howe's permission whipped the troops around him into a semblance of order and led a column up Bunker to stop Putnam's efforts to rescue the day.

In possession of Bunker, Clinton found that the Americans had taken cover in the cluster of houses on the seaward side of the Neck (where Robert Steele had found his rum). Clinton wanted to attack, and Lord Rawdon, with barely a dozen men left in his company, promptly volunteered, "which did him great honor," said the pugnacious Clinton. But he could not advance without Howe's permission, and he ordered the men to lay down a covering fire while he went back to get Howe's approval and bring up cannon.

By the time he reached Howe, Clinton's ideas had grown more grandiose. He wanted to carry out the remainder of their original operation and felt certain, if they continued the pursuit, they could still sleep in Cambridge that night. They had two fresh regiments, the Second Marines and the Sixty-third, which could lead the attack, and the rest of Howe's conquerors of Breed's Hill could follow.

Howe vetoed the plan. Too many of his officers were dead or dying in the tall grass behind him. The troops were too exhausted and most of their equipment was a quarter of a mile away, where they had flung it down before the third assault. Moreover, there was good reason to assume that the Americans would conduct the same kind of fighting retreat on the other side of Charlestown Neck, and they would be reinforced by fresh troops and militia from the nearby towns. Frustrated once more, Clinton could only expend his energy urging the artillery to Bunker Hill. The cannon quickly drove the Americans out of their houses on the Neck. At five o'clock, one hour and a half after William Howe began his advance from Morton's Point, the battle of Bunker Hill seemed to be over. But there were still bits and pieces of bloody epilogue.

On the slope of Breed's Hill Lieutenant Dutton of the Thirty-eighth sat down on the grass and pulled off his boots to ease his gouty feet. Two Americans came out of one of the few unburned houses on the outskirts of Charlestown and strolled toward them. Nervously Dutton's orderly pointed them out. "They are coming to surrender and lay down their arms," Dutton said, nursing his aching toes. It was perfectly logical. The battle had been won and according to conventional rules of warfare, any troops left on the field automatically became prisoners. The Americans came closer. Two shots rang out and Dutton and his orderly fell dead within twenty yards of their regiment. The Americans spun and ran, but Dutton's company cut them off and bayoneted them.

On Charlestown Neck, Major John Brooks, at last released by General Ward from staff duty, was coming into the fight with two companies when he met the first of the fleeing Americans. He struggled desperately to stop them and form some kind of order out of the mass of disorganized, often unarmed men, but it was useless. Farther up the road Colonel Gardner was being carried to his deathbed. He raised himself on his litter and forgetting his pain begged the Americans to regain their courage and form into some kind of order. No one listened to him either. These youngsters had seen and heard enough cannon and musket fire for one day and were intent on only one thing—putting distance between themselves and the British guns.

Captain John Chester's company came off the field in moderately good order, and Putnam found the other half of his own regiment, led by Lieutenant Colonel Experience Storrs, advancing down the Charlestown road as he came over the Neck. They were followed by Joseph Spencer's Connecticut regiment, also ordered too late to the field. Swept with a renewed sense of power by the sight of men who would obey his orders, Putnam promptly rallied them and decided to lead a counterattack. At this moment, the British twelve-pounders on Bunker opened up; the veteran campaigner rode across the Neck and took a long look at the British position. They were busily bringing up more cannon and were entrenched behind the flèche which they had built on April 19. Mournfully, Putnam decided he did not want to command an attack which could easily become a rout. He ordered his men to wheel and follow him to Prospect Hill, where he put them to work throwing up fortifications against a possible British advance. Prospect, just behind the Neck, commanded the Cambridge road. Putnam had begged Ward's permission to fortify it weeks ago. Now he got his way, without waiting for orders.

Meanwhile, in Cambridge, William Prescott was trying to organize his own counterattack. In Ward's study, he pounded his fist on the commanding general's desk and demanded three fresh regiments, with bayonets. He swore if he got them he would drive the British into the sea before nightfall. Ward wisely declined to cooperate. There were less than ten barrels of powder left in the American camp, and there were not three regiments left with enough organization to march. Gravely, the portly Puritan from Worcester thanked Prescott for his service. "You have done enough for one day, Colonel," he said. "See to your wounded and then get some rest."

In Medford, Major Andrew McClary gathered bandages for his wounded men and sprang back on a commandeered horse to bring them to a hospital set up on Ploughed Hill not far from Charlestown Neck. There he met his good friend Captain Henry Dearborn and together they had a drink. McClary was on fire with enthusiasm about the way the men had conducted themselves on the field, and the two friends talked and laughed excitedly together for fifteen or twenty minutes. Then the major decided that they should return to the Neck with Dearborn's company to make sure the British were not planning any sudden move on Cambridge. Dearborn was more than willing. He assembled his men and they marched down to the Cambridge side of the Neck. The British were still bombarding heavily, but McClary went forward. Dearborn begged him to be careful.

McClary laughed enormously. "The cannon shot hasn't been made that will kill me yet!" he said. He strolled casually through the steel onto the peninsula and for ten minutes boldly reconnoitered the British activities on Bunker Hill. They were obviously not planning any advance. In fact, they were already hard at work with picks and shovels, throwing up defensive barricades. McClary came back across the Neck. "He was returning towards me," Dearborn says, "and was within twelve or fifteen rods of where I stood with my company when a random cannon shot from one of the frigates passed directly through his body.

"He leaped two or three feet from the ground, pitched forward and fell dead upon his face." Dearborn was to fight with notable ferocity in almost every major battle of the Revolution. The largest part of the reason is in his farewell to Andrew McClary. "He was my bosom friend; we had grown up together on terms of the greatest intimacy. . . . I loved him as a brother."

Meanwhile, down on Morton's Point the grim business of transporting the British wounded to Boston began. Captain Harris gives a vivid picture of his journey to the hospital. His faithful grenadiers, three of them ignoring their own wounds, carried him out of musket range and placed him in the shade of a tree some distance from the beach. The first boats were already shoving off for Boston when Holmes, Harris' orderly, "running about like a madman in search of me, luckily came to the place where I lay, just in time to prevent my being left behind, for when they brought me to the water's edge the last boat was put off, the men calling out 'they would take no more.' "

Again Harris' popularity helped save his life. "It is Captain Harris," Holmes shouted. The boat turned back and took him in. In the middle of the river Harris was seized with a violent attack of nausea and shivering. He found a blanket in the bottom of the boat and in spite of the heat of the day, he wrapped himself up in it. In Boston he found coaches, chariots and wheelbarrows arriving at the waterside to help the wounded to the hospitals. Gage already had a fairly efficient general hospital set up in the Manufacturing House, a large abandoned factory. But he was now forced to hurriedly commandeer warehouses and empty barracks to handle the unexpected deluge of wounded. The quality of these quarters can be estimated by Harris' testimony. He tells of being carried into the "hospital" and offered a chair by a kindly old lady, who was serving as a nurse. As he began to sit down, he recoiled in horror; the thing was "crawling with bugs."

Senior officers such as Pitcairn and Abercromby were not taken to the hospitals. They were carried directly to their quarters. As they lifted Abercromby into the boat, he said: "If you catch Old Put, don't hang him, he's a good soldier." He had a flesh wound in the side and was not thought to be seriously hurt. But the primitive medical practice of the day was destined to kill him.

When Lieutenant Pitcairn reached the Boston shore, he saw his father would never survive a long carriage ride through the uneven Boston streets to his regular quarters on North Square. He therefore carried him into a house only a few doors from the Charlestown Ferry, on Prince Street. General Gage, who had already heard of Pitcairn's wound, asked his personal physician, Dr. Walter Hastings, to see if anything could be done. On the way Hastings met a loyalist named Ewing, who was a good friend of the stricken major. Hastings asked him to come along. "We found him," said Mr. Ewing, "lying on a bed with a sheet thrown over him. The doctor told him that General Gage was very anxious about him and that he had made the visit by his request. Pitcairn, with his usual courtesy, requested the doctor to thank the general for thinking of him in a time of so much trouble and added that he believed that he was beyond all human aid. The doctor asked him where he was wounded. He laid his hand on his breast and said: 'Here, sir.' The doctor attempted to raise the sheet for the purpose of examining the wound. The major kept his hand on the sheet and said, 'Excuse me, it is useless. My time is short. You cannot do anything for my relief. My wounds must cause death immediately. I am bleeding fast internally.'

" 'But let me see the wound,' said the doctor, 'you may be mistaken in regard to it.' And again, he attempted to raise the sheet. The major pressed it to his bosom and said, 'Doctor, excuse me. I know you can do nothing for me and do not argue the matter with me,' adding with a smile: 'It is not a fair argument between two persons, one of whom has but a few minutes to live, while the other, I hope, has many years of life before him. Let me say a few words to you about my private concerns.'

"The doctor then drew back. I bade Pitcairn farewell and left him," Ewing said. "The doctor informed me that the major died within an hour afterwards."

Bringing the rest of the wounded over was a long bloody job. Counting officers, there were almost 1,000 casualties and no transport but the clumsy rowboats. For almost twenty-four hours, all Boston, loyalist and patriot, stared from their windows or stood in their doorways, numbed by sights and sounds which brought home as no oratory ever could, the meaning of Bunker Hill. Even the most ferocious Whigs forgot their politics at the sight of those suffering officers and men. Along Prince Street by the ferry women rushed to their doors with bandages and pitchers of cool water for them. The doctors and druggists of Boston volunteered en masse to serve in the hospitals. Young boys went to the wharves, and when there were no more carriages or carts, they carried wounded officers through the streets on chairs.

The eye-witness descriptions are charged with the shock of their spokesman: "In the first carriage was Major Williams, bleeding and dying, and behind him three dead captains of the 52nd Regiment; in the second, four dead officers; then another with wounded officers." One Tory tells of meeting a young soldier: "His white waistcoat, breeches and stocks were much dyed of a scarlet hue: I thus spoke to him, 'My friend, are you wounded?' He replied, 'Yes sir, I have three bullets through me.'—He then told me the places where; one of them being a mortal wound; he then with a philosophical calmness began to relate the history of the battle; and in all probability would have talked till he died, had I not begged him to walk off to the hospital; which he did, in as sedate a manner as if he had been walking for his pleasure."

Almost as bad as the suffering of the soldiers themselves were the wails and cries of the women of the enlisted men. All night long, as the privates and corporals were ferried back and lifted into carts to take them to the hospital, the women crowded the nearby streets, sobbing and praying, hoping to see the familiar face for which they searched. Many were Irish, and their grief-stricken keening chilled the marrow of the distraught Bostonians. Nor were these "common women" the only ones who knew sorrow. Lieutenant Dutton's wife sat in her room, her two small children beside her, and heard the news she had dreaded all day.

All through the sweltering night the doctors toiled in the hospitals. They did their best, but they were hampered by a medical education which had not yet advanced much beyond the knowledge of ancient Rome, and in the matter of antiseptics, had slipped behind. The quality of the British army surgeons also undoubtedly left something to be desired, since they were paid only four shillings a day. Usually the surgeon was a Scotsman, who, like Tobias Smollet, entered the service without either examination or diploma, knowing little more than how to "bleed a patient, give an enema, spread a plaster, and prepare a potion." He had to supply his own tools, and who paid for splints, bandages, lint, trusses, dressings, ointments, drugs and other sickroom necessities was never clearly spelled out. Often it was the hapless doctor.

John Ranby, British Surgeon General in 1775, had issued a set of instructions to the regimental surgeons not long before Bunker Hill. They are a frightening picture of eighteenth-century medical procedure. For all gunshot wounds, declared Dr. Ranby, "the fingers should be used to dislodge a ball." Long forceps were "too dangerous." If the ball could not be reached with the fingers, it should be left to work its way out. For skull wounds and other wounds in which there was not much loss of blood, Ranby advised the surgeon to take some blood out of the unlucky soldier himself. Bleeding was then considered the ultimate in medical treatment.

Wounds were first cleansed with lint, either dry or wet with oil, and bandaged lightly. Later, they were to be washed with a "digestive"—a substance used to draw pus —and then covered with a bread-and-milk poultice, with oil for moisture. For the first twelve days, a "cooling regimen" of medicines and diet was recommended, on the theory that this lowered the danger of infection. The empiricists among the medical men of the time had noticed that a man ran a fever with an infection, and concluded, with somewhat superficial logic, that keeping him cool would lower the chances of the infection taking root.

Unfortunately there was little or no interest in using clean bandages or instruments. A worn-out flag was considered good material for a bandage. Since lint was expensive, surgeons used the same sponge for dozens of wounds, even if some were ulcerated. The same surgical knife, uncleaned, was used to probe wounds in a hundred men. It never occurred to a doctor to wash his hands before probing with his fingers for bullets. There were no anesthetics. Before operating a man was given a grain of opium or a slug of rum and a bullet to bite on. The surgeon general advised his men to be as gentle as possible, but added: "You should act in all respects as if you were entirely unaffected by their groans and complaints."

Amputations were the favorite operation. They were considered essential if a bone was splintered. Lieutenant Page of Howe's staff lost his leg before morning, thanks to this dictum. Joint wounds were also considered especially menacing, and amputation was deemed advisable for them. The surgeons understood enough about the circulation to stop bleeding with a tourniquet. Petit's screw tourniquet was a favorite because "once applied it can be used by the patient himself." The tourniquet was left on after amputation, and here, too, there was little understanding of what caused infection.

For head wounds such as Captain Harris suffered, there was an even more extreme procedure, known as trepanning. This consisted of boring a hole through the back of the skull and removing a section of bone, to relieve the pressure on the brain. The regimental surgeon performed this operation on the young grenadier captain sometime during the night. He obligingly set up some mirrors so that Harris could actually see his own brains while the doctor cut out the bone. The operation saved his life—or more accurately, Harris recovered—and in a letter home a few weeks later, the captain humorously remarked that he was glad he had had a chance to see his brains, since he could now definitely settle all arguments about whether or not he had any. Years later in India he was to demonstrate he had an ample supply when he conquered Tipoo Sultan and became Lord Harris of Seringpatam.

Putnam's old friend, Colonel Abercromby, was not so lucky. His flesh wound festered and he died four days after the battle. Many years before, Abercromby had written to Robert Rogers of the Rangers: "I am certain . . . it is better to die with the reputation of a brave man, fighting for his country in a good cause, than either shamefully running away to preserve one's life, or lingering out an old age, and dying in one's bed, without having done his country or his King any service." It could never have occurred to him that he would meet his fatal bullet from an American musket, which may well have been fired by one of those same soldiers from whom bravery was "no more than he expected."

There were some heartbreaking scenes in those British hospitals in Boston that Saturday night. One officer tells of Pitcairn's son coming in to have his own wound treated. His uniform was bloody and there were tears running down his face. A friend asked him if he were badly hurt and he shook his head. "I have lost my father," he said. Nearby him was a wounded sergeant who had served under Pitcairn for almost two decades. "We have all lost a father," he said softly. Sometime before morning one of the wounded grenadiers who had helped Harris to safety died. The captain carried a silver button from his uniform with him for the rest of his life, to remind him of his sacrifice.

There was also great bitterness. Again and again the doctors dug out of the wounded men pieces of glass and twisted, rusty nails, which reinforced the theory that the Americans were barbarians.

Dr. Grant, one of the regimental surgeons, voiced his indignation in a letter home and incidentally gave a grim picture of the fate of the British wounded:

"I have scarce had time sufficient to eat my meals, therefore you must expect but a few lines. I have been up two nights, assisted by four mates, dressing our men of the wounds they received the last engagement. Many of the wounded are daily dying and many must have both legs amputated. The provincials had either exhausted their ball, or they were determined that every wound should be mortal.

Their muskets were charged with old nails, angular pieces of iron, and from most of our men being wounded in the legs we are inclined to believe it was their design not wishing to kill the men, but to leave them as burdens on us to exhaust our provisions and engage our attention, as well as to intimidate the rest of the soldiery."

The doctors were hardly in a mood to understand that the desperate Americans used any substitutes they could find when they ran out of bullets. Over 250 of the British wounded were to die within the week. Lack of fresh meat and vegetables was to kill many more in the weeks to come. Margaret Gage donated all the vegetables and meat in Province House to the injured men, but it was a pittance compared to their needs.

While American doctors toiled over English soldiers in Boston, the traitor Benjamin Church was working just as hard over the American wounded in Cambridge. It had apparently never occurred to General Ward or anyone else that there would be some wounded in the battle, and only after 300 bleeding men poured into Cambridge were hospitals hastily improvised in many of the large private homes. Church was put in charge and he worked throughout the night, along with Warren's pupil, William Eustis, and Warren's younger brother, John, also a doctor, who had rushed from Plymouth when he heard news of the fighting.

Doctors were so scarce that they drafted four Harvard undergraduates as surgeons' assistants. The same surgical limitations and ignorance about antiseptic procedures prevailed here, as in Boston, but they managed to save a few good men. They operated on Captain Henry Farwell, who had given himself up for dead, and extracted the bullet from his back. The captain eventually took the bullet home with him for a souvenir and lived another forty years.

The American officers showed a commendable concern for their wounded men. Captain Abel Wilder personally took

Samuel Bradish of his company to the hospital. The young
soldier had been accidentally shot in the back of the neck by
one of his comrades. The bullet had come out his eye. Somehow he managed to walk off the field. In the hospital he
was at first ignored by the feverishly busy doctors. Captain
Wilder demanded to know why and was told it was a waste
of time. He would certainly die within a few hours. Wilder
hit the ceiling and demanded immediate treatment. The
doctor reluctantly obeyed, and Bradish made an amazing
recovery.

Other seemingly less serious wounds were fatal, probably
because of the ever-present infections. Seth Washburn's sergeant, John Brown, whom he had carried off the field with
two balls in his leg, died a few days later. During the stand-
up fighting of the retreat, a British bullet passed through the
body of one man and struck the man behind him in the
knee. The man with the body wound lived and the one with
the splintered knee died.

The doctors could do nothing for Colonel Gardner. He
lingered, in terrible pain, until July 5. On the day after the
battle, he was told that his son was outside, anxious to see
him. "Only if he has done his duty," said Gardner.

The same heroic spirit was displayed by James Prescott,
when he was told by his warrior brother William that his
son had died in the redoubt. "Did he behave well?" the
father asked.

"None behaved better," said the colonel.

"God be praised," the father said.

Over in Boston Captain William Glanville Evelyn, who
had been so certain, even after Lexington, that the Americans "were the greatest cowards in the world," sat down at
his desk and took pen in hand. He was unhurt, but he had
gone over to Charlestown with thirty-three men in his company and had come back with five. He dated the paper June
17, 1775, and wrote:

"As all men who have taken upon them the profession of Arms hold their lives by a more precarious tenure than any other body of People; and as the fatal experience of This Day shews us how particularly it is the case of those who are engaged in war, even with the most despicable Enemy, I think it is the duty of every Man who cares a farthing about the disposal of his affairs to declare in what manner he wishes to have them disposed of." The Americans were still despicable, but the captain thought it was time to make his will. He left all he had to his mistress, Peggie. A year later, he was killed in a skirmish at Mile Square in Westchester County, New York.

In Cambridge, John Warren worked over the wounded, with a mounting dread. Again and again, as he cleansed and bandaged a man, he asked him if he had seen his brother, Joseph. Almost every soldier told a different story. Some were certain that they had seen him taken prisoner. Others swore they had seen him, dead, beneath the locust tree behind the redoubt. (This was Willard Moore.) Finally, at dawn, young John could stand it no longer. He rushed to Charlestown Neck and tried to get across it to go over the battlefield. The British had a picket guard of 200 men in the road not far from the Neck and a sentry challenged him. Desperately Warren tried to explain he was a doctor on a mission of mercy. The sentry had his orders. The young doctor finally lost his head and tried to rush past him. The sentry savagely sank his bayonet into Warren's shoulder. Weeping, he returned to Cambridge.

Warren could have done nothing for his brother. But there were thirty other Americans who spent a pain-wracked night on Breed's Hill without medical aid. Moses Parker and Benjamin Walker with smashed knees, Private Frost with a bullet in the hip, Caesar Bason with his leg wound, James Dodge with an agonizing stomach wound. The British did not leave them there in a spirit of revenge. They had left many of their own enlisted men on the field all night.

Early in the morning Dr. John Jeffries, whom Warren had begged to join the cause only two nights ago in the darkness by the Boston shore, received permission to go over and care for the wounded still in Charlestown. He found the British had collected all the Americans in the redoubt, and he went to work on them promptly. He was setting Moses Parker's shattered leg when Captain Walter Sloane Laurie, in charge of the burial detail, asked him if he could identify the body of one American who looked important to him. Jeffries followed him around the redoubt and looked down on Warren's still form. His fine waistcoat was gone—a soldier had stripped it off him and sold it in Boston for £7. "It is Dr. Warren," Jeffries said.

Captain Laurie at first could not believe it. It seemed inconceivable that the president of the Provincial Congress should risk his life on the battlefield. He rushed to tell General Howe; it was the first good news Howe had heard since he landed on Charlestown; he slapped his thigh and swore that Warren was worth 500 American soldiers. Howe ordered the body searched and discovered a number of letters, which Warren had imprudently carried on the field with him. Other British officers flocked to see the dead hero, and one of the more bloodthirsty suggested that they cut off his head and carry it to Gage; beheading was, after all, standard treatment for rebels. But more moderate men prevailed. One of the officers was a freemason and he refused to allow a fellow mason's body to be desecrated. So Captain Laurie, who as the commander of the British company at Concord Bridge played no small part in starting the Revolution, reported to General Gage, "I stuffed the scoundrel in a hole with one of his fellows, and there may he and his seditious principles remain."

The American prisoners were brought over to Boston

the following day. They were not treated with anything approaching kindness. By now the full impact of the casualties had come home to the British, and these men were, technically, rebels, not enemy soldiers. For several hours they were left lying in the blazing sun on North Battery and then transported to the upper floor of the town's jail—hardly the best place to house wounded men.

The British took out some of their wrath on civilians, too. "Poor harmless Shrimpton Hunt," as a friend described him, was arrested because someone heard him say during the battle that he hoped the Americans would win. Samuel Gore landed in jail because he called to his sister to come see a procession of dead British officers. Peter Edes, who had led a cheering section near General Burgoyne on Copp's Hill, was seized and held without charges. One of the letters on Warren's body was from James Lovell, the young schoolteacher; it gave a very accurate estimate of the British strength in Boston. He was promptly seized as a spy. There was also considerable suspicion that he had persuaded his brother, Colonel Cleveland's clerk, to sabotage Howe's artillery by substituting the twelve-pound balls. The brother was not arrested, but he lost his job as clerk of the artillery department.

Most of the civilians were released for lack of evidence after sixty or seventy days in jail. They were not harmed physically, but they received a great deal of moral abuse from their captors. The military prisoners are a more tragic story. The British were, within the strict letter of the law, humane enough. They arranged for a doctor to see them regularly, and though they were all severely wounded, Gage considered them no worse off, on the second floor of the jail, than his own wounded, sweltering in the abandoned factories. Their surgeon declared that they had ample room, and their "lofty situation in the upper story of the jail gave them the benefit of every breath of air that was moving."

Burgoyne recommended that Gage release all the prisoners without punishment, telling them, "You have been deluded; return to your homes in peace; it is your duty to God and your country to undeceive your neighbors." But Gage, a man who lived by regulations and orders, doubted that he had the authority to dismiss rebels taken in arms.

John Scollay, the Boston selectman, provided the men with two nurses, bedding and most of their food, and Gage sent them bread and wood, when the weather turned cold. But the general unfortunately delegated the details to a pair of sinister human beings who were later to enlarge the scope of their sadism to a monstrous scale when Howe put them in charge of the prison ships in New York Harbor. William Cunningham, who had immediate charge of the jail as provost marshal, was British. Joshua Loring, Jr., was American, a scion of an old Boston family. Between them they profiteered on the prisoners' food and supplies and abused the sick and dying men with insults and the meanest kind of punishments.

One civilian prisoner, John Leach, wrote in his diary: "The poor sick and wounded prisoners fare very hard; are many days without the comforts of life. Dr. Brown told me that they had no bread all day and the day before. He spoke to the provost, who replied, 'let them eat the heads of the nails and gnaw the planks, and be d——d.' They have had no wood to burn for many days together to warm their drink, and dying men drink theirs cold."

Even for major surgery they were not permitted to leave the jail; Moses Parker and Benjamin Walker both had their legs amputated amid prison squalor and died within the next few weeks. On September 1, only ten of the thirty were alive. By those strange quirks of eighteenth-century medicine, Walker's loyal Private Frost survived his shattered hip, while his captain died of a leg wound. Frost was taken to Halifax in irons when the British left Boston; he escaped and stowed away aboard a ship which landed him in Rhode Island. He promptly volunteered again for service, but he was turned down because his wound had left him permanently lame.

Abigail Adams and her son, John Quincy, heard the news about their beloved friend and family physician Joseph Warren early on Sunday morning. They were standing by the road when a horseman came thundering by carrying messages about the battle to Connecticut, Rhode Island and the other colonies. They hailed him and were told that the Americans had been defeated in a great battle on Charlestown. Hundreds were dead and wounded and over a thousand British soldiers had fallen, but the Americans' greatest loss was Dr. Warren. He was dead.

"Dead?" young John Quincy said, staring up at his mother. "Who could kill Dr. Warren—why?" With a sob his mother drew him into her arms and he began to weep uncontrollably. From that moment, a violent antipathy for things British became a basic emotion in the young future president—not the least among the many embitterments which flowed from Bunker Hill.

Throughout the night of June 17, a number of New Hampshire troops refused to admit the battle was over, and on their own, without orders, they crept through the darkness to snipe at the British picket guard on Charlestown Neck. Gage's brother-in-law, Stephen Kemble, complained in his diary: "All night the enemy kept a popping fire on our Advanced posts, from Houses on the opposite side of Charles Town Neck, wounded several Men, and Killed one officer." Young Ensign Hunter, who remained with his regiment on Bunker Hill, remembered it as the worst night of his soldier's life. Along with the constant alarms, he was terribly shaken by the death of so many fellow officers and especially grieved by the loss of the best friend he had in Boston, Major Pitcairn. In spite of his doubts, he was to

come through many another fight unscathed and die in
bed at eighty-nine, General Sir Martin Hunter, the last
English survivor of Bunker Hill.

The British replied to the sniping with a ferocious cannonade from the ships and the battery on Bunker Hill.
They also poured shot into Roxbury again. All through the
morning Abigail Adams and her sorrowing son could hear
the guns booming from their farm in Braintree. The Americans were certain the British would attack again, and Israel
Putnam drove his men relentlessly to complete fortifications
on Prospect Hill. At dawn, Ward reinforced him with 1,000
Massachusetts and Connecticut troops drawn from Roxbury.

Putnam's son Daniel tells of going to see him early Sunday morning. "I found him," the boy said, "on the morning of the 18th of June about ten o'clock on Prospect Hill
dashing about among the workmen, throwing up entrenchments and often placing a rod with his own hands. He wore
the same clothes he had on when I left him on the 16th and
said he had neither put them off, nor washed himself since
and we might well believe him for the aspect of all he wore
bore evidence he spoke the truth."

New Hampshire troops were entrenching at the same
time on Winter Hill, which also guarded the road to Cambridge. Elsewhere in the American camp, men were furiously hammering out bullets and making cartridges, and
fatigue parties were swinging axes and shovels, both in
Roxbury and before Cambridge. For miles around the roads
were clogged with militia hurrying to answer the Committee of Safety's call for reinforcements and women and children fleeing from the nearby towns because the enraged
British were now said to be determined to put the whole
country to fire and sword, as they had destroyed Charlestown. Abigail Adams wrote to her husband: "It is expected that the British will come out over the Neck tonight,
and a dreadful battle must ensue. Almighty God! Cover

the heads of our countrymen, and be a shield to our dear friends."

But neither Thomas Gage nor William Howe nor John Burgoyne was thinking about coming out. Only pugnacious Henry Clinton had a plan to attack Roxbury with 1,000 men and sweep around to Charlestown Neck. Gage vetoed it, utterly and totally. With 1,000 men in the hospital, he could only think in terms of self-preservation. On Bunker Hill, Howe put working parties on a round-the-clock schedule to complete the defensive fortifications.

About noon, the British guns slackened off until only a few were firing—methodical, sullen booms—like the defiant roars of a sorely wounded lion. Finally, at three o'clock on that sultry Sunday afternoon, a rainstorm burst over the two armies. The cannon, unable to fire in the rain, abruptly ceased. With a crash of lofty thunder, which might have been applause from the God of Battles himself, the Battle of Bunker Hill was over.

15

AMERICANS are used to Fourth of July orations on the glories of Bunker Hill. It is difficult to realize now that throughout the Revolution and for several decades after, the fight was considered an ignominious defeat. Soldiers like Putnam and Prescott were plunged into the deepest gloom. In a letter to his family in Connecticut a few days after the battle, Captain John Chester heaped hot coals of criticism on the Massachusetts troops: "Our retreat was shameful, and owing to the cowardice and misconduct and want of regularity of the Province troops, though to do them justice, there was a number of their officers and men that were in the fort and a very few others that did honor themselves by a most noble, manly, and spirited effort in the heat of the engagement and 'tis said that many of them, the flower of the Province, have sacrificed their lives in the Cause. Some say they have lost more officers and men. Good Dr. Warren, God rest his soul, I hope is safe in heaven. Had many of their officers the spirit and courage in their whole constitution that he had in his little finger, we had never retreated.

"In short, the most of the companies of this province are commanded by a most despicable set of officers and the whole success of the battle with them depends on their virtue; for almost all, from the captain general to a corporal, are afraid to set a proper martial authority and say as affairs are situated they think their people will not bear it. But in my humble opinion they are very much in the wrong."

This depression was, however, temporary. As reports from Boston filtered into the American camp they soon realized that the basic purpose of the battle had been realized beyond their greatest hopes. The shocking British casualties utterly immobilized Gage and Howe. The British had lost 1,054 men—226 killed, 828 wounded—almost fifty per cent of their attacking force. Not even at Minden had Britain suffered so severely. Even more crushing were the casualties in their officer corps, the backbone of the army: 92 out of the approximately 250 officers in the fight. When the normal casualty rate was one in eight, it is easy to see why Gage was rocked back on his heels. American casualties were not light. They had 140 dead, 271 wounded and 30, all badly wounded, listed as captured. Prescott's regiment suffered the most, with forty-two killed and twenty-eight wounded. The Frye and Bridge regiments together counted another thirty dead, sixty wounded. These were the men who followed Prescott to Breed's Hill at midnight and stayed with him through the heat of the long day; they bore over one third the total American casualties.

There was, in the American casualty list, one irony which must have dripped like gall in the minds of those lords and members of Parliament who had seen the trouble in the colonies as a miasma created by the faction in rebellious Boston. Only one man among the American dead was from Boston. All the others came from those supposedly docile towns and farms far away from the center of seditious infection.

Gradually, as the Americans thought the battle over, a wry bravado crept into their cries of remorse and humiliation. Nathaniel Greene, the Rhode Island general, led the way. "I wish," he said, "we could sell them another hill at the same price." Other soldiers noted the good effect of action on the military discipline of the camp. "This battle has been of infinite service to us," one man wrote. "It has made us more vigilant, watchful and cautious."

"Our troops are in high spirits," another soldier declared, "and their resolution increases. I long to speak with them [the British] again."

Putnam had predicted precisely this effect, and he took quick advantage of the new spirit. Every day thousands of men toiled on fatigue, fortifying the roads, the shore line along Back Bay and the flank defenses at Roxbury and Charlestown Neck, until the siege lines were impregnable. Putnam and Prescott, incidentally, soon forgot the bitter words they exchanged on the retreat. A few months later, when the Americans were considering a frontal assault on Boston across Back Bay, Putnam volunteered to lead the deadly gamble, and Prescott insisted that he would go with him.

On the British side emotions ran in precisely opposite directions. William Howe expressed himself frankly in a letter to his brother, Admiral Richard Howe, written the next day in his tent on Bunker Hill. After a brief description of the fight, in which he gives generous praise to Clinton and especially to Pigot ("the little man deserves our Master's favor") he says: "But now I come to the fatal consequences of this action—92 officers killed and wounded —a most dreadful account . . . the General's returns will give you the particulars of what I call this unhappy day. I freely confess to you, when I look to the consequences of it, in the loss of so many brave officers, I do it with horror. The success is too dearly bought."

Many of his contemporaries blamed Howe's failure to

win the Revolutionary War on his experience at Bunker Hill. There is considerable evidence to support the argument, both in his actions and his words. Again and again in the two years he was commander in chief he failed to follow up smashing victories, or he let Washington slip away because he could not bring himself to send his men against the Americans when they were entrenched behind even the flimsiest walls. Many years later he was to write: "I invariably pursued the most probable means of forcing [the rebel army] to action but with one proviso, under circumstances the least hazardous to the Royal Army; for even a victory attended by a heavy loss of men on our part would have given a fatal check to the progress of the war, and might have proved irreparable." Before Brooklyn Heights, he relied on siege tactics rather than assault because "it was apparent that the lines must have been ours at a very cheap rate by regular approaches, I would not risk the loss that might have been sustained in the assault." At White Plains, Howe again defended his hesitation by explaining: "If I could by any maneuver remove an enemy from a very advantageous postion without hazarding the consequences of an attack, where the point to be carried was not adequate to the loss of men expected from the enterprise, I should certainly adopt that cautionary conduct." Even when the American army had withered away to a skeleton corps at Valley Forge and Howe was a few miles away in Philadelpha with an immensely superior and well-supplied force, he argued that the American weakness "did not justify an attack on that strong position during the severe weather." Surely this was not the daring colonel who had led the way up the Quebec cliffs. This was the baffled general who had stood among his slaughtered officers and men and stared up at the American fortifications on Breed's Hill, thinking: *A moment I never felt before.*

All Gage could do in his letter to Lord Barrington was report the bad news and point out that his gloomiest predictions had come true.

"My Lord:

"You will receive an account of some success against the rebels, but attended with a long list of killed and wounded on our side; so many of the latter that the hospital has hardly hands sufficient to take care of them. These people show a spirit and conduct against us they never showed against the French, and everybody has judged of them from their formed appearance and behavior when they joined with the King's Forces in the last war; which has led many into great mistakes.

"They are now spirited up by a rage and enthusiasm as great as ever people were possessed of, and you must proceed in earnest or give the business up. A small body acting in one spot will not avail. You must have large armies making diversions on different sides, to divide their force.

"The loss we have sustained is greater than we can bear. Small armies can't afford such losses especially when the advantage gained tends to little more then the gaining of a post —a material one indeed as our own security depended on it. The troops are sent out too late, the rebels were at least two months before-hand with us and your Lordship would be astonished to see the tract of country they have entrenched and fortified; their number is great, so many hands have been employed. . . . I have before wrote your Lordship my opinion that a large army must at length be employed to reduce these people and mentioned the hiring of foreign troops. I fear it must come to that or else to avoid a land war and make use only of your fleet."

Other British soldiers were neither so restrained in their feelings nor so terse with their hindsight criticisms of British tactics. "Too great a confidence in ourselves which is always dangerous occasioned this dreadful loss," wrote one officer. "We are all wrong at the head. My mind cannot help dwelling upon our cursed mistakes. Such ill conduct at the first outset argues a gross ignorance of the most common rules of the profession and gives us for the future anxious forebodings. I have lost some of those I most valued. The brave men's lives were wantonly thrown away. Our conductor as much murdered them as if he had cut their throats himself on Boston common. Had he fallen, ought we to have regretted him?"

Lieutenant Barker was disturbed by the prime tactical blunder of the day—the failure to use the men-of-war on the Mystic side of the peninsula. The next day he cruised with three floating batteries along the beach where so many of his friends in the light infantry had fallen and mused bitterly in his diary: "Had these boats been with us on Saturday at the time of the attack they could have been of great use as they would have taken a part of the Rebels' intrenchment in flank and in their retreat would have cut off numbers; instead of that they were on the other side and of no manner of use."

Other officers expressed great admiration for the courage of their adversaries. "Damn the rebels, they would not flinch!" said one lieutenant. Burgoyne himself, in one of his countless letters home, wrote: "The retreat was no rout. It was conducted with bravery and even military skill."

Elsewhere Burgoyne had much to say about the conduct of British troops. In a confidential letter to Lord Rochfort, secretary of state for the colonies, he gives him a report which is "not to pass even in a whisper . . . to more than *one* person. The zeal and intrepidity of the officers, which was without exception exemplary, was ill seconded by the private men. Discipline, not to say courage, was wanting. In the critical moment of carrying the redoubt the officers of some corps were almost alone; and what was the worst part of the confusion of these corps—all the wounds of the officers were not received from the enemy. I do not mean to convey any suspicion of backwardness in the cause of government among the soldiery, which ignorant people in England are apt to imagine; and as little would I be understood to imply any dislike or ill will to their officers. I only mean to represent that the men being ill grounded in the great points of discipline it will require some training under such generals as Howe and Clinton before they can prudently be entrusted in many exploits against such odds as the conduct and spirit of the leaders enabled them to overcome."

This was Burgoyne, the jealous subordinate, speaking, and it is a melancholy blot on his record that to advance his own position in America he vilified men who had shown courage beyond the expectation of the most brutal commander. In Parliament a year later, when jealousy no longer distracted his judgment, Burgoyne made up for the slander somewhat. When Colonel Isaac Barré charged that the enlisted men had "grossly misbehaved at Bunker Hill," because they detested the idea of fighting fellow Englishmen, Burgoyne sprang to his feet and declared: "No men on earth ever behaved with more spirit and perseverance, till they forced the enemy out of their entrenchments."

Other recriminations were hotly exchanged. "The wretched blunder of the oversized balls," said one officer, "sprung from the dotage of an officer of rank in that corps, who spends his whole time in dallying with the schoolmaster's daughter. God knows he is no Sampson, but he must have his Delilah." Colonel Cleveland, the Sampson in question, answered the charges with a querulous complaint of his own. In a letter to General Amherst he states that he sent sixty-six "rounds to each gun, not more than half was fired." He then says: "the men sent on purpose to carry the boxes of ammunition after the cannon went a-plundering and occasioned it to be said one of the guns wanted ammunition. A commanding officer of artillery cannot be in every place." The colonel's defense is difficult to believe; the only place the men could have gone "a-plundering" was Charlestown, which was in flames and infested by American snipers. To get to it the derelict artillerymen would have had to walk a half mile around the base of Breed's Hill and through Pigot's formations on the south side of the redoubt. Since plundering was also punishable by death, the accumulated obstacles, physical and moral, would seem to throw considerable doubt upon the colonel's alibi.

In England, ministry and Parliament were shocked by the heavy casualties. William Eden, ancestor of ex-Prime Minister Anthony Eden, said to Lord North: "Eight more such victories, and we will have no one left to report them." Pamphleteers and jingoist newspapermen came up with some wild explanations for the British losses. One man wrote: "American rifles were peculiarly adapted to take off the officers of a whole line as it marched to an attack." Another assured his readers "that every rifleman was attended by two men, one on each side of him, to load pieces for him so that he had nothing to do but fire as fast as a piece was put into his hand; and this is the real cause of so many of our brave officers falling." Others resorted to germ warfare claims: the Americans supposedly used "poisoned bullets" which made the slightest wound fatal. Others said the American redoubt was the work of several days and made it sound, in their descriptions, like a portion of the Great Wall of China. The *Gentleman's Magazine* even published a sketch of Prescott's little fort which tripled its size and gave it a dozen complex outworks and ditches that it never possessed.

In Cambridge the Americans decided there were some things about their side of the battle that needed explaining. There was considerable questioning, in all ranks, about the wisdom of selecting Charlestown peninsula as the place to fight a major battle. On June 20 the Provincial Congress appointed a committee of five to "enquire into the grounds of a report which has prevailed in the army that there has been treachery in some of the officers." The committee returned a vehement negative to this report and roundly declared that it was circulated by the cowards who had deserted before the shooting started.

Partially to appease this scapegoat-hunting spirit and partially to weed out some obvious rotten apples, the army began court-martial proceedings against all the officers accused of misconduct in the lines and behind them. Colonel Bridge, who fought in the redoubt with Prescott, was one of the first examined. In spite of the fact that he had been wounded twice, many of the men accused him of skulking under the walls of the redoubt and refusing to expose himself to enemy fire. The charges against him were dismissed.

Young Major Scarborough Gridley was not so fortunate. He was accused of cowardice and outright disregard of orders for his refusal to advance to Bunker Hill. He was found guilty and cashiered from the Massachusetts service. Probably out of deference for his famous father, the court-martial, headed by Brigadier General Nathaniel Greene, added: "On account of his inexperience and youth, and the great confusion that attended that day's transactions in general, they do not consider him incapable of a continental commission, should the general officers recommend him." The generals were not inclined to make the recommendation.

Gridley's younger brother, Captain Samuel, at least could say he had been on the battlefield, and he fared better before the court. His case was put off for almost two months, and when he was tried with cooler tempers, the charges against him were dismissed. Oddly, his lieutenant, Woodward, who was the chief witness against him, was court-martialed instead and booted out of the service. One suspects the fine hand of politics here, since the Americans were anxious to retain the services of Gridley *père*. Not, however, as head of the artillery, but for his genius as a military engineer.

The Gridleys' fellow artilleryman, Captain John Callender, was ordered held for court-martial on the complaint of Israel Putnam, who swore that he would quit the service if Callender was not condemned. Tried in such a highly prejudicial light, Callender was cashiered, and the official orders on July 7 dismissed him from all further service in the army as an officer. Callender protested the injustice of his conviction and now, at a distance, his complaint carries weight. A Massachusetts man, he was disinclined to obey Israel Putnam, as were several thousand of his fellows. He was deserted by his men and had the wrong-sized cartridges for his guns.

Determined to wipe out the disgrace, Callender enlisted in the ranks as a volunteer. At the battle of Long Island the captain and lieutenant of his artillery company were killed and Callender took command of the guns. He fought until the bayonets of the British were all around him. The British officer in charge of the attack was so impressed by his courage he forbade his men to touch him. Washington promptly ordered Callender's court-martial erased from the books and his commission restored.

Not even Captain Samuel Trevett, who had done his duty to the best of his ability, escaped the scrutiny of the generals. So incensed were the Americans against the artillery that he, too, was placed under arrest and confined to his quarters for several days. But there were no charges against him and he was quickly released.

Colonel Samuel Gerrish, who contributed so much to the confusion and so little to the courage on the brow of Bunker Hill, was also nominated for a court-martial, but General Ward refused the charge, citing the chaos behind the lines as a good excuse for the overweight colonel's refusal to advance. Several weeks later, Gerrish was commanding a waterside redoubt on Back Bay when it was bombarded by a floating battery. He made no attempt to repel the attack, declaring it would be a "waste of powder." His judgment would seem to have been correct—not a single British cannon hit the fort—but those who remembered his conduct on Bunker Hill promptly hauled him off to a general court-martial; he was found guilty of "conduct unbecoming an officer" and cashiered.

Colonel James Scammans who made the mistake of obeying Major Gridley and sat out the battle on Cobble Hill, was also tried for cowardice, but the charges were dismissed, since no one had any clear record of what orders were given or who gave them. He was able to prove he had obeyed his orders as he understood them; the court decided his intentions had been good, if his judgment was not. His fellow colonel, Mansfield, who dallied with him on the hill admiring Gridley's artillery practice, was not as adept at defending himself and was dishonorably discharged.

Having expelled these scapegoats, most of whom were at the very least guilty of incompetence, the Committee of Safety proceeded to issue an official report of the battle. Writing with one eye on public opinion, the patriots made their contribution to changing the name of the fight to Bunker Hill. Breed's Hill, they declared, was occupied "by mistake." The committee was still in the grip of the "don't strike the first blow" policy, and it was slightly embarrassing to admit that they had occupied the lower hill, which was so much closer to Boston. Occupying Bunker Hill could have been described as a purely defensive operation. Another impetus toward the choice of Bunker was the viewpoint of the young minister, Peter Thacher, who wrote the official report. He watched the fight from a house in Chelsea, across the Mystic channel. From there he did not see any of the fighting around Prescott's redoubt. All he saw was the repulse on the beach and at the rail fence, which was at the base of Bunker Hill.

The British early accepted Bunker as the battle name. In 1776 it was established usage in their journals and newspapers. For a long time many New Englanders continued to call it "the battle of Charlestown Heights." But these sticklers for the truth could not prevail against the general trend. When the Bunker Hill Monument Association was formed in 1823, the name became official. But the granite obelisk was erected on Breed's Hill. It was not the first monument. Years before Warren's Masonic Lodge had erected a small pillar there in his memory.

Once the sting of defeat had eased, by far the greatest American sorrow was the death of Warren. Abigail Adams, writing to her husband in Philadelphia, summed up the feelings of everyone: "Not all the havoc and devastation they [the British] have made has wounded me like the death of Warren. We want him in the senate; we want him in his profession; we want him in the field. We mourn for the citizen, the senator, the physician and the warrior. When he fell, liberty wept."

Warren's children were left penniless, but they were not neglected. Mercy Scollay gave graphic proof of her devotion to her handsome doctor by taking the two youngest, Richard and Mary, into her home and raising them herself for a number of years. The Continental Congress voted to educate the oldest son, Joseph, at the expense of the state, and the oldest girl Elizabeth, was educated by a local minister who assured Samuel Adams that "no gentleman's daughter has more of the advantage of schools than she has." In 1780 a movement, begun by an old friend of Warren's, inspired the Continental Congress to vote the children the half pay of a major general commencing from the time of Warren's death until the youngest child came of age. The name of the old friend who contributed $500 of his own money to the $7,000 the children received, was Benedict Arnold.

Warren did not die in vain. Beyond its immediate military results, Bunker Hill had enormous consequences in America and England. It convinced the wavering southern and middle colonies that England was prepared to wage all-out war to enforce her "ministerial" policy. John Coffin, a Massachusetts loyalist whose military ability eventually made him a full general in the British army, always regarded Bunker Hill as the event which controlled everything that followed. "You could not," he would say to American friends who visited him in London after the war, "have succeeded without it. Something in the then state of parties was indispensable to fix men somewhere . . . to show that the Northern people were in earnest. That, *that* did the business for you."

Bunker Hill also persuaded the waverers and heartened the patriots in every colony by demonstrating that the British army was by no means invincible. There is a tradition that George Washington first heard about Bunker Hill on the road outside Philadelphia, as he set out to assume command of the American army in Massachusetts. When the dust-covered messenger came pounding up to him with the news, the first question Washington asked was: "Did the Americans stand before the British fire?"

When told they had, he said: "Then the liberties of our country are safe."

Actually, Washington heard the details of the battle when he reached New York, and most historians feel his sweeping declaration about the safety of the nation is somewhat out of character. But from his later remarks on Bunker Hill the question of American courage was undoubtedly the first which leaped to his lips as it did for almost every other American. The optimists in the colonial ranks began arguing that if untrained relatively unorganized militiamen could fight the regulars to a standstill, an army better trained and led by experienced officers such as Washington would chase them into the sea. There was more than one fallacy in this thinking, and the Americans were to endure years of humiliating defeats before they learned enough about operating an army to chase the King's troops. In fact, many American military men have deplored Bunker Hill because it became a symbol which in later wars lulled America into an absurd confidence in the fighting qualities of untrained citizens. As late as World War I, the myth was inspiring statesmen to boast that defeating the Germans would be child's play because the moment Wilson declared war "a million freemen would spring to arms."

But in 1775, Bunker Hill, to use the providential language of those who look back, was the perfect rallying cry to both infuriate and unite the colonies. It banished any real hope of conciliation, although the moderates in the Continental Congress continued, by sheer momentum, to work on another petition to the King. But the congress also quickly and efficiently adopted articles of war for the army and organized a hospital service. Agents were directed to scour the continent for gunpowder and ammunition. Money was borrowed to buy army supplies, two million paper dollars were ordered printed and an appeal to the Indians was composed, asking them to remain neutral in the coming struggle. *"Brothers, Sachems Warriors. Open a kind ear. King George, persuaded by wicked counsellors, has broken the covenant chain with his children in America."*

In England the battle had a different, but equally momentous impact. The running skirmish along the Lexington road was possibly a misunderstanding, an accident in which blame could be distributed on both sides. But a battle fought behind barricades, with cannon and bayonet, could only mean one thing. The wavering Lord North collapsed and became a tool of the cabinet's war party. On July 26, he wrote to the King that it was now necessary to treat the rebellion as a foreign war and the Americans as an alien foe. The King agreed and ordered his ministers to draw up a Proclamation of Rebellion.

Only Lord Dartmouth clung to the cause of peace. He begged the King to withhold the proclamation until they heard from the Second Continental Congress. For a few weeks, he was successful. But the King's dislike for Dartmouth's policy was more and more evident. The colonial secretary began to absent himself from cabinet meetings on American affairs, and when the "Olive Branch" petition of the Continental Congress reached him, on August 24, it was already a lost cause. "Most Gracious Sovereign," it began.

> "Attached to your Majesty's person, family and government with all devotion that principle and affection can inspire, connected with Great Britain by the strongest ties that can unite societies and deploring every event that tends in any degree to weaken them, we solemnly assure your Majesty that we not only most ardently desire the former harmony between her and these Colonies may be restored, but that a concord may be established between them on so firm a basis as to perpetuate its blessings uninterrupted by any future dissensions to succeeding generations in both countries, and to transmit your Majesty's name to posterity adorned with that signal and lasting glory that is attended the memory of those illustrious personages, whose virtues and abilities have extricated states from dangerous convulsions, and by securing happiness to others have erected the most noble and durable monuments to their own fame . . .

Dartmouth saw, at a glance, that these earnest, pleading words would mean nothing to George III. Aside from the absurdity of asking him to repudiate his own ministers, the King could see them only as a clever ruse to gain time. The casualty lists from Bunker Hill spoke infinitely louder. There is no evidence that the King ever saw the "Olive Branch" petition. His methodical mind was already closed to the whole idea of peace. The day before, on August 23, he had issued the fateful Proclamation of Rebellion.

"Whereas many of our subjects in divers parts of our Colonies and Plantations in North America misled by dangerous and ill designing men and forgetting the allegiance which they owe to the power that has protected and supported them; after various disorderly acts committed in disturbance of the public peace to the obstruction of lawful commerce and to the oppression of our loyal subjects carrying on the same; have at length proceeded to open and avowed rebellion by arraying themselves in a hostile manner to withstand the execution of the law and traitorously preparing, ordering and levying war against us: And whereas there is reason to apprehend that such rebellion has been much promoted and encouraged by the traitorous correspondence, councils and comfort of divers wicked and desperate persons within this realm: To the end therefore that none of our subjects may neglect or violate their duty through ignorance thereof or through any doubt of the protection which the law will afford to their loyalty and zeal, we have thought fit by and with the advice of our Privy Council to issue our Royal Proclamation hereby declaring that not only all our officers, civil and military, are obliged to exert their utmost endeavors to suppress such rebellion and to bring the traitors to justice, but that all our subjects of this realm and the dominions thereunto belonging are bound by law to be aiding and assisting in the suppression of such rebellion and to disclose and make known all traitorous conspiracies and attempts against us, our crown and dignity. . . ."

The lines were drawn. Lord Dartmouth, America's last friend in a position of power, soon resigned, and reputation-hungry Lord George Germain, despiser of Americans and proponent of all-out war, became colonial secretary. On July 3, George Washington rode into Cambridge and Artemas Ward surrendered command of his New England soldiers, who now became the Continental Army of the United Provinces of America. Within the month George III and his war lords in London decided to recall Thomas Gage and replace him with William Howe.

Though Washington continued to refer to the British as the "ministerial army" and confessed the word independence still made him uneasy, he also said: "With respect for myself, I have never entertained an idea of an accommodation, since I heard of the measures which were adopted in consequence of the Bunker Hill fight. The King's speech has confirmed the sentiments I entertained upon the news of that affair; and if every man was of my mind, the ministers of Great Britain should know, in a few words, upon what issue the cause should be put. I would tell them . . . that we had done everything that could be expected from the best of subjects . . . and that if nothing else would satisfy a tyrant and his diabolical ministry, we are determined to shake off all connections with a state so unjust and unnatural. This I would tell them, not under covert, but in words as clear as the sun in its meridian brightness."

Down in Philadelphia, Benjamin Franklin, the man who had spent ten years hoping and working for peace, sat down and wrote a letter to an old friend in London.

"Mr. Strahan,
      You are a member of Parliament and one of that Majority which has doomed my Country to Destruction. You have begun to burn our towns and murder our People. Look upon your Hands! They are stained with the Blood of your Relations! You and I were long Friends. You are now my Enemy

                                                      and
                                              I am
                                                Yours
                                              B. Franklin."

A NOTE ON SOURCES AND METHODS

My purpose in writing this book has been to transform the story of Bunker Hill from a few pages in a history textbook to the magnificent drama of courage which it is. In pursuit of this "humanization of history," to borrow an inspiring phrase from Allan Nevins, I have allowed the actors in the drama to speak and feel and think as living men. But every conversation is rooted in historical fact. Although the exact words spoken are lost to us my re-creation of the scene is based on a close study of the available evidence—including the characters of the speakers.

For instance, the conversation between General Howe and General Clinton in the opening chapter, about the Americans entrenching on Breed's Hill, is based on notes found among Clinton's papers by that industrious historian of the first year of the Revolution, Allen French. Clinton's note read: "In the evening of ye 16th I saw them at work and reported it to Genls Gage and How and advised a landing in two divisions at day brake." With conversation this fact comes infinitely more alive. Similarly, in the American midnight debate on Breed's Hill, the words are lost, but the ones I have created are rooted in strong historical probability. An amazing number of conversations and interior monologues are well documented. For instance, the American Council of War which made the fateful decision to entrench on Bunker Hill has come down to us with most of the conversation recorded as participants remembered it. Putnam's moving words with his son, Daniel, before the battle are also recollections of the latter. Howe's "A moment I never felt before" is the General's own testimony. Nowhere has an incident been invented. Everything from the death of Asa Pollard to the loss of Isaac Livermore's rum is the testimony of eye witnesses.

Some details of Bunker Hill suffer from the confusion in which the battle was fought. The story of the American artillery's conduct, for instance, has never been fully narrated, in any previous account. Yet it is crucial to the understanding of the day. The version here is the result of much pondering and sifting of the sometimes conflicting evidence. Similarly there was debate about certain incidents. The anecdote of Major Small, for instance, was denied by many Americans. Small, on his part, told of trying to save Warren's life at the climax of the fight. Here I applied a simple test. Small's rescue by Putnam was supported by Daniel Putnam, who testified that the Major sent Putnam a gift the following day, with an effusive note of thanks. Small's attempt to rescue Warren has no support, except Small himself. I have left it out. Wherever a contested incident was unconfirmed by a contemporary, other than the teller of the story, I have omitted it.

I have deliberately avoided weighing pro and con the conflicting theories about Bunker Hill. To do so would have totally destroyed the battle's narrative drama. Probably Harold Murdock is the most original student of Bunker Hill. Thanks to him I have avoided many of the myths which have clouded the story of the battle for over a century. I have not, however, accepted Murdock's most daring suggestion—that there were not as many British attacks as tradition maintains. Murdock argued that the Reverend Peter Thacher, who wrote the American version of the battle within two weeks of its occurrence, added together two assaults at the Rail Fence, and one against the redoubt. Here I am inclined to follow the reasoning and documentation of Allen French who points out that Thacher, in spite of his inability to see the entire battle from his station across the Mystic, has told us that "what facts he did not see himself were communicated to him by Col Prescott . . . and by other persons who were personally conversant in the scenes which this narration describes." Since the three attack version was never contradicted during the lifetime of the men who fought at Bunker Hill, it seems foolhardy to challenge it, at this distance. However, I have conceded this much to Murdock's theory—the first two assaults were, from my reading of the primary sources such as the Prescott and

Howe account, probably so close together, that for the men in the ranks they were one continuous fight.

One of the few points where I seriously disagree with Allen French is in his discussion of the British preparation for the battle. Writing in 1934, French had none of our World War II experience with amphibious assault. The term had, in fact, almost disappeared from our military language. French sides with Clinton, who maintained in his memoirs that the British should have attacked immediately, perhaps at 6 A.M., certainly by 9. This omits all consideration that for the British Bunker Hill was a complex amphibious assault, against a foe who had a 3-1 advantage over them in manpower. (Clinton, we must remember was one of the "German Generals" in the British army, with all his experience in the strictly dry land warfare of the continent.) French suggests two alternatives for Howe—he could have landed in the rear, sealing off the peninsula at the Neck (Clinton's plan) or he could have landed on the Charlestown wharves.

> "American patrols may have been seen moving in the town that had been empty for so many weeks," French wrote. "For that reason, perhaps, was chosen a distant landing place. Far better for Howe to have forced a landing at the wharves, in the face of such slight opposition as provincial skirmishers could offer. Or better to have wet his men to the hips in landing on a flat shore. But no. This had to be done in decency and order."

Here we see repeated what one might call the "Colonel Blimp" explanation of British behavior at Bunker Hill. (Even Trevelyan agrees in part at least with this judgment against his countrymen.) I maintain it ignores all we now know about amphibious assault. To say that there were nothing but skirmishers in Charlestown is the language of hindsight. For all Howe knew, the Americans might have had a concealed battery of cannon waiting for him. Above all, it ignores the fact which obsessed Howe: the lack of covered flatboats for an effective assault. He had to choose a landing place which was as removed as possible from a surprise attack.

Because the Americans did not attack the landing is no reason for assuming that Howe should have known they *would* not attack it. We must remember that the British had already had one unpleasant experience with American audacity along the Lexington road. We have Lord Percy's testimony that in the heat of the fight many Americans advanced within a few yards to get a shot at him "though they were morally certain of being put to death." It was reasonable for Howe to assume that the same kind of reckless attack might be made on the landing force, if they chose a site which offered the Americans an opportunity to get at them.

As for ignoring the tide, and letting his men get "wet to the hips"—no one who had as much amphibious experience as Howe would consider such a thing when, all considered, there was no necessity for it. Men fight far better when they have not exhausted themselves floundering ashore through mud and water. Again, we have to recall that Bunker Hill was one phase of the overall British operation to break the siege of Boston. In Burgoyne's statement, "It became necessary to . . . attack on that side." But their plan—to smash the siege lines around Cambridge—remained essentially unchanged.

On the American side, I have made no attempt to rebut historians such as Christopher Ward who have castigated the whole idea of the American venture onto Charlestown peninsula and even more violently condemned the choice of Breed's Hill when the orders supposedly read Bunker Hill. French, Murdock, Martyn and others have condemned Israel Putnam for this choice.

Probably the most extreme statement was made by Charles Francis Adams:

"the affair of the 17th of June, 1775 . . . affords what might be called the 'balancing of blunders' between opposing sides, and of the accidental inuring of these blunders to the advantage of one side. Looking over the accounts of that battle and examining the ground upon which it was fought, it is difficult to understand how the Americans could knowingly have put themselves in such an untenable position; much more how the British should so utterly have failed to take advantage of the mistakes of their inexperienced antagonists."

There is no doubt that the venture was a daring gamble. But Putnam, Prescott and the other members of the Council of War were not military amateurs. They corresponded, in their experience and lively interest in things military, to the alert reserve officer of today. They were well aware of the risk, but they obviously thought it was worth taking. I think we should agree with them —*if we remember the real purpose of the expedition.* Most of the critics follow the line of reasoning in the wording of the Committee of Safety's resolution to fortify the peninsula—it was to be a defensive gesture, a refusal to allow the British to occupy another inch of Massachusetts territory. But the real purpose of the American expedition was to cripple the striking power of the British army in Boston, and abort their plan to break the siege. It was necessary, therefore, to choose a position which would leave the British no alternative but to attack. Bunker Hill did not satisfy this condition. As Samuel Swett and Richard Frothingham point out, it was simply too far away from Boston. From it, cannon, of the caliber available to the Americans, could neither shell Boston nor the shipping in the harbor.

French, Martyn and other writers have made Breed's Hill appear to be an impulsive as well as an idiotic choice. Samuel Swett offers sound evidence that it was deliberate. He quotes contemporary witnesses to prove Putnam was thoroughly familiar with Charlestown Peninsula, and had gone over the ground at least twice in the month preceding the battle, once in the company of the American army's chief engineer, Colonel Richard Gridley. Moreover, I think there is valid reason for arguing that it was, militarily, the best choice.

Bunker Hill lacked the ready made flank defenses which the houses of Charlestown and the swamp at the base of Breed's supplied. It would have been difficult to defend with the men Prescott and Putnam had at their disposal against the kind of flanking attack Howe would have undoubtedly planned.

I have also avoided almost all discussion of the vast but largely pointless controversy which erupted in later years about the command at the Battle of Bunker Hill. New Hampshire men, led by Henry Dearborn, maintained that no one commanded and accused the by now deceased Putnam of playing the coward as much as Colonel Gerrish. Massachusetts men declared that Prescott was in command of the expedition and Putnam was a mere volunteer. Now that the partisan heat has died down, I think it is obvious that Putnam was in nominal command, but the disorganized undisciplined state of the newborn American army made almost all those who were not from the state of Connecticut disinclined to recognize it.

SELECT BIBLIOGRAPHY

Adams, Charles Francis; *The Battle of Bunker Hill from a strategic point of view;* in the American Antiquarian Society Proceedings, Vol. 10, pp. 387-389; 1895

Adams, Charles Francis; *Familiar Letters of John Adams and his wife Abigail Adams, during The Revolution;* Hurd; Houghton; 1876

Alden, John Richard; *General Gage in America;* Louisiana State University Press; Baton Rouge; 1948

Anderson, Troyer Steele; *The Command of the Howe Brothers during the American Revolution;* Oxford University Press; New York and London; 1936

Baker, Henry Moore; *New Hampshire in the Battle of Bunker Hill;* The Rumford Press; Concord; 1903

Bancroft, George; *History of the American Revolution,* 3 Vols.; R. Bentley; London; 1852

Barker, John; *The British in Boston;* Cambridge; 1924

Becker, Carl Lotus; *The Eve of the Revolution;* Yale University Press; New Haven; 1921

Belcher, Henry; *The First American Civil War,* Vol. 1; Macmillan and Co. Ltd.; London; 1911

Bernardo, C. Joseph and Eugene H. Bacon; *American Military Policy: Its Development Since 1775;* The Military Service Publishing Co.; Harrisburg; 1955

Bolton, Charles Knowles; *Letters of Hugh, Earl Percy from Boston and New York, 1774-1776;* C. E. Goodspeed; Boston; 1902

Booerstin, Daniel Joseph; *The Americans: The Colonial Experience;* Random House; New York; 1958

Bowen, Catherine Drinker; *John Adams and the American Revolution;* Little, Brown; Boston; 1950

Bradford, Alden; *A Particular Account of the Battle of Bunker, or Breed's Hill, on the 17th of June, 1775;* by a citizen of Boston; Cummings, Hilliard and Co.; Boston; 1825

Brown, William Wells; *The Negro in the American Rebellion;* Lee and Shepard; Boston; 1867

Carman, W. Y.; *British Military Uniforms;* Leonard Hill, Ltd.; London; 1957

Carrington, Henry Beebe; *Battles, Maps and Charts of the American Revolution;* A. S. Barnes and Co.; New York and Chicago; 1881

Chichester, Henry Manners; *The Records & Badges of Every Regiment and Corps in the British Army;* William Clowes and Sons Ltd.; London; 1895

Child, David Lee; *An enquiry into the conduct of Israel Putnam in relation to the Battle of Bunker Hill, and remarks upon Mr. Swett's sketch of the Battle;* Printed by T. G. Bangs; Boston; 1819

Clarence, C. W.; *A biographical sketch on the life of Ralph Farnham of Acton, Maine;* Boston; Sept. 20, 1860

Clarence, John; *Bunker Hill, Battle of 1775;* Broadstreet Press; New York; 1868

Clarke, John, Lieut. of Marines; *Bunker Hill, An Impartial and Authentic Narrative of the Battle;* Printed for the Author and sold by J. Millan; London; 1775

Clinton Papers, William L. Clements Library, University of Michigan

Clinton, Sir Henry; *The American Rebellion; Sir Henry Clinton's Narrative;* edited by William B. Willcox; Yale University Press, New Haven; 1954

Coffin, Charles; *History of the Battle of Breed's Hill;* Portland; D. C. Colesworthy; 1835

Coffin, Charles, compiler; *The lives and services of Maj. Gen. John Thomas, Col. Thomas Knowlton, Col. Alexander Scammell, Maj. Gen. Henry Dearborn;* Egbert Harvey and King; New York; 1845

Commanger, Henry Steele and Richard B. Morris; *The Spirit of Seventy-Six;* Bobbs-Merrill; New York; 1958

Coolidge, George A.; *Brochure of Bunker Hill, with Heliotype Views;* J. R. Osgood and Co.; Boston; 1875

Cuneo, John R.; *Robert Rogers of the Rangers;* Oxford University Press; New York; 1959

Cutter, William; *The Life of Israel Putnam;* George F. Cooledge; New York; 1850

Dearborn, Henry Alexander; *An oration pronounced at Boston on the fourth day of July, 1811;* Monroe & French; Boston; 1811

De Fonblanque, Edward Barrington; *Political and military episodes in the latter half of the 18th century;* Derived from the life and correspondence of the Right Hon. John Burgoyne; Macmillan and Co.; London; 1876

Devens, Charles; *An oration delivered at Charlestown June 17, 1875, in commemoration of the Battle of Bunker Hill;* J. Wilson and Son; Boston; 1876

Dorson, Richard Mercer, editor; *American Rebels: Narratives of the Patriots;* Pantheon; New York; 1953

Drake, Samuel Adams; *Bunker Hill Story in Letters from the Battle Field by British Officers Engaged;* Nichols and Hall; Boston; 1875

Drake, Samuel Adams; *General Israel Putnam, The Commander at Bunker Hill;* Nichols and Hall; Boston; 1875

Drake, Samuel Adams; *Old Landmarks and Historic Personnages of Boston;* Roberts Bros.; Boston; 1876

Edes, Peter; *His Diary while a prisoner of the British;* edited by Samuel Lane Boardman; Printed for the De Burians; Bangor; 1901

Ellis, George Edward; *Chronicle of the Siege (of Boston);* In the Boston, Mass. City Council; March 17, 1876

Ellis, George; *History of the Battle of Bunker Hill from Authentic Sources;* Lockwood, Brooks and Co.; Boston; 1875

Ellis, George Edward; *Sketches of the Battle of Bunker Hill and Monument;* C. P. Emmons; Charlestown; 1843

Ffoulkes, Charles John; *Sword, Lance and Bayonet;* The University Press; Cambridge (England); 1938

Fisher, Sidney George; *The Struggle for American Independence,* Vol. 1 and 2; J. B. Lippincott Co.; Philadelphia; 1908

Fisher, Horace Newton; *The Object at Bunker Hill;* Bunker Hill Monument Association Proceedings, 1907

Force, Peter; *American Archives Series 4;* Washington; 1836-1846

Fortescue, J. M.; *History of the British Army;* Vol. 2; London; 1899-1920

Freeman, Douglas Southall; *George Washington* (Vol. 3); New York; 1951

French, Allen; *The Day of Concord and Lexington;* Little, Brown; Boston; 1925

French, Allen; *General Gage's Informers;* University of Michigan Press; Ann Arbor; 1932

French, Allen; *Siege of Boston;* Macmillan and Co.; New York; 1911

French, Allen; *The First Year of the American Revolution;* Houghton Mifflin; Boston; 1934

Frothingham, Richard; *Battle of Bunker Hill;* Little, Brown and Co.; Boston; 1900

Frothingham, Richard; *History of the Siege of Boston;* C. C. Little and J. Brown; Boston; 1849

Frothingham, Richard, Jr.; *Life and Times of Joseph Warren;* Little, Brown and Co.; Boston; 1865

Frothingham, R.; *The Command in the Battle of Bunker Hill, with a reply to Remarks on Frothingham's History of the battle, by S. Swett;* C. C. Little and J. Brown; Boston; 1850

Fuller, Maj. Gen. J. F. C.; *Decisive Battles of the United States of America;* Harper and Bros.; New York; 1942

Fuller, Maj. Gen. J. F. C.; *British Light Infantry Tactics;* London; undated

Gibbes, Robert Wilson; *Documentary History of the American Revolution;* Banner Steam-Power Press; Columbia, S.C.; 1853

Gluckman, Arcadi; *U. S. Muskets, Rifles and Carbines;* Otto L. Ulbrich Co.; Buffalo; 1948

Goold, Nathan; *Colonel James Scammons's 30th Regiment of Foot during the Battle of Bunker Hill;* reprinted from the Maine Historical Society's Quarterly; Portland, 1899

Green, Samuel A.; *Col. William Prescott and Groton Soldiers in the Battle of Bunker Hill;* Cambridge; 1909

Hatch, Louis; *The Administration of the American Revolutionary Army;* Longmans Green and Co.; New York; 1904

Heath, William; *Heath's Memoirs of the American War;* A. Wessels and Co.; New York; 1904

The Historical Magazine, III; *Bunker's Hill;* (June, 1868); 321-442.

Howe, Sir William; *General Sir William Howe's Orderly Book at Charlestown, Boston and Halifax; June 1775-May 1776;* Collected and edited by Benjamin Franklin Stevens; Printed in London by Benjamin Franklin Stevens; 1890

Howe, William Howe; *The narrative of Lieut. Gen. Sir William Howe in a committee of the House of Commons;* Printed by H. Baldwin; London; 1780

Hudleston, Francis Josiah; *Gentleman Johnny Burgoyne;* Bobbs-Merrill; Indianapolis; 1927

Hudson, C.; *Doubts Concerning Bunker Hill;* J. Munroe and Co.; Boston and Cambridge; 1837

Hulton, Ann; *Letters of a Loyalist Lady;* Harvard University Press; Cambridge; 1927

Humphreys, Colonel David; *The Life and Heroic Exploits of Israel Putnam;* Silas Andius and Son; Hartford; 1833

Hunnewell, James F.; *Bibliography of Charlestown, Mass. and Bunker Hill;* J. R. Osgood and Co.; Boston; 1880

Hunter, Gen. Sir Martin; *Journal of;* Edinburgh; 1894

Lancaster, Bruce; *From Lexington to Liberty;* Doubleday; New York; 1955

Livingston, William Farrand; *Israel Putnam;* C. P. Putnam; New York and London; 1901

Lushington, S. R.; *Life and Services of Lord Harris;* London; 1840

Martyn, Charles; *The Life of Artemas Ward, First Commander-in-Chief of the American Revolution;* New York; 1921

Massachusetts Historical Society Proceedings: Various

A Memorial of the American Patriots Who Fell at the Battle of Bunker Hill. . . . Boston; Printed by order of the City Council; 1890.

Miller, John C.; *Triumph of Freedom: 1775-1783;* Little, Brown and Co.; Boston; 1948

Millis, Walter; *Arms and Men;* G. P. Putnam's Sons; New York; 1956

Montross, Lynn; *The Reluctant Rebels, The Story of the Continental Congress;* Harper; New York; 1950

Moore, George Henry; *Historical Notes on the Employment of Negroes in the American Army of the Revolution;* C. T. Evans; New York; 1862

Morsman, Oliver; *A History of Breed's (Bunker) Hill Battle;* Truman W. Haskell; Sacket's Harbor, New York; 1830

Murdock, Harold; *Notes and Queries on a Famous Battle;* Houghton Mifflin Co.; 1927

Murdock, Harold; *The Nineteenth of April, 1775;* Houghton Mifflin Co.; Boston; 1923

Namier, Sir Louis; *Personalties and Powers;* New York; 1954

Namier, Sir Louis; *The Structure of Politics at the Accession of George III;* London; 1957

Nell, William Coger; *The Colored Patriots of the American Revolution;* Wallcutt; Boston; 1855

Palmer, John; *America in Arms;* Yale University Press; New Haven; 1941

Pecham, H.; *The War for Independence;* University of Chicago Press; Chicago; 1958

Pitcairn, Constance; *History of Fife Pitcairn;* London; 1905

Potter, Israel Ralph; *Life and Remarkable Adventures of Israel R. Potter;* Henry Trumbull; Providence; 1824

Pulsifer, David; *Account of the Battle of Bunker Hill;* A. Williams and Co.; Boston; 1872

Putnam, Colonel David; *A letter relative to the Battle of Bunker Hill and General Israel Putnam;* in the Connecticut Historical Society Collection

Putnam, Alfred Porter; *General Israel Putnam and the Battle of Bunker Hill;* Salem; 1901

Robson, Eric; *The American Revolution in its Political and Military Aspects, 1763-1783;* Oxford University Press; New York; 1955

Sabine, Lorenzo; *The American Loyalists;* C. C. Little and J. Brown; Boston; 1847

Scheer, G. and H. Rankin; *Rebels and Redcoats;* World Publishing; Cleveland; 1957

Scull, Gideon Delaplaine, editor; *Memoir and Letters of Capt. W. C. Evelyn;* Printed for private circulation by J. Parker and Co.; Oxford; 1879

Stiles, Ezra; *The Literary Diary,* Franklin B. Dexter, Ed; New York; 1901

Swett Papers, New York Historical Society

Swett, Samuel; *History of the Battle of Bunker Hill;* Monroe and Francis; Boston; 1826

Swiggett, Howard; *The Forgotten Leaders of the Revolution;* Doubleday; New York; 1955

Thacher, James, M.D.; *The American Revolution, given in the form of a daily journal;* Bainitz; Cincinnati; 1857

Toner, Joseph; *Contributions to the Annals of Medical Progress and Medical Education in the United States before and during the War of Independence;* Government Printing Office; Washington; 1874

Trevelyan, Sir George Otto, Bart.; *The American Revolution;* Longmans Green; New York and London; 1899

Van Doren, Carl; *Benjamin Franklin;* The Viking Press; New York; 1952

Van Tyne, Claude Halstead; *The Causes of the War of Independence;* Houghton Mifflin; Boston; 1922

Wade, H. and R. Lively; *This Glorious Cause;* Princeton University Press; Princeton; 1958

Wallace, Willard M.; *Appeal to Arms;* Harper; New York; 1951

Ward, Christopher; *The War of the Revolution: 2 Vols.;* The Macmillan Co.; New York; 1952

Webb, Samuel B.; *Correspondence and Journals,* Worthington C. Ford, Ed.; New York; 1893

Wheildon, William H.; *New History of the Battle of Bunker Hill,* Boston; Lee & Shepard; 1875

Willard, Margaret Wheeler, Ed.; *Letters on the American Revolution, 1774-1776;* Houghton Mifflin Co.; Boston; 1925

Winsor, Justin; *Literature of Bunker Hill;* Boston; 1893

Winthrop, Robert Charles; *Address and speeches on Various Occasions;* Little, Brown and Co.; Boston; 1852

Index

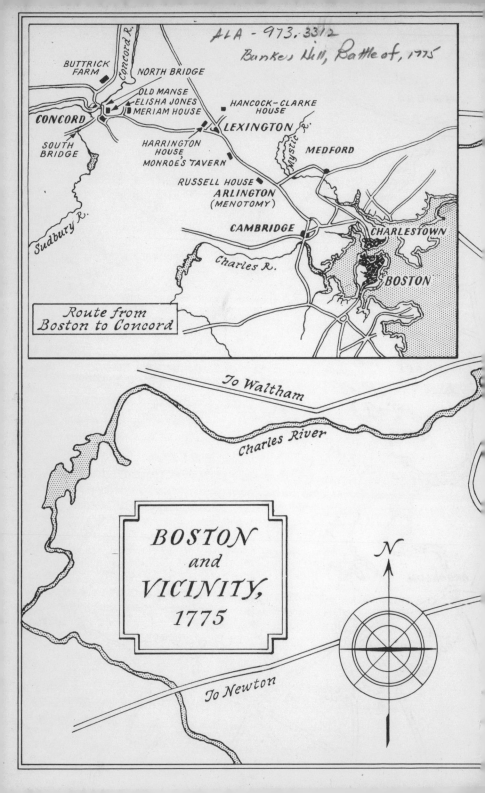

ALA - 973.3312
Bunker Hill, Battle of, 1775

Route from Boston to Concord

BUTTRICK FARM
NORTH BRIDGE
Concord R.
OLD MANSE
ELISHA JONES
MERIAM HOUSE
HANCOCK-CLARKE HOUSE
CONCORD
LEXINGTON
SOUTH BRIDGE
HARRINGTON HOUSE
MONROE'S TAVERN
Mystic R.
MEDFORD
RUSSELL HOUSE
ARLINGTON (MENOTOMY)
Sudbury R.
CAMBRIDGE
CHARLESTOWN
Charles R.
BOSTON

To Waltham

Charles River

BOSTON and VICINITY, 1775

N

To Newton